Social Semiotics for a Complex World

Social Semiotics for a Complex World

Analysing Language and Social Meaning

Bob Hodge

polity

First published in 2017 by Polity Press

Polity Press
65 Bridge Street
Cambridge CB2 1UR, UK

Polity Press
350 Main Street
Malden, MA 02148, USA

ISBN-13: 978-0-7456-9620-1
ISBN-13: 978-0-7456-9621-8 (pb)

A catalogue record for this book is available from the British Library.

Library of Congress Cataloging-in-Publication Data

Names: Hodge, Bob (Robert Ian Vere) author.
Title: Social semiotics for a complex world : analysing language and social
    meaning / Bob Hodge.
Description: Malden, MA : Polity Press, [2016] | Includes bibliographical references and
    index.
Identifiers: LCCN 2016009985 (print) | LCCN 2016023476 (ebook) | ISBN
    9780745696201 (hardback) | ISBN 9780745696218 (pbk.) | ISBN 9780745696232
    (Mobi) | ISBN 9780745696249 (Epub)
Subjects: LCSH: Semiotics--Social aspects. | Social interaction. | Semantics.
Classification: LCC P99.4.S62 H64 2016 (print) | LCC P99.4.S62 (ebook) | DDC
    302.2--dc23
LC record available at https://lccn.loc.gov/2016009985

Typeset in 10.5 on 12 pt Plantin by
Servis Filmsetting Ltd, Stockport, Cheshire
Printed and bound in Great Britain by Clays Ltd, St. Ives PLC

For further information on Polity, visit our website: www.politybooks.com

Contents

Preface

This book has a practical aim. It offers ideas and approaches for readers who want to understand and cope better with their world. Its angle on problems and solutions is its emphasis both on analysing language and meaning as key to understanding society and on society as key to understanding language and meaning. Its basic premise is that meanings are part of every problem and every attempted solution. Language and meaning are crucial for effective action. Analysing them matters.

Social semiotics is a uniquely powerful, inclusive framework for this purpose. It analyses meaning in all its forms, across all modes of language and practice. No other approach can match its scope, in today's multimodal world as in the past. The book is oriented to practice, its ideas and methods always embedded in real-life situations, problems and responses. Its concepts, ideas and models come from many theories. Social semiotics here does not describe and illustrate a well-known body of ideas and apply them. In this book analysis is a laboratory for theory, and theory develops tools for analysis.

The book is not intended as definitive, either about linguistics or about social semiotics. It is embedded in my personal journey, researching such public themes as globalization, digital culture, critical management and postcoloniality and private themes such as love, madness and the meaning of life. I address many different readers because these themes are important to so many people. Many will be university students, from first years to postgraduates. Some may be in linguistics, wanting to understand how language and meaning connect with society. Others may be in sociology, aware of the ever-present role of language and meaning in every issue that engages them. Others may study other fields, such as psychology, philosophy,

English, and cultural or media studies. All need a one-stop shop on language and social meaning.

I also write with general readers in mind: thoughtful, intelligent citizens grappling with problems that are usually generic as well as personal. The internet has supported the emergence of a new class of such citizens, sometimes called citizen-scientists, who use the net to cross traditional boundaries between experts and non-experts.

I use a minimum of jargon and explain all specialist terms. I use many accessible examples – mini-stories raising complex issues, mostly available from the internet. To move between my two purposes, exploratory and didactic, *I italicize key points as they arise in the flow of exposition.*

* * *

Disciplines are socially embedded modes of producing meaning. All students should know about the history and assumptions of disciplines they study. To set the scene for this book I use my personal history with social semiotics to reflect on disciplines and interdisciplinarity.

My story began with the 1968 student 'revolution', which swept through European and American universities, erupting into my studies of literature and classics at Cambridge University. This worldwide movement went viral across the globe without an internet. America played a key if ambiguous role. Its war in Vietnam was a catalyst for young people everywhere to recognize and protest against imperialism. Its civil rights movement was inspiring. The feminist slogan 'the personal is political' changed the agenda. French, German and Italian theory was liberatory, interacting with practice in exciting new ways.

The movement targeted the dominant academic system, but its goals included wider social change and a key role for academic knowledge in achieving it. Forty years later those are still my goals, though I now see many more problems with achieving them.

Disciplinarity then seemed a device to divide and rule. The interdisciplinarity I wanted could not just combine tightly bounded existing disciplines. It needed a more fluid space in which to follow connections and build new practices.

I was drawn to the reflections of the Italian Marxist Antonio Gramsci on why his own revolution in 1930s Italy failed. His concept 'hegemony' opened a door for me into unsuspected realities. Hegemony acted through 'intellectuals' to produce 'the "spontaneous" consent given by the great masses of the population to the general

direction imposed on social life by the dominant fundamental group'
(1971: 12). Gramsci was imprisoned in the 1930s by the fascist dicta-
tor Mussolini, so he was fully aware of the role of material force, 'the
apparatus of state coercive power which "legally" enforces discipline
on those groups who do not "consent" either actively or passively'
(ibid.). I knew that the repertoire of conceptual tools to dismantle the
current hegemony must include political, economic and social analysis. I immersed myself in a search across the social sciences.

I also knew the tools to attack hegemonic systems must include
ways of analysing the texts and processes through which hegemony
acted to create 'spontaneous' consent and apparent 'legality'. I saw
that as my task. I was trained in interpretive disciplines, classics
and literature, but it seemed obvious that linguistics, the official
'science of language,' was essential. So I turned to linguistics. Noam
Chomsky inspired me in this thinking. His courageous politics
impressed me, beginning with his critique of American power and
'the new mandarins' (Chomsky 1969) – unscrupulous ideologues
of state policy employed in American universities. In his new role as
activist the world's greatest linguist taught himself political science.
Chomsky's linguistics (1957, 1965) also excited me. I was not sure
how his politics and linguistics came together, but I was sure they did
and would, in a powerful analytic tool.

In 1972 I went to the new interdisciplinary university of East Anglia
in England, specifically to develop 'English studies', an approach
later called 'cultural studies'. I was fired up with the promise of
Chomsky's linguistics in a matrix of critical approaches. There I
met Gunther Kress. Gunther had studied under the British linguist
Michael Halliday, and he brought Halliday's work into our mix. We
grafted linguistics, drawn from the full range of current schools, onto
the Marxist tradition of critical theory (Hodge and Kress 1974; Kress
and Hodge 1979; Fowler et al. 1979). The result was first called
'critical linguistics' and later rebranded 'critical discourse analysis',
CDA (Fairclough 1989).

Chomsky and Halliday co-existed happily in the pages of our book,
but not in linguistics in the world outside. I sadly watched the wonderful enterprise of linguistics become mired in polemics, so virulent
that people referred to 'the linguistic wars' (Harris 1993). Chomsky's
exciting vision solidified into a fiercely defended orthodoxy, excluding former followers such as George Lakoff (1968) and alternative
traditions such as Halliday's (1985).

Linguistics has been frozen in a cold war for four decades. It is
long past time for peace to be declared. One task I set myself in this

book is to use social semiotics for that purpose. Social semiotics creates a space in which the social function of the opposition between Chomsky and Halliday and their followers is seen as a struggle for position. Social semiotics can then do what it also does well. As a meta-discipline, it places the different proposals about language, meaning and society of these two great linguists in a more dynamic context. The result is not a synthesis but a new, more powerful, comprehensive linguistics in which different or complementary ideas interact and evolve.

I once told Halliday that I aimed to reconcile the opposition between his and Chomsky's linguistics. He smiled sceptically and said: 'I wish you luck with that.' I do not know Chomsky personally, so I have not asked him what he thought, but I suspect I would be lucky to get even a sceptical smile.

Chapter 4 addresses this theme directly, and it weaves into other chapters. I hope both men will read this book and feel respected. But more important is that no one looks to linguistics for insights into language, meaning and society and thinks they have to choose between the two. *No ideas are better for being kept 'pure', quarantined from interaction with other competing systems of ideas.*

The 'linguistics wars' mirrored and were implicated in another set of 'wars'. In the 1980s there was talk of a 'linguistic turn' in philosophy and social sciences. Ironically, this movement was not a turn to the current discipline of linguistics but a decisive turn away. Given currency by Lyotard (1984), 'the linguistic turn' became a slogan for 'postmodernism', presented as radically opposed to 'modernism' and 'positivism', in a series of 'wars' across academia: 'culture wars', 'science wars'.

Common to these different fields are the concepts of system and structure, a hotly contested legacy from Saussure (1974). They have been understood in different ways, in battles that have divided disciplines and departments. The constructed 'war' between 'structuralism' and 'poststructuralism', and of both with 'empirical' or 'positivist' sociology, tore sociology apart in the 1980s, and the influential sociologist Anthony Giddens wrote the obituary of both: 'Structuralism, and poststructuralism also, are dead traditions of thought' (1987: 195).

But this obituary was premature. Both tendencies are alive and well in different incarnations. In practice, structuralism needs to incorporate more of what it excluded: dynamism, process, causality, uncertainty. Conversely, poststructuralism has discovered more structures not fewer, more forms and functions at more levels, more

tasks for new forms of structuralism. Poststructuralism complements and needs structuralism; it does not replace it. Nor can either
be indifferent to 'facts'. Likewise positivist sociology cannot ignore
the processes by which those 'facts' are constructed and established.

Social semiotics is good at analysing metaphors (see, e.g., Lakoff
and Johnson 1980), and 'war' illustrates the point. Declarations of
war, natural and metaphoric, are semiotic acts which usually construct semiosic conditions in the interests of the declarer. In war,
'truth is the first casualty'. That is a common effect of declarations of
war, real and metaphoric.

Sun Tsu, in China in the sixth century BC, wrote: 'All warfare
is based on deception' (1963: 18). He had two contradictory
deceptions in mind relevant to the 'linguistic wars'. One common
deception in war is that contending parties have no real interests in
common, no reasons for peace. Another deception is that 'our' side is
totally united. I use social semiotics in this book to see through both
deceptions and to disrupt the conflicts they produce and legitimate,
whether these are between Chomskyans and Hallidayans, linguists
and sociologists, structuralists and poststructuralists, or participants
in Bush and Blair's 'War on Terror'. This is not to deny the reality
of difference and conflict everywhere in social and biological life.
Paradoxically, the war model replaces the complex reality of multiple
differences and conflicts with a misleading binary, a single conflict
between homogeneous combatants.

* * *

By 1980 Gunther Kress and I had relocated from East Anglia to different communication and cultural studies departments in Australia.
There we became more aware of the role of new media in political and
social life. An exclusive focus on verbal language risked our analyses
missing the shifting new major sites of action. We recognized that our
critical enterprise had to take on board semiotics, to study verbal language alongside all codes in all media. The explosion of 'new media'
only underscored that message. But we remained clear that verbal
language was still central in the organization of power and meaning
in contemporary society. Verbal language was not obsolete. We still
did CDA, but with more options. CDA still needed linguistics, but
linguistics with a semiotic basis. Our enterprise kept its social imperative. We wanted stronger ways of analysing language and meaning
involved in social issues and problems. We saw the emphases on
semiotics and society as complementary. From this reasoning, social
semiotics was born (Hodge and Kress 1988).

Semiotics has a complex place in linguistics. Partly this was because of the Swiss linguist Ferdinand de Saussure, a founding father of both linguistics and semiotics. Saussure (1974) saw linguistics as part of semiotics, an overarching framework for all forms of language, verbal and non-verbal. But most linguists restrict semiotics to non-verbal sign systems, understood as totally different from verbal language. For them, semiotics becomes a marginalized, irrelevant theory of marginal forms of language. Social semiotics restores Saussure's original vision and takes it further.

Outside linguistics, semiotics had a different history. A 'semiotics revolution' flourished in the 1960s and 1970s, with such famous exponents as Barthes, Lévi-Strauss, Derrida, Foucault, Eco, Metz, Goffman, Geertz and Hall. At first it was celebrated but not much used, then it fell increasingly out of fashion. But important recent writers still give their work a semiotic scope. Innovative theorists such as Donna Haraway (1991) and Bruno Latour (2005) use this scope to rethink the ontological basis of new developments in science and technology. After the counter-revolution, semiotics is surging back. This book is part of that new movement.

In its earlier phase, semiotics developed an impressive repertoire of ways of analysing meanings. Why were these not more commonly used? I feel they seemed too specialized. Semiotics became too formalist, demanding too much work from new users. Many analytic tools were formed in structuralist semiotics and seemed discredited by poststructuralism. Damagingly, the search for meaning drifted from the centre, and meaning was detached from the study of social forces. Social semiotics in this book does not emphasize formalism. It is a demotic strategy for pursuing meaning in all forms and contexts, always to understand society better.

In linguistics and CDA, work by Gunther Kress and Theo van Leeuwen has been revolutionary. In their theory of multimodality (2001) they pointed out the omnipresence of multimedia texts in contemporary life, where meanings come via different modes, only one of which is verbal. In a radical insight, they showed that even print media, previously seen as the bastion of verbal language, in practice used other semiotic codes such as composition. Likewise spoken language itself is fundamentally multimodal.

Multimodal analysis is proving irresistible because of the intrinsic limitations of monomodal analysis for today's problems. Social semiotics provides a basic framework for theory and analysis of meaning in all modes, in linguistics and CDA as in other social sciences. Conversely, the many other languages revealed by semiotics, from

non-verbal languages such as intonation to languages such as art, film
or architecture, cannot be understood apart from verbal languages.

* * *

Many problems we face today have familiar faces: injustice, violence,
exploitation, oppression, discrimination, alienation, madness. Social
semiotics is part of a long tradition, but it also looks for new and better
solutions. A book for the second decade of the twenty-first century
must take stock of the current situation. Are there game-changing
developments in what is happening in society and language? New
challenges? New problems? New analytic resources?

All social sciences today are tackling the need to understand globalization as a set of forces and changes – political, social, economic,
environmental and cultural. The causes and effects of problems
regularly cross boundaries that were previously treated as fixed and
absolute. So do the resources to deal with them. With hindsight, it is
now clear that those boundaries were always less absolute than they
seemed, and the flows were always there. In this book I deal with
semiotic conditions and consequences of globalization in particular in chapter 8, but the theme affects every analysis. My examples
come from a small number of key sites, always analysed in global
contexts. To help readers to follow particular sites, these are listed
in the index.

Choices of site reflect power structures in the English-speaking
world, currently dominated by the USA and the UK. In a different book this imbalance might be taken to endorse the dominance
of the dominant. In my case it responds to the need of those from
the margins – settler colonies like Australia and Canada, developing
nations like India, China and Mexico – to use critical social semiotics
to understand the meanings of the dominant better than the dominant do themselves.

Intimately related to globalization is another game-changer, the
advent of new information technologies. Social semiotics needs to
take account of the subtle and obvious ways in which new media
interact with issues of language, meaning and society. The challenge,
as with globalization, is to maintain complex, comprehensive, flexible
theories, not opt for simplistic responses.

I do not have a separate chapter on the semiotics of the digital
world, though chapter 6 addresses some main themes. The theme of
digital versus analogue meanings and technologies weaves through
every chapter, a significant addition to ways of understanding the
nature and limits of the 'digital revolution'. The index provides a

guide to the many analyses which deal with some aspects of analysis in a digital world.

I draw on recent developments in science as new resources for social semiotics. My fascination with science and mathematics began before I knew about linguistics, and my first job was teaching maths and physics in school. For me the hidden hostility I experience between the cultures of sciences and humanities needs addressing and resolving as much as the 'wars' in linguistics and sociology. In this book I draw freely on ideas from science in my interdisciplinary mix.

Especially relevant are the new alignments and alliances between science, technology and society called 'chaos theory' and 'complexity science'. From 1990 I began to bring these together with social semiotics, aware that most colleagues in CDA or social semiotics were reluctant to do the same. More than twenty years later I am more sure than ever how important this connection is, more clear about where and why the links exist.

I am also aware how careful I need to be in bringing these ideas to non-scientists. Social scientists are rightly wary of writers who use the prestige of science to give weight to ideas supposedly from science. I do not 'apply' these theories to language, society or thought. Rather, I pick up phenomena in social, linguistic and mental life already recognized in academic works or in the public mind, characterized by turbulence, contradiction or complexity. These are usually poorly explained by linear theories but illuminated by specific ideas from chaos and complexity. Analysing these features of language and society in careful empirical detail can generate appropriate versions of these theories, rather than illustrating them.

This approach does not impose chaos or complexity on phenomena; it just loosens assumptions of stability and order imposed by linear theories. Linguistics needs to include non-linear concepts to deal with the hyper-complexity of language and society today.

* * *

I call this social semiotic practice a whole-of-linguistics approach to a whole-of-language object. This sees all the distinct branches of linguistics as aspects of a single, complex whole that is other than the sum of these parts. At the same time, these components are complex wholes at their own level. They integrate their own components at lower levels. Each of these does the same to lower levels, and so on. A whole-of-linguistics approach attends to the new possibilities of any whole but never loses the parts.

I also use a whole-of-linguistics approach to open up pathways between the present and the past. Many academic disciplines draw a boundary around the present state of knowledge as if it is all that anyone now needs to know. Those obsessed with being up to date insist that all references should be later than 2000: everything else is superseded. I believe this is a dangerous misconception, with pernicious effects on teaching and scholarship. My whole-of-linguistics conception includes many ideas and thinkers from the past. Many are largely forgotten, but they are vital parts of the intellectual gene pool for linguistics and social semiotics.

Sir Isaac Newton, a very great scientist, described his achievements by stating that he was a dwarf who could see further because he was standing on the shoulders of giants. Playing with this metaphor, I observe that some dwarves are bigger than others, and Newton was a very big dwarf. I also suspect that what Newton called giants were often heaps of dwarves seen from a distance.

I use this idea to guide the strategy of this book. I reach back to the long roots of the study of language, meaning and society, going back to thinkers from the past who made major advances to human knowledge. I do not do justice to other dwarves, but this strategy still helps recover the inexhaustible depths of this tradition.

*   *   *

This book combines an invitation to linguistics with an account of social semiotics. Sarah Lambert, then with Polity, asked me for a book to help social scientists appreciate the value of linguistics and to help linguists see new possibilities for their discipline. I agreed enthusiastically. But the tensions involved in this attempt illuminate the current state of linguistics. To bring out some of these I suggest how my book could be used alongside traditional introductions to linguistics – where the two could complement each other and where they might diverge.

I admire Bill McGregor's introductory text on linguistics (2009), and I use it to see how these two texts and approaches might work in tandem. His introduction corresponds to my chapter on key concepts. He lays out theory, as I do. He goes back to Saussure, as I do. He points out the need for alternative frameworks, as I do. The main difference is in emphasis. 'Total linguistics' includes more theory and more divergence than does McGregor. But his readers could read my chapter with profit, and vice versa. His chapter on phonetics and phonology is basic for linguistics. I do not have a single chapter on this theme, but theories of multimodality provide a rich context for describing sound systems. McGregor follows with two chapters on words. This is more than in most introductions to linguistics. I have one chapter on words. Again, this is a relation of complementarity. McGregor has one chapter on syntax. I have one on grammar. The topics are treated differently, but our chapters are complementary.

But our projects tend to diverge as our books progress. We both have chapters on meaning. McGregor gives more importance to meaning than most other introductions to linguistics, yet meaning is studied in linguistics mainly as 'semantics', a narrow, formalistic study of a small number of aspects of meaning. For social semiotics, meaning is fundamental, understood in a wider sense, and it permeates all parts of the study of language. In the two books, 'meaning' is both the same and not the same concept.

Likewise, McGregor treats the social in four solid chapters, 30 per cent of the book. This is more than in most other introductory texts. But the account of social theory is thin, and there are no social theorists in his bibliography. In his crucial first part, language is understood as an autonomous system outside society. But for social semiotics the social is present in every act of meaning. Again the theme appears across both traditions – the same but not the same. Beginning readers might have problems bridging the difference, but if they could it might be transformative.

There is a similar challenge with my multimodal approach. McGregor, as a linguist, focuses mainly on verbal language, as a largely distinct object for an autonomous discipline. For social semiotics, verbal language is hugely important but not independent of other semiotic modes, in theory or practice. I claim that it offers a better account even of verbal language. Can this claim be inspiring for students of linguistics? Or is it too big a challenge?

My complexity approach is likely to be challenging in the same way. I try to show that traditional linguistics always acknowledged some degree of complexity, and that complexity theory has a place for linear analysis. But to cope with the scale of complexity of language and meaning I argue that the science of language and meaning needs to become far more fuzzy, more complex and multidimensional. Could creative teaching bridge the two perspectives in a single course, assisted by a book as good as McGregor's in dialogue with mine?

Traditional linguistics still does some things very well. Linguistics books are treasure troves of different languages. McGregor's is a fine example, referring to no fewer than 236 languages, including English.

CDA tends to analyse only one language. I analyse nine, including English, but compared to traditional linguists I seem narrow and ethnocentric. However, my analyses integrate complex interplays of language and social meanings, so I need a first-hand grasp of how that language worked in that context. My respect for the many differences across languages confronts the demand to understand language–meaning–society as a complex whole. I work with more than one language, but far fewer than the many languages and contexts in McGregor's book.

I mainly used three languages in this way. Classical Greek is a now dead language whose otherness confronts all modern European languages with their own lost history. I spent many years trying to master Chinese with sufficient understanding of its social meanings. My main guide in this task was Kam Louie, a good friend as well as a collaborator (Hodge and Louie 1998). I also use Spanish as a reference point. This is one of the current triad, with English and Chinese, of global languages. It is also the first language of Gabriela Coronado, anthropologist, linguist and acute observer of both English and Spanish. With her help I have been able to reflect on subtle processes of the two languages in the interlingual conditions which characterize language in use today.

* * *

I have many debts to acknowledge. Gunther Kress has been a dear friend, profound guide and supportive collaborator for many years. Without his interaction and influence I would never have appreciated what linguistics could be, under that and other names. Gunther's frequent collaborator, Theo van Leeuwen, has been a friend with whom I should have liked to work more, had circumstances permitted. Through Gunther I came to know and admire Michael Halliday personally as well as through his work.

As this book will show, Halliday's lifetime contribution to linguistics has made a crucial difference. So have some of his followers. Here I make special mention of the late Ruqiaya Hasan, David Butt and Jim Martin, as well as innovative scholars such as Annabelle Lukin, Wendy Bowcher, Ed McDonald, Alexis Don and Peter White. Other linguists have been helpful in recent times. Chris Hart convinced me of the merits of cognitive linguistics. Ingrid Piller showed me the rich texture of intercultural studies. Jan Blommaert showed me the importance of a globalization perspective.

In a different relationship, but still admitting a real debt, I wish to acknowledge Noam Chomsky. I heard him speak only once, at

Cambridge in 1971 as I recall, but the impact of his work has been immeasurable. My first encounter with his writings in 1969 produced an inner revolution. He converted me to linguistics. My subsequent struggles with the later Chomsky have been important and formative, too, even if at times I was insufficiently respectful. In this part of my journey I owe most to Stephen Crane, who patiently re-educated me to appreciate Chomsky's greatness.

My education in chaos and complexity theories owes most to two people. Vladimir Dimitrov, mathematician, mystic and lover of Spanish poetry, challenged me to go more deeply into a chaos theory of language. Lorena Caballero added biology to the list of sciences I needed to understand from a complexity perspective.

Among my formative influences, I especially thank my three children. Anna Notley provided me with many fascinating semiotic examples and read many of my works with insightful and inspiring comments. John Hodge contributed a level of critical social commentary over many years from which I am still learning. Jennifer Sultana's reports from the front line as an inspirational teacher of ancient history and English have kept me in touch with what education should and can be.

In writing this book I owe four special debts of gratitude. Rodney Williamson, a good friend and valued colleague, drew on his exceptional range in linguistics and social semiotics to give me a generous, detailed critique of a draft. Teresa Carbó gave a warm, acute, meticulously scholarly commentary on the first chapters, as well as on the book's concept. John Thompson, the author of influential books, was a formative critic of my writing and a creator of Polity Press as home for the work I try to do. I enjoyed working closely with Sarah Lambert, Polity's linguistics editor, and with Jonathan Skerrett, who ably took over from her.

Gabriela Coronado's contribution has been beyond acknowledgement. She provided insightful commentaries in the early stages as I was trying to formulate my ideas and a host of illuminating ideas as the book was progressing. She gave detailed commentaries on every chapter, as unerring with my faults in English as though she was the native speaker. At crucial points in my argument, when I felt I had lost my way, she shone a kindly spotlight on my confusions. I cannot thank her enough, as linguist, colleague and much, much more.

PART I

Principles and Practices

1

Key Concepts

This chapter outlines some basic principles of social semiotics in a complexity framework. A complexity framework is essential for social semiotics. Complexity is built into the foundations of social semiotics and has always been there. Each key term – language, meaning and society – refers to a complex system already studied by one or more disciplines. I add to the complexity by presenting language, meaning and society as an even more complex system formed from intersections and relationships between these three systems.

Complexity is often seen as a newfangled ('postmodern') idea, yet it has deep roots. At its heart is a powerful idea that goes back to Aristotle's *Metaphysics*: 'The whole is other than its parts' (1935: 1045a.8-10). I analyse this phrase at greater length in chapter 5. Here I note only how deceptively simple it is, yet how far it resonates. Aristotle's beautiful idea links science and linguistics, semiotics and sociology, ancient and modern theories. In the chapter that follows I try to write as simply and clearly as Aristotle did about complex ideas.

Key terms

The social semiotic imagination

The term 'social semiotic imagination', adapted from the influential book by the sociologist C. Wright Mills, is not a technical term, but it captures the essence of the practices I describe in this book. Mills (1959) challenged his readers by connecting imagination with 'sociology' (understood as science with therefore no connection to 'imagination'). For him, 'imagination' was a basic capacity for seeing, interpreting and changing complex social relationships as meanings. He wanted to cultivate 'the vivid awareness of the relationship between experience and the wider society' (1959: 8). In my adaptation of his concept, those relationships are understood as countless multiscalar networks, starting from details of everyday life and ultimately connecting with invisible social forces and movements such as capitalism, racism and injustice. Mills's sociological imagination made sense of these details as signs. That is basically what social semiotics does, too.

I illustrate this social semiotic imagination with a news story that unfolded as I began writing this chapter. In Oslo, Norway, on Friday 22 July 2011, Anders Breivik set off a car bomb, killing eight people. He then travelled to Utøya, an offshore island, and killed sixty-eight others. I was in Australia at the time. I saw the news on TV, read it in print, and followed it up on the net.

I have never been to Norway, but I am a global citizen for whom terrorism matters. In this context I asked: What is the meaning of this senseless act? What meanings drove Breivik to do such a thing? To answer these questions I looked at the smaller component meanings, made up of everyday words and sentences. *Minute analysis of everyday acts of meaning is indispensable to address big questions about big meanings, and vice versa.*

I knew about this event only through the media. This adds a second object for my semiotic imagination. They are my sole sources for what went on – 'ideational meanings', as Halliday (1985) calls them. The social role of media, what Halliday calls their 'interpersonal function', complicates the uncovering of this deep meaning of the globalized world I live in.

The headline of the first article I read on the theme came from the front page of *The Australian*, a paper in the right-wing Newscorp group:

1.1 Toll to rise as Norway faces the twisted logic of a mind intent on killing (*The Australian*, 25 July 2011)

The headline was accompanied by an image of the explosion which killed eight people. In this multimodal newspaper text, key information carried by the visual channel was omitted in the verbal. I used semiotic imagination to wonder why.

In this case I saw a larger pattern. The phrase 'toll to rise' is a transformation of 'the toll (numbers) of dead will rise'. Transformations, a term associated with Chomsky (1957), are rich sources of semiotic questions. Do they think that more people will die, or have they not counted them all yet? Why not mention 'dead'? One effect of this is to shift attention from the large numbers of dead to the 'mind' of the murderer, from social issues to individual psychology.

I compared this text with a template I carry in my mind about this theme, in which two terms are structural: 'massacre' and 'terrorist'. I restore these two problematic terms and ask: Why did this newspaper, known for its links with conservative politics, avoid these potent terms here? This was clearly a 'massacre', and 'terrorist' has been applied to many incidents with far fewer deaths. Was it because Breivik was right wing, and not Muslim? At this time I chose not to follow this line into the 'twisted mind' of the right-wing media. The question of Breivik's 'twisted mind' interested me more, part of larger questions about terrorism. What did he mean by this act? To begin to answer this question I took one sentence from his 1500-page manifesto, published online just before the event:

1.2 Once you decide to strike it is better to kill too many than not enough, or you risk reducing the desired ideological impact of the strike. (Breivik, 23 March 2011)

Reading this sentence semiotically, I noted the social meanings. The phrase 'desired ideological impact' creates a complex relationship with 'you'. From Breivik's manifesto I constructed this reader as a 'Knight Templar', as Breivik called his followers in his crusade. I went outside his text to check if these followers really existed. They probably did not. This input from reality then became part of the meaning I gave this text. Breivik's followers existed only in his fantasies. The social meaning was a conversation with himself, in which he split into two, leader and follower.

This meaning is only an inference, my guess. But meanings in social use are typically contested, not fixed and certain, and guessing is normal in semiotics. The immediate context of my interpretation contains two competing sets of meaning, mine and Breivik's – or, more precisely, my guess at what Breivik meant and my guess about the deeper sense of his statement.

The word 'desired' illustrates the role of transformations in semiotic analysis. I interpret it as a transformation of an underlying fuller sentence, 'you and I desire . . .'. In this implied fuller form, 'you' (his imagined Knight Templar reader) and 'I' (Breivik) unite in their/our common desire to kill large numbers of people. This is only what Breivik's twisted mind 'desired'. He co-opts his reader into an imaginary position, as someone outside himself who wants his advice. In my analysis at this point I hold at least two versions of 'meaning' in tension. I am interested in what he 'means', but I am also interested in what his words mean to me in my diagnosis of his 'twisted mind'.

This discussion shows three features of the social imagination:

1 *Big meanings about the state of the world are used to identify signs and instances in the environment.*
2 *Single small concrete instances allow analysis to relate elements to each other and to hypothesized deeper meanings.*
3 *Analysis identifies many questions to investigate further, and to weigh against each other in a complex provisional judgement.*

Language, meaning, society

Language, meaning and society are key terms for social semiotics, but they also have meaning in everyday English and in linguistics. In this section I show how social semiotic understandings of them can come from and co-exist with their meanings in other contexts.

1 *Language*   'Language' is one of the top 1000 words in everyday use according to the *Oxford English Dictionary* (*OED*). *OED* defines language as 'The system of spoken or written communication commonly used by a particular country, people, community, etc.' 'System' is part of the definition. So is connection with society, though not with 'meaning'. The *OED* adds four more strands of meaning. One is modern – computer languages. The other three go back to the seventeenth century – 'languages' of animals, non-verbal communication, and other human signifying systems.

Mainstream linguistics as represented by the *Oxford Dictionary of English Grammar* (*ODEG*; Chalker and Weiner 1998) defines language as 'The method of human communication, consisting of words, either spoken or written'. This monomodal theory does not include the idea of 'system', unless 'method' implies it, and it does not refer to society or to social uses of language. Everyday English has a more semiotic understanding of language than mainstream linguistics.

'Discourse' is an alternative word for forms of language, the defining term in 'critical discourse analysis'. It does not make the *OED* top 1000 words, but it captures language in action better than 'language' does.

'Discourse' has other advantages over 'language'. The American linguist Zellig Harris (1950), Chomsky's teacher, used 'discourse' to include large stretches of text above the level of the sentence, something mainstream linguistics needed. Halliday used 'discourse' and 'text' for a similar purpose. Michel Foucault (1971) connected it to bodies of knowledge associated with language, thus opening up the term to a role in analysing the sociology of knowledge. I see no compelling reason why mainstream linguistics should not embrace 'discourse'.

2 *Meaning*   To my surprise, 'meaning' is not in the *OED*'s top 1000. *OED* lists two main meanings for 'meaning'. One is broad, dealing with big meanings: 'The significance, purpose, underlying truth etc. of something'. This strand includes 'Something which gives one a sense of purpose, value, especially of a metaphysical or spiritual kind.' The second strand is more restricted: 'The sense or signification of a word, sentence, etc., of language, a sentence, word, text, etc.: signification, sense'.

OED reflects a split in the field of meanings of 'meaning'. Differences of scale construct a gulf between disciplines of 'big meanings', such as philosophy or religion, and small meanings of linguistics. Everyday English includes both kinds of meaning while still registering the gap.

The linguistic *ODEG* has a surprisingly limited concept of meaning: 'What is meant by a word, phrase, clause, or larger text'. But what is meant by 'meant'? The definition includes different scales of linguistic form, the scale studied by linguistics plus the scale studied by other disciplines, but not the idea that meanings, whatever they are, may be bigger or smaller.

But, as we saw in the Breivik case, 'big' and 'small' meanings form a continuum. Small meanings at the levels of word, sentence, text and discourse are not different kinds of meaning. Big meanings of ideology and religion are constituted by the same system, with massive social effects. All kinds of meaning need a common theory. *Analysis should be multiscalar to move between big meanings and big effects and the many smaller meanings which sustain them.*

3 *Society*   Both 'society' and 'social' make the *OED* top 1000. This indicates a big meaning. Society is 'The aggregate of people living together in a more or less ordered community'. This indirectly includes a concept of system through the mention of 'order', but there is no reference to means of communication to hold societies together. *ODEG* has no specific entry for 'society'.

Social semiotics can take this range of meanings of its key terms from everyday English and linguistics and understand them in new ways that remain connected to their previous uses. It understands the terms as elements of a three-body system, in which each term is continually modified and becomes more complex by interacting with the other terms over many cycles.

This strategy draws on Henri Poincaré's idea of three-body systems (1993). The 'three-body problem' arose as a problem for Newton's great synthesis. Newtonian maths could not predict the behaviours of the earth, moon and sun. In 1889 the King of Sweden offered a prize for a solution. Poincaré won the prize by showing why it could *not* be done, and in the process he developed the mathematics of 'indeterminate chaos'. Relatively simple systems, even with only three components, acted on by only two forces, gravity and momentum, cannot be predicted with certainty over a long term.

Social semiotics recognizes strong reciprocal links between these key terms. Everyday definitions of 'language' and 'meaning' recognize connections with society, but not as strongly as social semiotics. As Halliday wrote: 'Language is as it is because of the functions it has evolved to serve in people's lives' (1976: 4). Those functions are mediated through meanings. Halliday distinguished between social and referential functions and meanings. These categories overlap. All meanings have social effects, to some extent, though some do so more prominently. Likewise, all meanings refer to or invoke reality, material or social, some more directly than others.

Meaning is at the centre of social semiotics' complex, reciprocal three-body system. Meanings are known only through language of some kind, and language exists to carry meaning. Language and meaning facilitate and shape social relations, which supply tasks and functions that shape language and meaning. *Analysis of language is a gateway to analysis of meanings, social and referential. Analysis of meanings is a portal into social processes and the versions of reality that drive them.*

Semiotics and meaning

Everyday English has a broader, more semiotic understanding of meaning than current linguistics, and many everyday practices help find and negotiate meanings. I want to reframe linguistics to have a better theory of meaning and a stronger practice of analysis.

But semiotics has similar problems to linguistics. Semiotics includes many valuable ideas and analytic tools, but meaning has a paradoxical place there. Social semiotics must settle accounts with semiotics itself to fulfil its potential. That means technical discussions which some readers may find difficult or tiresome.

Some problems and contradictions come from the basic premises of semiotics' two 'founding fathers', the American philosopher and mathematician Charles Peirce (1839–1914) and the Swiss linguist Ferdinand de Saussure (1857–1913).

I begin with Saussure. His work is binary (dualistic) and full of dichotomies (dividing topics into two parts), as can be seen in his theory of linguistic signs: 'The linguistic sign unites, not a thing and a name, but a concept and a sound-image' (1974: 66). He says 'unites' but insists that that bond is 'arbitrary', a problematic term I discuss later. His first move cuts 'things' (reality) from 'signs'. His second move cuts one part of the sign, the concept (equivalent to 'meaning'), from its carrier, sound images in speech. The effect of this double dichotomy was to remove both meaning and the realities it referred to from linguistics and semiotics. Saussure devoted thirty pages to a highly original discussion of phonology (sound systems) but none directly to meaning. This impoverished account of meaning has been a damaging legacy to his followers, in linguistics and semiotics alike.

Peirce was born eighteen years before Saussure but died a year after him. A scientist and philosopher, not a linguist, he introduced the complexity that semiotics needs. Western thought since Descartes in the seventeenth century has reflected or wrestled with what has been called Cartesian dualism – splits between body and mind, matter and spirit. Saussure's dichotomies reflected the splits. Peirce aimed to resolve them.

In a proposal similar to Poincaré's three-body model, Peirce (1956) argued that meaning is a three-way relationship between a piece of reality, the object or referent; a sign; and an idea produced in an entity which interprets or processes it, which he called the 'interpretant'. He called the process 'semiosis', a vital term for social semiotics to draw attention to processes, not just to signs and texts. 'Discourse' carries a similar sense of process. In linguistics, Halliday (1985) proposed a function he called 'textual', weaving language and meaning together in social practice.

Peirce did not remove the boundary between matter and mind, but he foregrounded processes which cross it. Peirce's scheme was not equivalent to Saussure's. Saussure's model (1974) locked reality on one side of the Cartesian wall and then ignored it. Peirce's semiosis continually crossed it. Peirce's model frees semiotics from an exclusive concern with text as its primary object, to include social and cognitive processes which constitute every act of meaning. For Peirce, *semiosis is the same process whether interpreting material reality, reading texts, or moving between the two.*

For instance, in the Breivik case I use the same process to read the print and visual texts and use both as guides to reconstruct the event and meaning they are about. By seeing them as basically similar processes, I do not blur them together. On the contrary, I can compare meanings created in the different forms and different stages of the process and criticize any of them in this framework. For example, distortions introduced by the press are themselves meanings.

Neither Saussure nor Peirce focused on social dimensions, so their theories should be adapted to include them. Saussure insisted that language is a social fact, though he needed better social theories to build that premise into his theory. Peirce's concept of semiosis as infinite flows of meanings is like the social processes of the internet, though he did not make that connection.

This discussion has not tried to produce an amalgam of Saussure and Peirce. The dialectic between them generates ideas for social semiotics that neither thinker envisaged. From this discussion I propose a provisional sense of 'meaning' as a key term in the language–meaning–society complex: *meaning is an inflection of reality, carried by language as a socially shared resource, underpinning every social action and reaction.*

System

'System' plays a fundamental yet problematic role in social semiotics. The word comes from Greek *systema* (from *syn-*, together + *istemi*, arrange into a complex whole). The concept underlies Aristotle's idea that an arrangement of elements becomes a new entity ('other than its parts') with distinctive properties. This idea has become central in modern complexity theory. For instance, a 'complex adaptive system' has 'emergent properties', different from the properties of component elements (Gell-Mann 1994).

Semiotics has a proud but undervalued place in the history of the concept of system. Linguistics in its time made significant contributions to general theories of systems. These later theories now can be used to recover that history and give a firmer basis to the concept in linguistics and social semiotics.

Saussure's contribution to ideas of system was vital but problematic. A core concept for him was 'value' – his term for the place of elements in systems: 'Language is a system of interdependent terms' (1974: 114). Saussure used 'value' with its role in economics in mind, comparing linguistic signs to coins, and generalized: 'Being part of a system, it is endowed not only with a signification but also and especially with a value' (1974: 115).

Saussure had two terms, value and signification. Value connects with systems, signification with processes connecting language and reality. In this formulation, Saussure does not use either–or thinking to separate 'signification' (meaning) and 'value'. Although he emphasizes 'value', he still includes 'signification'. His exact words signify his uncertainty, which in this case is as admirable and important as his main meaning.

In a famous example, Saussure contrasted French *mouton* and English *mutton/sheep*. As he points out, *mouton* refers to the same woolly animals as 'sheep' (the same signification) but as a single word it has a different value to the two English words, and hence, for him, a different meaning. This brilliant insight draws attention to a sub-system of meanings English speakers use unconsciously. The difference is also grounded in differences in reality and in social contexts. The words mutton and sheep reflect differences in dead/cooked and living animals. The different values grow out of and mark differences in reality. Those differences reflect inherited cultural differences between French and English, still active in the present.

So value does not oppose signification (relation to the world of objects), it inflects it. Since reality is cut up differently by speakers of the two languages, the two words refer to or signify not the same reality, but different portions of that reality. Signification is not opposed to value, as Saussure half thought. *Signification is meaning, and value plays a key role in making meaning.*

Saussure proposed a related pair of categories. Strings of signs in texts formed what he called 'syntagmatic' structures (Greek *syn-*, together + *tag-*, ordered). Adding Peirce's general concept of semiosis, we can say that these forms in text correspond to elements in reality ordered in space and time. Syntagmatic elements are parts of a whole and are modified by their place. They too have a kind of 'value'. *'Syntagmatic' refers to all linked structures on every scale in every semiotic mode, in texts and realities alike.* 'Syntax' comes from the same roots, but in linguistics it is restricted to sentences, clauses and phrases.

Syntagmatic structures and systems generate meanings through intersections with another plane Saussure called 'associative'. Others call this 'paradigmatic', from lists in grammar such as verb forms, and I follow that usage. But Saussure's term was more complex and inclusive. He envisaged many axes intersecting at every semiotic site. Only one of these was a linear, ordered taxonomy such as a paradigm. The rest were 'associations', spontaneous non-linear systems.

Saussure insisted that these two planes are interdependent. Their relationship is key to the production and analysis of meaning. Combining this idea with Peirce's concept of semiosis, I propose a general model, in which *meaning at every point is determined by the socially motivated interaction of values in syntagmatic and paradigmatic systems (versions of reality and classifications of that reality) to connect that semiotic structure with a world of objects.*

Analysis using these terms is simple and powerful. I illustrate from Breivik's text. 'Ideological impact' is a small syntagm linking two words and meanings and changing each: -al attached to 'ideology' changes the form and value of both elements in this syntagm. Its meaning here is anchored by its reference to the massive carnage and the worldwide publicity. 'Impact' in the syntagm can refer equally to the two, so it means both. Breivik's choice of the word 'ideological' triggers a paradigmatic opposition between social and material forces, in which he seems to have chosen social effects and ignored material ones. That then becomes his inflection of reality, his meaning. This exemplifies what *The Australian* called 'twisted logic', a deformed paradigmatic structure in which the difference between material and social realities is simultaneously asserted and ignored.

The two great complementary figures in modern linguistics, Chomsky and Halliday, had different emphases on syntagmatic and paradigmatic structures. Chomsky called his revolutionary work '*Syntactic* Structures' (1957) implying greater interest in syntagmatic than paradigmatic structures, but in practice he studied the interaction of both. Halliday called his model '*Systemic* Functional Linguistics' (1985), using 'system' for paradigm, associating meaning with choice. But he also said many illuminating things about syntagmatic forms.

I emphasize this complementarity in two social semiotic points:

1 *Paradigmatic and syntagmatic structures are so interdependent that all linguistic and semiotic analysis or description must continually refer to both.*
2 *Relations of semiosis and signification intersect with paradigmatic and syntagmatic structures in social contexts to produce social meaning.*

Counter-systems

I complement this semiotic history of 'system' with a brief reference
to its role in Marx's thought. Marx saw capitalism as a system. In a
discussion of social relations he used armies as an illustration: 'The
relationships within which individuals can constitute an army and act
as an army were transformed [by new technologies] and the relations
of different armies to one another also changed' ([1849] 1972). Here
the properties of a whole (the army) are different from those of individuals. They are formed by relationships, which include relationships between humans and non-humans in a way that foreshadows
Bruno Latour's concept of actor-networks, which link humans and
technology (2005). Lower-level systems, armies, are part of a higher-
level system.

In contemporary theories, systems come in several forms. Hard
systems are mainly made by humans. Marx is mainly describing what
would be called 'soft systems', loosely organized sets of elements. But
sometimes systems are so fleeting and loosely organized that I call
them 'amorphous'.

Marx's concept of class is also a system term – the organization
of relations between individuals whose options and behaviours are
affected by their class membership. But Marx was clear that the
degree of cohesion which held elements together as a class/whole was
variable and fluid: 'separate individuals form a class only insofar as
they have to carry on a common battle against another class' (Marx
and Engels [1845] 1976: 85). *Boundaries between wholes and parts are
created and dissolved under pressure of social forces.*

Marx emphasizes 'transformation' as system-wide change. In linguistics, 'transformations' are associated with Chomsky. I discuss
Chomsky's theories of transformation at greater length in chapter 4.
Here I quote an early formulation: 'A grammatical operation T
operates on a given string . . . with a given constituent structure and
converts it into a new string with a new derived constituent structure'
(1957: 44). Chomsky's statement carries the core point: *transformations are systemic and act on systems within systems.* Marx's words
remind us that *transformations are a crucial focus for dynamic analyses of
systems,* in society as in language.

Marx is important in the history of systems thinking. He was early
to recognize its role in social causality but did not overvalue it, as
Saussure tended to do. Marx noted how elements in a system are
acted on by lateral forces (other elements in that system) and by vertical forces (systems or elements from higher or lower levels). Where

for Saussure systems were all-powerful, for Marx *systems are amor-phous assemblages* (see Deleuze and Guattari 1988) *of material factors that shape and act in social struggles.*

The sociologist John Law elevated a counter-systems orientation into a principle of method for the social sciences: 'Imagine what it might be like to remake social science in ways better equipped to deal with mess, confusion, and relative disorder' (2004: 2). Linguistics remade in this way would have a greatly expanded range of more relevant structures and systems to study, within a social semiotic framework.

Multidimensionality

Multidimensionality is an intrinsic part of complexity paradigms. Halliday (1956) introduced the term to refer to the interaction of more than one axis at a given point, as happens all the time in social semiotics. The concept can be applied to the co-action of syntag-matic and paradigmatic planes or the intersection of different modes in multimodality. Language and meaning in social contexts are always multidimensional. At the moment of production, meaning is different for producers and receivers, even those with much in common. In divided societies differences are greater, exacerbated by differences of time, place and ideology.

Multimodality

The work of Gunther Kress and Theo van Leeuwen on multimo-dality (Kress and van Leeuwen 2001, 2006; Kress 2010) has been a game-changer for social semiotics and the study of language, meaning and society. It is transforming critical discourse analysis and systemic functional linguistics. I believe it is only a matter of time before it transforms all forms of linguistics.

The starting point for Kress and van Leeuwen was their recogni-tion of the dramatically changing media environment, in which print modes rapidly lost their long-standing dominance, and new multime-dia forms flourished. All analyses, they saw, now need a multimodal approach in order to study the many semiotic modes in use.

Others had noted the massive changes of this multimedia revo-lution. Kress and van Leeuwen's distinctive strength came from their base in social semiotics, from which they saw important conti-nuities as well as discontinuities in media systems. They came to the profound conclusion that even a seemingly monomodal form, such as the previously dominant print media, has in practice always been multimodal, to a degree. The multimodal revolution is new, and it has been with us since human history began.

I use a small example to illustrate the value of the term. In September 2011, the US actress Demi Moore engaged in a public break-up with her then husband, Ashton Kutcher, via tweets. I learned about it from a print article in the Australian women's magazine *New Idea*, which followed the story from online sources using Demi's tweets, which they reproduced as pictures. Couples have broken up throughout history, but this particular event could not exist as a social form without the interplay of many semiotic modes, by all participants, at all levels. Multimodal analysis is not optional here. *It is essential to track the various meanings as they cross different levels, including boundaries between private and public, which in most semiotic regimes are more carefully separated.*

This is not just a fact about film stars like Demi Moore. It is a general situation today, produced by new media technologies and new uses of those technologies. Different semiotic modes available form a system which can be transformed in different epochs by a process similar to what Marx ascribed to the effects of new technologies on the army system.

New Idea rephrased one of Demi's tweets:

1.3 Last Tuesday she Tweeted a picture of herself with her eyes shut, and the caption 'I see through you'. (*New Idea*, 10 October 2011: 15)

This whole article is multimodal in a way that is now commonplace, weaving together words and images, many carried by the multimodal resources of the internet.

If we focus closely on specific modes, separately and as they interact, we note a significant discrepancy between the words and the image, as transmitted through tweetpics. Demi's words say 'I see through you', implying that she sees that Ashton is lying, but the image shows her with her eyes closed. This photograph communicates two main meanings. Demi closes her eyes, which acts out a conventional meaning, in effect translating a common phrase in English. However, the photograph also shows her looking pale and thin. This is a different kind of sign. Her physical state is how she is and also signifies her distress and anguish.

Words and images are two distinct modes, but we can drill down with each to reveal more modes. Verbal language comes in three modes – spoken, written and electronic – each a different system, each with different social reach. Demi wrote, 'I see through you', a written form which, however, transmits the direct and intimate language of speech. It then appears in the public domain as a media text. *This passage between successive modes is serial multimodality.* The same applies to the relation between the photograph and Demi's body. The photograph represents Demi's body, showing that it is indeed thin and that she is indeed very unhappy. But photographs can be altered in various ways. They have a lower truth value.

The Canadian Erving Goffman's emphasis on interaction can enrich this analysis. While he is usually classified as a sociologist, he made significant contributions to social semiotics. He analysed 'the presentation of self in everyday life' (1959) in terms that illuminate this exchange. Goffman saw exchanges like this as games, in which participants try to create meanings about themselves to create 'impressions' and see through the impressions of others.

In modern societies where many people are relative strangers, manipulation has become so widespread that people become better at it and have greater distrust of the messages of others. In this situation words, though part of the dominant mode, become the least-trusted mode, since they can be so easily faked. Demi, for instance, might say many things which Ashton might distrust or dismiss.

Some signs are harder to fake. Goffman distinguishes between signs which are given, more under control of the producer, and those that are 'given off', with less or no conscious control. Demi's look of distress is partly 'given off', but actresses could fake it. Thinness and pallor are harder to fake but not impossible for method acting. This status of signs is a continuum, in which values shift in response to the state of the game. Demi may be really distressed, and really thin and pale, but Ashton may still feel that she is exaggerating to manipulate him. What Ashton thinks, in this stage of the semiotic relationship, then becomes part of the meanings in the exchange. Their signs are dialogic.

This illustrates an important aspect of multimodality: *messages in different media may be different or contradictory, and their relationship to each other is itself potentially a meaning: a syntagm formed out of their difference.* Unlike static, meaningless typologies, dynamic multimodal systems constrain and give meaning to exchanges. Such systems are slowly shifted by the weight of multiple interactions. *The current state of multimodal systems signifies social and semiosic relationships in the group.*

Types of signs

Theories of multimodality rest on prior theories dealing both with what signs are and their main types and functions. Here the problems created by the founding fathers are especially acute. Peirce and Saussure both classify signs, but their classifications are too different to be easily harmonized. Eco (1976) reviewed their different ideas critically and proposed some alternatives. I basically agree with Eco but with more radical criticisms and more radical solutions. Social semiotics needs a simple, powerful new theory of signs starting from first principles.

I start with an influential statement of Saussure's. Principle 1 in his theory of signs stated: 'The linguistic sign is arbitrary' (1974: 66). The phrase 'linguistic sign' is singular, implying that linguistic signs are simple, homogeneous things, more like stop signs. From a complexity perspective I ask whether that is so.

Eco prefers the term 'sign-function'. Voloshinov (1973) argued that the minimal unit is the utterance, because it combines social and semiotic elements. A theory of signs is far more than a theory of individual significant objects like traffic signs. *It is about the complex relationships between language, meaning and reality in social contexts.*

Saussure distinguished between 'arbitrary' and 'motivated' signs. His 'arbitrary' signs have no link between words, meanings and referents. So the sound of *mouton* is nothing like the concept of sheep. English 'sheep' is no closer. But Saussure did not recognize that his second principle opened up a different analysis: 'the linear nature of the signifier' (in speech) (1974: 70). That is, order (of words, sounds) is intrinsic to verbal language. Order, then, is a motivated basis for signifying systems of verbal language.

Kress and van Leeuwen (2001) developed this insight into a foundation of multimodal theory. They saw qualities of spatial organization such as composition and layout as crucial signifying systems that had decisive effects on verbal meanings. The same is true of spoken language. For instance, intonation patterns studied by Halliday (1985) are motivated signs that affect meaning and interpretation. Saussure's first principle, then, is wrong in the absolute terms he used. *Signifying systems in verbal language are full of more or less motivated signs.*

Peirce (1956) proposed three classes of sign. Two are useful for semiotic analysis because they flesh out the category 'motivated'. 'Indexical' signs are materially related to the reality concerned, part of it or causes or effects (e.g., Demi's pale face signifies her grief).

These are similar to Goffman's signs 'given off'. 'Iconic' signs resemble a reality, as drawings or images do, like Demi closing her eyes. Peirce extends the scope of iconic signs to include diagrams and algebraic formulae, not just pictures. Peirce's third class of sign, conventional, seems similar to Saussure's 'arbitrary', so it seems easy to put the two systems together. But, as both recognized, all signs become conventionalized with use. Conventionalization is something that happens to all signs to differing degrees, not a quality that defines only one kind.

Repeated use of a given relationship between signs, meanings and realities for a given community establishes a conventional bond supported by that community, which allows the initial 'motivated' bond to be weakened until it becomes invisible, seeming 'arbitrary'. This has happened to most though not all the vocabulary of all spoken languages, which as a result are able to express social meanings (whose language it is) over referential meanings. It happens to non-verbal sign languages. But 'motivated' relationships remain important for important parts of every language. For instance, languages of politeness work with more motivated forms of meaning to carry social meanings.

This leaves greater need for linguistics and social semiotics to understand how relatively motivated meanings work in all modes and all social exchanges. Peirce's two terms are a start but they are not enough. Eco (1976) criticized both founding fathers. In the process he brought in another pair of key terms – analogue and digital – from media studies, where they were key terms in debates about media technologies. Eco criticized Peirce's 'icon' because it had too many meanings. Eco was right. But from a complexity perspective that is what the term needs. Eco preferred 'analogue' as opposed to 'digital', the new master code of the cybernetic age. Peirce sometimes called his icons 'analogue' signs, so it makes sense to bring the two terms together.

Following this reasoning, I propose a new pair of fundamental generative categories underpinning all ways of meaning.

1 *Analogue systems of meaning relate complex forms or structures to each other across domains of language, meaning and reality.* Some principle of resemblance motivates this relationship, so the meanings can be called 'motivated'.
2 *Digital systems of meaning are produced by binary operations, usually repeated as by digital computers.* However, modern computers are only a modern instance of fundamental processes in semiosis

and thought. All judgement and discrimination, human and non-human, follows a binary pattern, separating elements from each other. The starting point for the binary process may be motivated, but many repeated actions produce chaotic, apparently arbitrary outcomes.

3 *These two ontologically different systems work in tandem in semiosis.* Analogue forms frame digital processes, which are organized to mimic analogue forms. Digital processes act on analogue forms as wholes or parts, producing transformations.

4 *All signifiers are changed by repeated use in a semiotic community to become more conventional and arbitrary.* They interact with a range of modes and technologies of perception in different contexts of use to make up mature multimodal systems.

The 'digital revolution' is a major challenge for social semiotics today, needing a stronger multimodal theory. The pattern underlying this set of changes is best seen as *multiple transformations between two irreducible semiotic modes, not the triumph of one over the other.* Conventionalization then becomes a third dimension, in terms of which we can map the full range of the meanings thrown up in this 'revolution'.

The dialogic imagination

Complexity approaches typically allow causes, forces and meanings to co-exist, interacting with each other to produce potentially infinite, open sets of possible outcomes. This concept of language, meaning and society was captured well in Mikhail Bakhtin's concept of the 'dialogic imagination' (1981), developed in Stalinist Russia in the 1920s. That dysfunctional totalitarian state ruled through a one-directional exercise of power and meaning. Bakhtin emphasized plurality of languages and meanings through his concepts of *heteroglossia* (different languages) and *polyphony* (many voices). His concept *intertextuality* similarly saw meaning passing through networks of texts. Bakhtin called the one-way language of power 'monologic' as opposed to 'dialogic' communication, in which meaning changes as it passes between participants, in a chain with no single moment or meaning as fixed point. In contrast, monologic discourse attempts to close off all meanings and impose the single unchanging dominant meaning of the powerful.

Like Mills, Bakhtin used 'imagination' in two ways. He saw a reality buried beneath the surface of everyday life. He also used this vision to critique that repression. This dialogic principle can be described as *affirming the effects of interaction on meaning, to produce dynamic multiplicity or resist closure.*

To build on Bakhtin's theory of dialogism I draw on Freud, especially his analyses of jokes, dreams and behavioural texts. He distinguished between manifest (surface) and latent (hidden) content, a model analogous to Chomsky's 'surface' and 'deep' structures linked by transformations. Freud's deep/latent structure is dialogic, competing meanings from internalized selves, including voices of authority and desire. His manifest content is not exactly monologic but skewed in response to the dominance of the dominant. Freud argues that a joke arises when a small amount of text from the id, the subverted self, irrupts into the main text and takes it over.

I illustrate my fusion of Freud and Bakhtin by analysing a joke:

1.4 A drunk loses the keys to his house and is looking for them under a lamppost. A policeman comes over and asks what he's doing.
'I'm looking for my keys,' he says. 'I lost them over there.'
The policeman looks puzzled. 'Then why are you looking for them all the way over here?'
'Because the light is so much better.' (Zapata 2008)

The manifest content of this joke is a dialogue. However, that fact does not explain why it is a joke and what it means. The first paragraph sets the scene from a rational 'Ego' perspective. In paragraphs 2 and 3 this rational logic co-exists with the drunk's logic. In paragraph 4, the punch line, the drunk's logic emerges in its pure form, the logic of Freud's Id, who is also a person, marginalized and drunk, but still a citizen.

This version of the joke comes from the blog of an American junior media executive, Dushka Zapata, who uses it to rebuke her colleagues for their tunnel vision. She does so by relating the two dialogues in a complex way. She assumes her colleagues would identify with the policeman, not the drunk, but she implies that they are really more like the drunk. The point of the joke, however, is not that the policeman is right either. He is foolish for being tricked by the drunk, who is smart for having tricked the policeman. Zapata herself is neither character, but both, existing in the dialogue.

In the Demi Moore text, different meanings in the dialogue come from different semiotic modes, visual and verbal. As in the joke text, the two overlap around seeing, but in the verbal text rational Demi claims to 'see (through Ashton)', while the visual shows her with her eyes shut, seeing nothing. A third, supposedly rational Demi takes the picture and sends it to Ashton and her followers.

From these brief analyses I propose an analytic guide: *in situations marked by inequality of power, the meanings of the non-powerful are normally distorted or repressed. Analysis should reverse the dominance of the meanings of the powerful and restore the dialogic content.*

Complexity

New forms of science and definitions of 'science' emerged in the late twentieth century, often referred to by the labels 'chaos theory' and 'complexity science'. In this book I do not treat these ideas as a coherent body of work or 'paradigm'. I use them in similar ways to John Urry (2005), as a multidimensional resource for social sciences which weaves together ideas that are scientific and deal with high levels of complexity and uncertainty.

If problems for analysis typically involve interrelations between language, meaning and society, it is best to look for them in the complex reality of social action. Analyses of complex objects should not rest on unreal premises of simplicity. As Zapata's joke warned, if you are looking for a key you should look where it might be, not where the light is good.

Cybernetics

'Cybernetics' is an integrating thread across sciences and humanities. The concept was launched in 1948 by the mathematician Norbert Wiener (1948). This is not normally called 'chaos' or 'complexity' theory, yet it scientifically explains most paradoxes that make 'chaos' and 'complexity' theory so exciting. 'Complex adaptive systems', a key idea for complexity science (Gell-Man 1994), are cybernetic products. They often respond to chaotic phenomena: complexity as cure for chaos, not its cause. Yet escalating catastrophes are also products of cybernetic systems. *Cybernetics is key to non-linear causality in social and semiotic systems.*

Wiener's theory integrated physical and social sciences, biology and engineering around the common theme of systems of control. After its initial success as a revolutionary interdisciplinary proposal, cybernetics tended to fragment into its previous parts and became less visible. In biology it is a basic concept. In technology it framed the explosion of devices, large and small, that underpin 'cyberculture' and the digital revolution. Donna Haraway (1991) used the term 'cyborg' (cybernetic-organism) to signify new relations between humans and machines and a new consciousness.

In elementary cybernetic systems such as steering ships ('cybernetics' came from Greek *cybernetes*, a ship's pilot), pilots 'read' signs, small and large, of waves and wind, and calibrate them against a template of what they should be. Small changes to the steering system achieve large effects, such as turning big ships around. Cybernetic systems use connections across different parts of a system to achieve non-linear effects, which do not mirror a given cause or sum of causes.

Far-from-equilibrium dynamics

Earlier forms of cybernetics were especially interested in systems that maintained steady states, 'homeostasis', as when pilots hold their course in spite of turbulence or cross-winds. This is best achieved by what is technically called 'negative feedback' – that is, feedback which cancels out tendencies to depart from the given state or route. Biologists found a fascinating array of homeostatic mechanisms essential to all forms of life.

However, homeostasis and negative feedback loops are only part of the story, as the chaos theorist Ilya Prigogine insisted (Prigogine and Stengers 1984). Even elementary cybernetic systems need positive as well as negative feedback in the technical sense. 'Negative feedback' damps processes down, while 'positive feedback' magnifies them. 'Positive feedback' does not always have benign outcomes. It can be explosive and destructive, pushing towards chaos. Yet it is equally essential in cybernetic systems. The pilot's slight pressure on the rudder must be magnified by positive feedback mechanisms. Life processes are enabled by catalysts, such as enzymes which allow us to metabolize food. The explosive journey from fertilized egg to embryo and healthy organism needs a mix of positive and negative feedback.

Prigogine developed an overarching term, far-from-equilibrium dynamics. This term is ambiguous, depending on whether it refers to 'soft' cybernetic systems or to amorphous systems that are hard to see or describe. Prigogine argued that systems behave very differently close-to-equilibrium. Connections are slow and structures simple. Closer to 'the edge of chaos', complex dynamic forms can emerge. Life itself needs to be close to this edge of chaos.

Cybernetics and far-from-equilibrium dynamics combine in many important ideas in 'chaos theory'. Edward Lorenz (1993) developed the idea of 'sensitivity to initial conditions' (also called, more poetically, the 'butterfly effect'). This described chaotic, far-from-equilibrium conditions in a cybernetic network containing many positive feedback loops, where causes are so small, complex and variable that before the event it is impossible to know which factors will prove decisive. In Lorenz's metaphor, a butterfly flapping its wings in the Andes might afterwards be found a decisive factor, multiplied through the system, in producing tornados in Montana. For social semiotic analysis, *'butterfly effects' are indexical signs of far-from-equilibrium conditions.*

Another link between 'chaos theory', cybernetics and language is Lotfi Zadeh's concept of fuzzy logic, as expressed in his 'Principle of Incompatibility':

> Stated informally, the essence of this principle is that as the complexity of a system increases, our ability to make precise and yet significant statements about its behaviour diminishes until a threshold is reached beyond which precision and significance (or relevance) become almost mutually exclusive characteristics. (1973: 28)

This principle carries a warning for all disciplines with highly complex objects. Given that meaning is a highly complex system of systems, *key terms to describe patterns and behaviours need to be fuzzy, complex, multivalent terms in a multivalent logic.*

A final concept I introduce here is *fractal,* invented by the mathematician Benoit Mandelbrot (1977, 1993) from Latin *fractus,* 'broken', hence an irregular shape, an analogue form. Mandelbrot found many different fractals in physics and biology, and they are common in social semiotic life. Mandelbrot was interested in the way this quality often applies across different scales. *Fractals are cybernetic forms,* whose output is a modified form of a previous input, positive feedback, which produces endless difference around similarity, 'self-similarity'. *Fractals are multiscalar.* They are *analogue forms produced by digital technologies,* remarkable examples of *highly complex order that arises only in complex, chaotic conditions.*

Interdisciplinarity

As I point out in the preface, disciplinarity is an important object for analysis for this book, since most of my readers are formed in disciplinary systems. Social semiotics can reflect productively on such systems.

'Discipline' comes from Latin *disciplina,* which carries complex analogue meanings, including teaching practices and relationships. Embedded in *disciplina* is *discere*, 'to learn', and *puer*, 'child'. This is learning understood as transmission of knowledge from teachers who know everything to pupils who know nothing. Whatever its merits for child learning, this model is less suited to a research community of independent adult learners. Modern systems of disciplinarity still have qualities from these origins. They rely on and reinforce the power of teachers over taught. Since that power is based on certain knowledge possessed by teachers, they are conservative. Those with power defend their monopoly of knowledge.

A common alternative to disciplinarity is 'interdisciplinarity'. 'Inter-' (Latin for 'between') *potentially transforms the meanings of 'disciplinarity' by creating a Bakhtinian dialogue between disciplines, a space between them.* But that move can be resisted by upholders of disciplinarity, who can maintain the primacy of 'disciplinarity' in this picture.

'Transdisciplinarity' (Latin trans, 'across' or 'changing') implies a more dynamic relation to disciplinarity, as well as more space for change.

Meta-disciplinarity (Greek meta, 'after', 'above') implies an even more dynamic relation to disciplinarity, suggesting a more profound reflection on disciplinarity.

These root meanings make the latter two terms stronger alternatives than interdisciplinarity. Yet they still repeat disciplinarity in their deep structure, and, like all words, they can still be appropriated by groups with greater social power, as disciplines still have today.

Instead of words, I explore meanings. In an old tale attributed to the Buddha in the sixth century BC, a king summoned nine blind sages to his court, and gave them a test. Each had to touch an elephant, and describe what they saw.

> 1.5 When the blind men had each felt a part of the elephant, the king went to each of them, and said to each: 'Well, blind man, have you seen the elephant? Tell me, what sort of thing is the elephant?' (Buddha 1948)

But each described an apparently completely different object. The one who touched the head described it as like a pot. The one who touched the ears said that it was like a winnowing basket, and so on. There were nine blind men, but no consensus.

The Buddha drew some lessons:

> 1.6 Just so are those preachers and scholars holding various views blind and unseeing. In their ignorance they are by nature quarrelsome,

wrangling and disputatious, each maintaining that reality is thus and thus.

The Buddha is a religious leader, not a sociologist, yet this parable needs little change to apply to disputes between schools and disciplines today. Stories are analogue forms, as are concepts like 'disciplines'. *The story as analogue sign contains more meanings than were encoded in it.*

The story is intriguingly close to a common form of psychology experiment, in which experimenters blindfold subjects to demonstrate the unreliability of perception. From another point of view, the Buddha invented a model for critical discourse analysis. I draw further lessons from the parable. I see a semiotic impoverishment in the blind men's method. Deprived of one sense, sight, they use only one other, touch, to replace it. Did they not smell the beast or hear its cries? They needed multimodal semiotics.

They also needed a social theory of meaning. But Buddha's king did not encourage them to have one. He was brusque and authoritarian and isolated each sage. I identify a subtext here, about distorting effects of power on the production of knowledge. Each blind man emphasized the uniqueness of his contribution in order to impress the powerful. But the elephant itself is more than the sum of the parts they felt (trunk, tusks, etc.). The elephant is a complex, dynamic whole, intelligent, strong and mobile. A whole on that scale had to be imagined in order to interpret the details. The individual blind men/ scholars turned their sensory impressions, their empirical data, into coherent accounts, fitted into the wholes defining their discipline. The more coherent their descriptions, the further they went from the truth about elephants.

This has lessons for disciplinary systems. Disciplines typically have high boundaries around the group and its world of meanings and weak connections with reality and with other versions of it. If their object is part of a wider whole, disciplines lose sight of the connections. There is a price to pay when interconnected elements from one whole are taken over into another whole, another system. *The demands of a whole can suppress and distort its parts, leaving whole and parts alike less effective.*

In the parable, individual observations are distorted when tidied up into the system of each blind man/school. This form hinders the necessary conversations across groups. It impedes a collaborative search for truth. So too with specialist terminology that typically accompanies disciplinary knowledge. Students and scholars need *open, fuzzy terms and definitions, sharing findings, opening debates, not attempting to close them.*

Deep time

Space and time are the fundamental dimensions of the physical universe, but structuralist approaches, including semiotics, have had problems with time and history. These problems reflect the ambiguous legacy of Saussure. *Saussure distinguished what he called diachronic structures from synchronic structures* (from Greek *chronos*, 'time' + *dia*, 'across', *syn*, 'with' or 'at the same time'), and argued that synchronic structures were a more scientific object of study.

Semiotics and the social sciences have suffered from a split between historical and contemporary studies. Marx defined his theory as *Historical* Materialism, but most social sciences tend to operate around a split between contemporary and historical studies. Social semiotics needs to recover the dimension of time in all its complexity.

Paradoxically, Saussure knew more about diachronic studies than about the synchronic studies he was inventing. He was oppressed by his awareness of the relentless change in the sounds of language and acutely aware of how arbitrary was the process, how complex the transformations leading back forever into the past. The complexity is a challenge, not a barrier. Saussure's tradition is one resource for social semiotics to cross it.

I begin my diachronic analysis with the striking fact that Buddha's words, written 2500 years ago in Pali, a dead language, still have such impact and relevance to English speakers. What 'meaning' is transmitted, how is it managed, with what resources and costs?

The first resource is cybernetic. Buddha's text crosses vast tracts of space and time to reach me, but at every point individuals and institutions act as feedback loops, transmitting and correcting this text and the social meaning of 'Buddha', saturated with social and referential meanings. As a result, Buddha's meanings reach many more people today than in his own time, with greater impact. It is a semiotic butterfly effect. There are nearly 500 million Buddhists today (Johnson and Grim 2013).

This is a 'big' meaning that gives purpose to existence. Such meanings are often separated from the 'small meanings' studied by linguists – words, sentences and texts. As the Buddha's meanings show, the two kinds of meaning in practice travel together. Big meanings survive over time because they are big. They become bigger because they have survived so long.

Buddha's text is in verbal language, full of conventional signs which are eroded by time, as Saussure knew. There are no living speakers of Pali, the language of the text, but it uses words to create sentences which paint a picture, a story, analogue meaning. This can then be painted in other words, in other languages. Buddha's text chains analogue and conventional signs together. Multimodal packages are more durable than any mode on its own.

The original language of this text, Pali, was closely related to Sanskrit, an ancient language that played a key part in what is arguably the greatest breakthrough in the proud history of linguistics. In 1786 Sir William Jones, an English judge in newly colonized India, delivered a speech to the Orientalist Society to demonstrate that Latin and Greek, the prestigious languages of Europe's two founding civilizations, were closely akin to Sanskrit, ancestor of Hindi, the language of colonized India (Jones and Cannon 1993). Jones postulated the existence of an original mother language, now known as Indo-European, the common ancestor of English, Celtic and Germanic languages, among others. Indo-European is currently estimated to have been spoken 6000 to 8000 years ago. Descendant languages are spoken all over the globe.

The comparative method Jones used to establish this tree structure of language families pre-dated Darwin by fifty years. It was cutting-edge science of its day. The linguistics that grew from his work flourished for a century. Language trees can be reconstructed because meanings persisted over time, not the same but recognizably related. In the same way and by similar methods, evolutionists track relations between biological species, genera and classes back many millions of years.

Discontinuities

Modern studies of globalization track meanings across a vast scale in space, but they usually shrink time. Comparative philology tackled language and meaning across large areas, including colonizers and colonized, but its reach in time was far greater. It would seem obvious to combine the two fields to create a single vast space–time continuum.

Saussure's theory of synchrony and diachrony provides an insightful explanation of why this is so difficult in practice. He tried to explain diachronic structures as a series of synchronic structures, but found that he could not. *Synchronic structures are incommensurable with diachronic structures.*

A seemingly similar phenomenon can perhaps be seen in Heisenberg's 'uncertainty principle'. Heisenberg proved that, at quantum levels, the more precisely the position of some particle is determined, the less precisely its momentum can be known, and vice versa. Position here corresponds to synchronic states, momentum to the diachronic plane. Saussure independently discovered a similar incompatibility between synchronic and diachronic description in the slow chaos of language.

Quantum mechanics observes other boundaries which may have something comparable in society and language. Different states of particles are separated not by a continuum but by discrete parcels or quanta of energy. To pass up from one level to another requires a jump, consuming energy, while descending levels releases energy. By analogy, it may be that a fully interdisciplinary system is at a higher level and requires energy to reach it from a discipline. Conversely, to enter a discipline from an interdisciplinary field may release new energies.

The age of globalization may be presenting new problems for time and history. David Harvey (1991) influentially talked of the space–time compression of postmodernism: the tendency for processes to be faster and distances less. If this is happening it may be seen as a sign of far-from-equilibrium conditions.

In a similar vein, Michel Foucault (1972), a historian of ideas and institutions as well as a semiotician, noted a paradox in contemporary histories. On one hand, he saw an ever greater fragmentation of the past, creating ever more boundaries. On the other, broad sweeps of time were becoming more important. Braudel's 'long duration' (1996) saw history as a series of layers for different actors on different scales, up to vast stretches of geological time. It may be the case that *time becomes more problematic in far-from-equilibrium conditions, and far-from-equilibrium semiotics is needed to frame adequate analysis of non-linear time and history.*

Complexity approaches bring out uncertainties of language, meaning and society within a given situation, yet they also reveal surprising continuities over vast distances, resolving as well as creating problems. Many people fear complexity and cling to simplifications as defences against loss of control. Paradoxically, the opposite often happens. *Using complexity wisely gets things done. Denying complexity makes it more powerful, less manageable.*

Conclusion

I offer six points to guide analysis of issues and problems for linguistics and social semiotics:

1 *Language, meaning and society together form a highly complex differentiated and interdependent system on many levels, a system of systems.*
2 *Meaning is a fuzzy term incorporating many levels and kinds of meaning, big and small. Meanings are socially inflected versions of reality which play a crucial role in language–meaning–society systems.*
3 *Semiotic systems interact with social forces and processes, operating through many cybernetic loops with sometimes massive non-linear, unpredictable effects in far-from-equilibrium conditions.*
4 *In these complex systems, many different codes and modes interact in multimodal systems and processes, in which conventionalization and the distinctive properties of analogue and digital forms play fundamental roles.*
5 *Fractal patterns link configurations of power and solidarity across all levels, from micro-levels up to the global.*
6 *Crossing dynamic worlds of flows there are also deep discontinuities, forming often unsuspected barriers for analysis.*

2

Some Notes on Method

This chapter is a guide to problem-driven strategies for analysing language, meaning and society. It looks at ways to identify sites where language and meaning intersect with social issues and problems, where concepts from the previous chapter were born and can be used. But meanings are everywhere, all social, all encoded in language. All problems are posed in and solved or made worse by interweaving language and thought, always in social contexts. Where to start?

I do not present social semiotics as a single, grand method. Instead I reflect on my own experiences of doing social semiotics, responding to specific problems, embedded in interdisciplinary contexts. I add personal reflections that I hope will stimulate my readers. Rather than concentrating on one social semiotic method, I exemplify a social semiotic imagination, deployed on common problems and methods. I sometimes draw on large projects for examples. At other times I suggest possible studies that might use these methods and themes. I put these speculative proposals in boxes.

I argue against some common limiting conceptions of social research in the social sciences. Research methods are usually divided between macro- and micro-studies, 'qualitative' and 'quantitative'. Meaning is usually studied in only one option, qualitative micro-studies. I use social semiotics as a meta-discipline to reconfigure this map and develop methods where analysis of language, meaning and society enhances quantitative and qualitative research across all scales. The methods I look at in this chapter are individually well known. Social semiotics contributes six things to this toolkit:

1 it deepens and broadens their analysis of meaning;
2 it connects meaning with social issues;

3 it expands what can count as evidence;
4 it finds richer connections between methods and processes;
5 it recognizes more complexity, contradiction and chaos;
6 it combines these features in a flexible strategy which is greater than the sum of its parts.

The semiotic imagination

Making it strange

A major paradox for understanding and analysing language and social meaning is that all native speakers have a profound knowledge of their language in all semiotic modes, verbal and non-verbal, but they normally cannot explain it well, either to themselves or to others. The two halves of the paradox generate key problems and strategies for linguistics and social semiotics. Chomsky drew creatively on linguistic intuitions of native speakers as the royal road to knowledge of language, yet our own language can be so familiar that we cannot see it. What we know in this way seems mysterious and hard to study, since it exists inside minds. How do we access it?

As a strategy I adapt a term from the early twentieth-century Russian literary theorist Viktor Shklovsky (1991) – *ostranenie* ('estrangement', 'defamiliarization'). Shklovsky argued that, as perception becomes automatic, as is normal, processes become unavailable for conscious reflection. Estrangement challenged this unconsciousness. Paul Gee (2010) uses the 'making strange tool' in his helpful guide to discourse analysis. I use it in similar ways.

I illustrate the technique with an example I came across while semiotically grazing the media. On 20 July 2010, US President Barack Obama held a televised press conference with British Prime Minister David Cameron. To 'make it strange', I imagine how this might seem to extra-terrestrial anthropologists, from say a planet of the star Electra in the Pleiades system. I see the Pleiadeans taking notes as they observe two upright animals facing a larger group. Like Earth ethnographers, they are multimodal analysts. They record both animals as almost motionless, 2 metres apart. The animals stand in front of identical structures (later identified as 'lecterns'). They are covered by what seem identical pieces of cloth, including blue cloth around their necks (a 'tie'). The Pleiadeans see the one on the left nodding its head vigorously, occasionally moving an arm, a stream of sounds coming from an orifice in its face. The other animal half crouches, its two arms rigidly holding the sides of the 'lectern', looking at the first.

'How could these be the rulers of this world?' one of my imagined Pleiadeans asks her companion. 'And could this be how they rule their world? Through what they call "language"? What a crazy theory!'

'Completely absurd!' the other anthropologist replies. 'But our best scholars say it seems the only explanation.'

The two Pleiadeans would be even more perplexed when they read the first animal's opening words in the White House webpage:

2.1 Good afternoon, everybody. Please have a seat.

This is how you rule this world? Were they meant to take the seats? Was this a bribe: I will let you take these chairs home if you obey me? Yet it had an immediate impact, unlike anything else in the speech. All animals in front of the pair sat down as though pulled down by a force-field. Perhaps this language thing did have power after all.

The next part of the speech would bewilder them again:

2.2 It is my great pleasure to welcome Prime Minister Cameron on his first visit to the White House as prime minister. We have just concluded some excellent discussions – including whether the beers from our home towns that we exchanged are best served warm or cold. My understanding is that the prime minister enjoyed our 312 beer and we may send him more. I thought the beer we got was excellent – but I did drink it cold. (Laughter)

'Making strange' shows how invisible is most of the main action, *inside minds that produce and process meanings, in cognitive acts held together by social relationships*. Without this key, there is nothing to get hold of to study. Actions on their own are meaningless, incomprehensible.

The example illustrates the *complex, non-linear causality which links language to effects via meaning*. The Pleiadeans want to understand language for its use-value, because of the causal role they think it plays in the actions and activities of the people they have come to conquer or befriend. What more adequate hypothesis about causality can I tell them?

In this speech the only piece of language with a clear effect is the command. But even the order that is obeyed is surrounded by conditions, as speech act theorists note (Austin 1962). When the US president tells the press corps to sit down they do it fast. We know because of our internalized system of speech acts that Pleiadeans saying this would be treated as aliens and shot by security guards. What is true of commands is equally true of other speech acts. They rest on internalized conventional systems of meaning.

To explain the causality at work here in terms the Pleiadeans might understand I use a cybernetic model (Wiener 1948). The power of Obama's words is multiplied by countless complex systems of linkage, too vast and complex for him to know or control.

This instance illustrates the non-linear causality of cybernetic systems in complex conditions. The text as quoted expresses niceness, seemingly to create solidarity, not power. Yet it negates that power in order to make it more acceptable and more effective. The system runs on contradictions. This makes it unstable. If Obama was felt to be insufficiently polite, that could be interpreted as rude and hostile and greeted with hostility. If he was judged excessively polite, he could be interpreted as hypocritical or even sarcastic, with a different, still hostile response. *Outcomes are unpredictable in cybernetic systems in complex conditions.*

I made my baffled Pleiadeans linear thinkers, relying on objective observations, to make three points. *Language and social meanings operate through complex systems with non-linear causality.* The key to understand them is *not in external behaviours alone but also in meanings inside heads.* Yet, as a final problem, *these meanings are inaccessible except to observers who already know what they are or by asking people what they mean and trusting what they say.*

The ethnographic imagination

Part of the knowledge the Pleiadeans want is captured in Chomsky's concept of 'competence' (1965). His term referred to the extraordinary levels of tacit knowledge of their language possessed by native speakers. Halliday has a complementary emphasis on language in use. Dell Hymes (1972) added 'communicative competence' to include competent native speakers' knowledge of language in use.

But ethnography came first to this theme. It formed itself around the concept of the *ethnos*, often translated 'culture', a vast, mysterious but potent object. 'Culture'/*ethnos* is a highly complex analogue form. Ethnography assembled a set of powerful analytic tools to study it.

Ethnography is always a social practice. Edward Said (1978) influentially dissected what he called 'Orientalism' as a discourse. Orientalism included linguistics and anthropology as strategies to sustain European imperialism over 'the East' (Arab and Asian nations) in a 'Western style for dominating, restructuring and having authority over the Orient' (1978: 3). Similar tactics and structures applied to native peoples in America, Africa and Australia. 'Critical ethnography' (Clifford and Marcus 1986) denounced these practices in the past, seeking a new more ethical ethnography.

Said's critique is now part of social semiotics' toolkit. But social semiotics as meta-discipline can reanalyse ethnography's theory and practice to find ways the tools can still work, less ideologically and to better effect. The bathwater of ethnography was dirty, but there was a baby.

Recently I was in Mexico airport and took semiotic/ethnographic notes. I arrived from Los Angeles and entered passport control accompanied by Gabriela Coronado, a Mexican citizen and my wife. The room was large, with a high roof. I observed two large signs: *Mexicanos/Mexicans* on one, *Extranjeros/Foreigners* on the other. Beside each was a passage formed by moveable ropes, zig-zagging to a series of desks, each headed by a uniformed official. It seemed much the same as LA airport which I had just left: International-Airportese.

This seems a banal event with a thin set of signs. However, even the thinness of the signs is itself a sign. The behaviour of all these passengers was remarkably controlled by these few signs. Everyone joined a queue, no one pushing in front of anyone else. The barriers were flimsy, easily pushed aside, yet no one did so. *Semiotic and material conditions weave together as a functional, meaningful whole.* That is how semiotics works. We (international passengers) do most of the work. We read signs well and willingly obey. Our obedience signified obedience as one meaning. We assumed and created a harmonious, linear social world. We did so without thinking. The automatic reproduction of signs we have learned was part of the reassuring meaning we constructed. I know because I did it myself.

Verbal language plays a role. There were four words in two languages with two meanings, classifying the many nationalities present into two: Mexicans and non-Mexicans. I observed a small multimodal sign. The Spanish-language version of words was above the English. This signifies that Spanish here is more important than English. I connect this small sign to a bigger object of cultural meaning.

These brief pieces of text have their own complexity. They are single words, apparently without syntax, yet they are interpreted as analogue signs. They could be understood as commands: 'Mexicans (queue here)'. This command is communicated multimodally, inscribed in bodies that see what others are doing and join the queue. There are other prior statements presupposed: 'Identify yourself (as Mexican or foreigner)'. Behind this is another presupposition: 'Accept the authority of this airport to define you and control your behaviour'. *These major social meanings are unstated and invisible yet have decisive social effects.*

I accompanied Gabriela in the Mexican queue. I self-defined myself as partly Mexican, as a member of a Mexican family. The sign did not imply this fuzziness, but when I reached the customs officer I found he accepted the redefinition as I expected. He looked up from his computer and smiled at me. I know that computers are the master code in this multimodal cosmopolitan system. The database said that I was acceptable, a global citizen. I passed through. Gabriela caused brief confusion when she presented her Australian passport. But the potential rupture was quickly repaired when she explained her situation in perfect Spanish with a Mexico City accent. Redundancies in the multimodal system saved her.

Each 'I' who goes through is a single body, with a single identity. But 'intersectional analysis' (Cunneen and Stubbs 2004) sees me as the intersection of at least three systems – class, gender and ethnicity/nationality. As white and male, I belong to the dominant, Anglo but non-Mexican. Gabriela is white and female, and Mexican/non-Anglo. Here the categories non-Mexican/Anglo are sites of instability.

The ordinariness of this performance conceals how much semiotic work it rests on. This work connects with many larger themes. As I go through customs to book a taxi I encounter another reality. Mexican airport taxis are controlled because of the well-known threat of robbery or kidnapping by taxi drivers. If I extended the unit of analysis to include this phase, this would incorporate key contradictions of modern cosmopolitan Mexico.

I want to understand the *ethnos* as a complex social fact. But this *ethnos* shifts from site to site. In the airport I shared the *ethnos* of global passengers, some Mexican, and I used this competence to detect traces of the Mexican *ethnos* which co-exists in this space, under conditions that are part of my analysis.

As I go out into Mexico City I look for other Mexican versions of the *ethnos*, interpenetrated by different forms of US and global culture. The lessons of Orientalism warn me not to claim I know this *ethnos* better than Mexicans. However, there are profound differences among Mexicans and potential alliances with outsiders. *Social and political analysis is part of post-Orientalist ethnography.*

As a possible project I could assemble a set of places of entry to Mexico to include this airport, the heavily policed road border with the USA, and places where Mexicans enter the USA illegally. At every level, *boundaries and transitions are rich sources of social meaning.* Comparative ethnography could bring different inflections of the *ethnos* in sites where Mexican meanings are stronger or weaker compared with those of the global/US dominant.

Reframing linguistics

Revisiting linguistics fieldwork

I argue that social semiotics and critical discourse analysis (CDA) should look to linguistics for methods and insights. I also argue the converse. Social semiotics as a meta-discipline can identify limitations or distortions in traditional linguistics and help overcome them.

In the early twentieth century, American linguistics developed tools adapted to its major tasks in its then context: an Orientalist study of American Indian languages and cultures. To become usable in other contexts, the tools and practices need to be detached from that system and reimagined in new forms for new tasks and practices. *Disciplines in given contexts are analogue forms, systems linking practices, tasks, contexts and outcomes.*

Also in the early twentieth century, anthropology and linguistics in the USA were closely aligned, especially in the school founded by Franz Boas (1911), which included Edward Sapir (1921) and Benjamin Lee Whorf (1956). But anthropology and linguistics had drifted apart by the 1950s. Post-war anthropology across the world critiqued its fieldwork practices. Linguistics, however, shifted interest away from fieldwork. A survey by Paul Newman (2009) found that most US linguistics departments taught fieldwork methods in some form, but one-third reported no adequate training courses.

At the heart of linguistics method, its gift to anthropology, is the distinction between 'emic' and 'etic' description (Pike 1993). This reflected the difference between analogue and digital meanings. 'Phon*etics*' is a comprehensive, objective description of the sounds of human languages. 'Phon*emics*' describes the sounds of a language as elements in unique systems, in which each element has significant relationships to all other elements. 'Emic' descriptions throw light on systems of all kinds, linguistic and cultural. These systems are the mysterious objects of ethnography. Their coherence was seductive, leading ethnographers and linguists to exaggerate coherence. They ignored heterogeneity in the systems and conflicts between their users. As critics of Orientalism pointed out, this method of analysis was blind to differences and effects of power.

One powerful linguistic technique for finding emic structures is called 'minimal pairs'. To research a phonological system, linguists ask informants to compare two words with a single difference of sound. This allows their system to be built up as a system of differences. At the same time, the perception that the difference is minimal leads to the recognition that these elements are otherwise similar in a single system. In social semiotic terms the method is digital, used to reconstruct analogue forms (phonological systems, the *ethnos*).

This principle underlies a family of methods, starting with Jones's comparative analysis of related forms between Sanskrit, Greek and Latin. Jones analysed forms such as Sanskrit *pita*, Greek *pater*, Latin *pater*, Old English *faeder*, English father. In these clear cases he argued convincingly that these words had the same meaning because they referred to the same thing. Jones also made the powerful inference that, because many words from different languages were consistently related, the languages as a whole had the same genetic relationship. Minimal pairs of this type were motivated indexical signs marking stages of a transformation of sets of sounds, and thence whole language systems, producing dynamic maps of relationships between major languages.

Chomsky developed a powerful method that rests on a similar principle. He used his linguistic imagination to invent examples that seemed close to correct but were not, and he marked the wrong half of these minimal pairs with an asterisk – *. Chomsky's asterisks are usually seen as marking all ungrammatical forms, but in practice, like minimal pairs, they are ambiguous, signifying not acceptable, but interestingly close.

Similar forms at any level can be analysed closely, from modes to meanings and contexts, from small items to languages, ideologies and cultures, using digital analysis (binary terms) to project analogue meanings.

Language, culture and reality

I illustrate these concepts at work in the most famous article written by Whorf (1956: 138–9), who was a remarkable yet also typical linguist. He shows what linguistics then did and also what it could have done, then and now, within new contexts, with a new theoretical framework.

In some respects Whorf was Orientalist. Newman reports that working with 'a native informant' is still at the heart of linguistics fieldwork methods. Whorf did not mention it, but he relied mainly on just one Hopi speaker, then living in New York, with whom he worked for six years, between 1932 and 1938 (Carroll 1956). He never publicly acknowledged this informant. But in other ways Whorf did linguistics differently. He began with a conventional goal for linguistics, to describe a language, Hopi. He then revealed another goal: to 'stand aside from our own language' to understand other languages. We commonly see these through the lenses of our own, he said. But we do not understand our own either, from inside it. His solution is to study an 'exotic' language, 'for in its study we are at long last pushed willy-nilly out of our ruts' (Whorf 1956: 138). Although 'exotic' seems an Orientalist word, Whorf inverted the Orientalist gaze. *Difference here is not a barrier to understanding others. It becomes part of a strategy to respect others and understand ourselves.* This is not 'relativism' as commonly understood. It is 'making strange', a strategic, respectful use of difference.

Buried in Whorf's practice was a revolutionary innovation in method: his use of his intuitions about his own language as primary data. In anthropology this came to be known as 'auto-ethnography' (Denzin and Lincoln 2008). In linguistics it underpins Chomsky's use of 'intuitions' as a native speaker to build and test hypotheses about language as a system: 'Suppose that we assume intuitive knowledge of the grammatical sentences of English and ask what sort of grammar will do the job of producing these in some effective and illuminating way' (Chomsky 1957: 13).

Whorf compared two language families to generate statements which could be said in one but not the other. In the process he could have marked aberrant forms with Chomskyan asterisks. He used this method at many levels, from large scale (a language, a culture) to very small (minute features of linguistic or cultural systems). Because it is driven by perception of difference, it may seem to take difference for granted. But differences become significant only when two forms or systems are put together in the first place. His method is better seen as *a dialectic between sameness and difference, a capacity to perceive sameness in difference and difference in sameness.*

Whorf's emic descriptions were overlaid with an etic grid, drawn from his extensive knowledge of related and different languages – for example, 'Where possible state avoidance of commonly found categories, e.g. no plural, no gender' (1956: 129). He also continually compared his own language, English, and the language he was studying – comparative emics. In practice he used *a series of double perspectives, emic and etic, analogue and digital, whole and part, English and Hopi, universalistic and relativistic*. His purpose was not to impose English onto Hopi, but to recognize how strange English looks through Hopi eyes. This led to remarkable insights into English that are a still untapped resource for linguistics and CDA. The example he gives, plurals, illustrates the point. He noted that 'we say "ten men" and also "ten days"' (1956: 139), but according to his Hopi informant the two are distinct. They form a minimal pair in Hopi but not English.

Whorf here *referred to reality as an arbiter of difference*. This contradicts the so-called Sapir–Whorf hypothesis attributed to him: that language constructs reality, which is otherwise inaccessible to analysts. The actual Whorf notes the distinction in reality that underpins the Hopi distinction. Hopi and English speakers alike see ten men and count them, but English speakers can count 'days' only after they have objectified them, turned them into 'imaginary plurals' (1956: 139).

The linguistic feature is small, but its implications are profound. It connects with a similar pattern of objectification endemic in 'Standard Average European' (SAE) languages, as Whorf called them, the languages of England and Spain, which colonized and despised the indigenous peoples of the Americas. Whorf's diagnosis converges with that of Marx (1972), who saw a similar process, 'commodification', as a foundational premise in capitalism.

Critical linguistics as practice

During 1973, Gunther Kress and I worked intensively on the theory that was to become critical linguistics, critical discourse analysis. I use one example to illustrate some principles and practices at that stage in social semiotics' emergence.

Our first analysis in *Language as Ideology* (1979) was intended to be exemplary: an eleven-page analysis of a complete 486-word text, a *Guardian* editorial of 20 December 1973. First I note the date. It implies what was in fact the case, that this analysis was a nearly instant response to immediate events. English miners took industrial action that winter, and their ban on overtime was biting. Edward Heath's Conservative government legislated a 'three-day week' in response, a government equivalent of going slow.

Kress and I wanted our analytic method to be responsive. With hindsight, I now see that this analysis of a naturally occurring corpus could be complemented by a longer-term analysis with a larger corpus. We could not know it then, but the miners won this confrontation, and the Conservatives lost power. But in 1984–5 Maggie Thatcher learned from Heath's failure and smashed the miners, weakened the unions, and radically changed British political culture. It is not that we were wrong, just that *diachronic analysis can introduce chaotic twists and turns.*

We focused on political functions of specific linguistic forms, but our methods were closer to traditional linguistic analysis than we emphasized. We analysed the editorial as a corpus, describing and itemizing the dominant forms as a functional grammar of the text. Constructing corpuses is a crucial but often neglected aspect of analytic method for CDA (Carbó 2007). In a similar move to Whorf's we referred to reality, asking what linguistic forms the situation could be expected to produce, and we noted discrepancies. We treated linguistic forms and processes as meanings and operations on meaning and read their social meaning against our understanding of the political situation.

I illustrate the editorial's language from its first paragraph:

2.3 A three-day week for industry is extremely hurtful. A sudden blackout for a whole city the size of Leicester or Bradford is worse. It can kill people. (*The Guardian*, 20 December 1973)

We noted first that this editorial was supposedly about actions taken by the sides in conflict, but it has few of the forms that express causality in English, especially transitives. These are mostly displaced from the surface, as with 'is . . . hurtful' (for 'hurts'). On the rare occasions it appears, as in 'It can kill people', the subject is not a person but an abstract thing ('a three-day week'). Another part of this pattern was the fact that action was always associated with the miners, not the government.

Instead of action statements, the editorial is full of statements of judgement or evaluation (e.g., 'is hurtful'). Those acts of judgement are then turned into imaginary objects of the same kind that Whorf noted is typical of SAE languages like English. The 'three-day week' is an example of something the Hopi could not say and could not think existed as an entity.

A similar analysis now with the benefit of hindsight might ask different questions and use a larger corpus. For instance, in the light of the collapse of the left under Thatcher's later ruthless attack on the miners, we might both see greater significance in *The Guardian*'s representation of the government as powerless and study changes in a corpus from 1973–4 and 1984–5. Given this newspaper's position as the voice of the progressive left, the analysis may illuminate Thatcherism as a phenomenon that did not yet exist when we wrote. No analysis is tied to a specific interpretation or use.

Rethinking CDA

Many students have found Norman Fairclough's model (1992: 10) useful for analysing language and power. It is a simple, clear guide to practice. I adapt it to make it more semiotic, to make it more widely usable, to illustrate continuities between linguistics, critical linguistics and CDA over this time.

Without changing Fairclough's model I note that 'text' can function in a multimodal framework. I also note that, from a semiotic perspective, interactions and social action are both carried by semiotic modes, non-verbal behavioural codes, allowing all of Fairclough's levels to be analysed in the same terms, as multimodal social meanings. Fairclough inserts 'text' in the processes of interaction, between the production and the interpretation that constitute it. This is the dialogic principle which is basic for social semiotics. Basic, too, is the idea that the two *semiosic processes, production and interpretation, affect each other and the text itself as components of a common system.*

Fairclough distinguished between *cues* in the text guiding interpretation and *traces* of processes of production. In the Kress–Hodge analysis it would have been helpful to mark these two different orientations. For instance, the predominance of clauses of judgement is arguably a trace of habitual modes of thought. The accusatory directness of 'It can kill' is probably a cue.

CDA in Fairclough's model consists of three phases: description (of texts), interpretation (of texts and contexts) and explanation (of relations and social action). For social semiotic purposes I reframe this list. *'Description' should not be 'mere' description, but always analytic, used of all levels.* Likewise, *'interpretation' is deployed on social actions and contexts as well as texts.* Here social semiotic methods of tracking meaning come into play. Finally, *'explanation' connects*

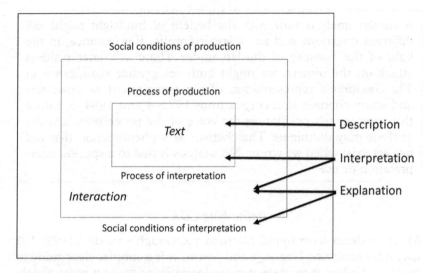

Figure 2.1 A three-dimensional model for discourse analysis
Source: Based on Fairclough (1989: 25–6)

individual elements with major analogue signs in the context, guiding belief and action.

Anomaly

According to Thomas Kuhn's theory of scientific revolutions, anomalies play a paradoxical role. No scientific paradigm accounts for all observed facts, he claims. There are always 'anomalies' (Greek *a*, not + *nomos*, law). But even when scientists are 'confronted by severe and prolonged anomalies' they normally do not abandon paradigms (Kuhn 1962: 77). Instead they devote massive efforts to re-examining the terms of the anomaly, changing everything except the paradigm's core premises. Anomalies generate research. When paradigms finally change, it is a direct effect not of the truth of the anomaly but of the paradigm community's crisis of belief.

In cybernetic terms, this history signals homeostatic social processes that correct anomalies until a tipping point is reached when resistance collapses. Every system has anomalies which ultimately reveal its limits and internal contradictions, the site where its logic generates alternative logics that can replace it. Alternatives will be resisted by homeostatic forces and may never appear in recognizable or feasible forms. But *focus on anomalies is a key heuristic strategy for social semiotics.*

Discovery spirals

Fairclough lists explanation as an important goal for analysis. Discovery is equally important. Social semiotics is a hermeneutic practice, part of a trend that entered sociology relatively recently (Thompson 1984), as part of the 'turn' to meaning. The concept 'hermeneutic circle' was influential in philosophy (e.g., Heidegger 1971) and social sciences (e.g., Gadamer 1989).

Here I adapt a version of this model, which Leo Spitzer (1948) called the 'philological circle'. He combined linguistics, the historical linguistics he was trained in, and literary studies and called the combination 'literary stylistics'. This is currently a minor sub-discipline of linguistics. In this section I combine Spitzer and CDA in a general social semiotic model to analyse many kinds of text and problem.

Spitzer (1948) usually started from an intuition. Thus 'the first step, on which all may hinge, can never be planned.' He noticed 'an aberration' of language in a major literary text, so close to ungrammatical as to justify a Chomskyan asterisk, but saw it instead as a trace of emerging new forms. Small anomalies can signify major fissures. They can be studied in a small amount of text, in focal texts. Spitzer guessed the meaning and rationale and connected these to ideas of the author and the age. He then returned to details of the text, marking and collecting other examples, aberrant or not, which showed a similar pattern, to expand the material for analysis. Figure 2.2 shows the amount of text for analysis growing systematically with each return of the spiral to produce a heterogeneous corpus. *Spitzer oscillated between small and large scale in a hermeneutic spiral crossing a common fissure across language, meaning and society.*

Spitzer drew on ideas from the nineteenth-century philosopher Hegel (1977), who understood history as a succession of turning points in an unfolding dialectic of what he called the *Zeitgeist* ('spirit of the age'). Marx attacked Hegel's metaphysical version of history (Marx and Engels [1845] 1976). However, Marx's view of history was also dialectical, and 'turning' or 'tipping' points make sense in contemporary chaos theory. Spitzer's model can complement Fairclough's in a hybrid model that is more sociological and materialist than Spitzer's own, more systematically multiscalar than CDA.

Social semiotics, like CDA, starts from a complex, multiscalar object composed of interactions between language, meaning and

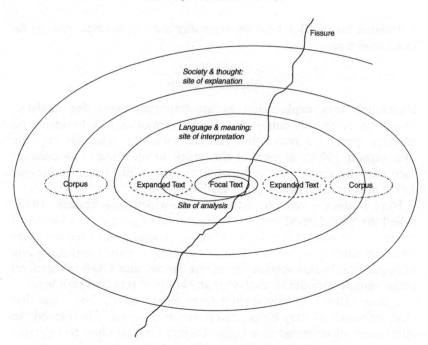

Figure 2.2   Spitzer's hermeneutic circle
Source: Based on Spitzer (1948)

society, text plus event. Spitzer's spiral form is useful to guide research. So is his idea that *the trigger for the journey is the perception of anomaly.*

Spitzer's work gives a new perspective on the role of 'critical'. As its name implies, CDA is definitionally critical. Spitzer valued the literary works he studied, and critical activists could apply his appreciative orientation to texts by many agents in any given struggle – e.g., victims of oppression, participants with valuable insights, Gramsci's 'organic intellectuals' (1971). *To engage in social struggles, social semiotics needs a range of strategic options, appreciation as well as criticism.*

Both models have only three levels. But society and text exist on far more than three scales. Different dimensions intersect at all levels *and need multiscalar maps and fuzzy strategies to track them.* Some strategies begin with larger scales and move in towards smaller scales. Others begin with smaller scales and move outwards towards larger scales. Fractal theory is a strategy to track patterns across many different levels in both directions. *Both orientations need to be combined, oscillating between larger and smaller, smaller and larger.*

As a brief example of the hermeneutic spiral, I take the case of Obama's tie. Watching and rewatching the video, I was troubled by the fact that both Obama and Cameron wore blue ties. This was a difference which seemed not to make a difference. As I thought more about it I realized what I felt was wrong. Cameron was a conservative. Blue as a colour signifies political conservativism, so the colour was right for him. But why did Obama wear a blue tie? It was almost ungrammatical for him. My first interpretation was that he was specifically negating semiotic carriers of difference and the system which created them. I returned to the text in my hermeneutic spiral and found him doing something similar with presents. Although he ended with difference (in temperature), his other categories converged: symmetrical gifts, both alcoholic beverages, both beers, of low economic value, gifts that were not really gifts. Following the spiral into the wider context, spatial and temporal, I connected it with his conscious political project, to minimize political differences with his Republican opponents. In 2015, as I write this, five years later, the fate of that project seems an ever more intractably divided political landscape.

But the lack of fit between the meaning of Obama's anomaly and this outcome does not show that Spitzer's spiral does not work. On the contrary, the two meanings, Obama's project and the Republican response, are significant as mirror images of each other. By the ferocity with which it was rejected, Obama's healing project showed how much it was needed. Hermeneutic analysis in a Marxist framework does not show a 'spirit of the age' replicated in reality, as in Hegel's model. *It discovers deep meanings produced in struggle and possible new outcomes that may never emerge.*

When things go wrong

In Chomsky's influential formulation 'linguistic theory is concerned primarily with an ideal speaker-listener, in a completely homogenous speech community' (1965: 3). He distinguished between 'competence', as an ideal construction of the knowledge of this 'ideal speaker-hearer', versus 'performance', how language is actually used, and he argued that the study of 'competence' could develop models to explain 'performance' better. Social semiotics shows the inverse is true as well. 'Performance' is also crucial to understanding 'competence'. We must explore *'when things go wrong'*, to use Carbó's evocative phrase (2004), *to discover how systems really work, as key to selecting what to analyse, and why.*

Clifford Geertz (1973) was an influential figure straddling linguistics, anthropology and social semiotics who embedded his term 'thick description' in brilliant analyses of social meaning in practice. The metaphor 'thick' refers to the number of semiotic modes and frames of reference involved in the description. At the heart of 'thick description' is the reason it is necessary. Geertz was fascinated by apparently minor incidents which explode. Such events have inexhaustible reverberations, because they cannot be captured by dominant frames of meaning and systems of control. Unlike the anomalies on which Spitzer focused, they are events surrounded by texts rather than texts signalling fissures in the world around them. But Spitzer's and Geertz's approaches are complementary.

I built on Geertz's ideas with input from ideas from chaos and complexity to develop a method I called 'critical incident analysis' (Hodge and Matthews 2011). From chaos theory came the proposition that, *when systems are far-from-equilibrium, they can go 'critical', as in states of nuclear meltdown, reaching a 'tipping point', subject to cascades of criticality* (Bak 1996). In such states there can be butterfly effects, small causes which trigger major catastrophes or surprising breakthroughs. They typically cross the boundaries of categories which normally contain them.

Critical incidents are social phenomena, not semiotic forms. Critical incident analysis provides a model of situations as guide to what incidents best repay analysis. They are not tied to kinds of discursive processes or ways of analysing them. Yet the critical incident model is useful in deciding what to analyse with thick descriptions and how to interpret the results.

For illustration I use another text from my Obama corpus, from another ceremonial occasion at the White House, on 10 January 2011:

2.4 President Obama and First Lady Michelle Obama stood silently on the South Lawn of the White House at 11 am Eastern Time with more than 200 White House staffers. A chime rang three times, and those assembled bowed their heads. (Nakamura and Branigin 2011)

This act commemorated six people killed by 22-year-old Jared Loughner, in Tucson, Arizona, two days before. At the time his target, the Democrat Congresswoman Gabrielle Giffords, was alive but in a critical condition.

In this case the massacre, not this ceremony, was the critical incident, *but events and reactions form a single explanatory unit.* The incident is an inverse image of Obama's press conference with Cameron. In my thick description of that conference, the main action seemed to take place in words, unobtrusively supported by many other semiotic systems. In this ceremony, reported in the mono-modal form of a news story, no words were used. But multimodality is crucial to the incident and its analysis. Loughner used actions, with few words. His 'meanings' came from the barrel of a gun, a message disconnected from words. This incident triggered a crisis of reality systems in language.

There is also a crisis of social categories, the basic paradigmatic categories that normally manage difference in a society. The terms that would describe Loughner and his target were opposites, a digital, binary structure split down the middle. He was young, male, socially marginal and conservative. Giffords was mature, a woman with power, politically on the left. A social meaning of Loughner's act for him was that these qualities were irreconcilable. Another meaning, expressed by the semiotics of the action, was that words, the domi-nant code, could not express or bridge the opposition. Problems of social structure interacted with problems of code to multiply the crisis.

Thus far I am treating the report as reliable and transparent, but it is a thin description in print mode. In this case, since the theme was the threat to the prevailing multimodal system, we need to infer the context. For instance, the text does not include the verbal command someone must have issued to get the silence. Nor does it include the media processes which take these images into millions of American homes.

Thin description has a place when beginning to analyse critical incidents, but thicker description needs to take over.

Recuperation

A crucial phase in analysing critical incidents is to look diagnostically at strategies of recuperation. Cybernetically, Obama's action was designed to cancel the disruptive effect of this unassimilable meaning/act. The legal system also responded quickly to recuperate the inci-dent. The accused was reported as answering the judge's question in a firm voice in the first court hearing, which began the process of incorporating this incident into society's terms and rituals. Again the media played a supporting role, seeking Loughner's motives through the words and clues that society needed to believe that he must have given to those who knew him:

2.5 Bryce Tierney, a friend of Jared Loughner, said: 'Loughner had held a long-held grudge against Giffords since he attended a campaign event – possibly in 2007 – and did not get an answer to a question he asked her. Afterwards Loughner repeatedly called Giffords a "fake"' Tierney said. (Nakamura and Branigin 2011)

Again I thicken this description, drawing on sociolinguistic research of everyday discourse. Tierney is quoted as calling the shooter 'Loughner'. Calling someone by their surname in standard American English signals social distance (Brown and Ford 1961), the same distance as with 'Giffords'. We can infer that Tierney was not such a close friend or that important things have been lost in the transition from speech to writing. Or both. There are other signs of editorial intervention, by the reporters or the newspaper, constructing a reassuringly rational friend for this pathologically friendless person.

This incident might have had enough momentum to change US gun laws, as Obama hoped. But critical incident analysis includes the cybernetics of how they were finally contained, by whom, and how.

To begin to follow this line of research I used internet searches to build a corpus around this incident, to include the National Rifle Association (NRA), the US pro-gun lobby, whose cause was damaged by this incident and which needed to repair the discursive damage. In this case, as in all other mass shootings to date, NRA strategies proved sufficient to neutralize the impact of this incident, in spite of the best that Obama could do.

It is a major challenge for social semiotics to examine the success of US pro-gun law lobbyists in neutralizing such monstrous anomalies to their position as the twelve deaths in Columbine High School in 1999 and the twenty-six deaths in the Sandy Hook Primary School in 2012. The NRA's first tactic was silence, followed by attempts to shift blame. Wayne LaPierre, CEO of the NRA, began a speech on 1 October: 'We continue to pray for [the victims] and wish them well', before blaming 'the media' for 'making a celebrity out of the deranged killer' (Stein 2011). The inclusive 'we' blurs boundaries between the NRA and the 'God-fearing' majority. 'Deranged' turns a compressed, disputed narrative about his motives into Loughner's defining characteristic. This characteristic, madness, then serves to separate him from the rest of society, all supposedly sane. Social analysis then appears, but only in the form of media critique.

Loughner is not a Chomskyan 'ideal speaker'. Yet his performance reveals another side of the same systems that Obama exploits with such skill. We cannot understand a system that produces such contradictory results without studying situations where 'things go wrong'. We *need to understand the meanings of non-ideal agents* (mad, marginalized and incompetent or ruthless, cunning and amoral) who also exist in massive numbers, whose system it also is. *We also need to recognize the force and effect of other non-ideal agents* whose tactics and meanings sometimes prevail.

Hidden meanings and everyday life

In this section I combine two themes that often come together in social semiotic investigations: everyday life and the hermeneutic search for hidden meanings. In an influential work, Henri Lefebvre saw everyday life as a neglected site for Marxist analysis, as the 'intersection of illusion and truth, power and helplessness, the intersection of the sector man [*sic*] controls and the sector he does not control' (1947: 40). *Social semiotics plays a valuable role where hidden meanings erupt into social life*, when even skilful social agents find their 'competence' stretched.

I illustrate with the following text, from a telephone conversation I had with a woman I name Helen. She described an incident at her office Christmas party:

2.6 I said I'd got through the year without making any lawyer jokes, and my manager looked a bit strange.

As normal for social semiotics, I explain the immediate context. Helen had been in this job for only a year. She is an accountant, working mainly with lawyers in a community legal centre for people with low incomes, with a woman manager.

I treat Helen's account as a thick description of the context. For instance, she says 'my manager', giving neither first name nor full name plus title. This paradigmatic choice has social meaning. The set of terms oppose boss to friend/acquaintance, signalling a relationship of power rather than solidarity. Yet this is countered by the choice of 'my', not 'the'. The result is a contradictory signal about the relationship according to Helen. It includes both solidarity and power.

Helen's problem is a joke that went wrong. It is a small-scale critical incident. Her joke pivots around implied negatives, which paraphrase brings out:

2.7a I have got through the year without telling any lawyer jokes. ←
2.7b I have not told any lawyer jokes for a year.

The surface form de-emphasizes the negative, though it is still understood. It turns the adverbial phrase 'for a year' into a main clause which begins the joke, 'I have got through the year without . . .' As Whorf might note, this sees time as a metaphor of space.

As well as local instances of negation, the whole joke hinges around negation. This statement is a joke about lawyers, so Helen is making a lawyer joke at the very moment she denies she is doing so. For a Spitzerian analysis, the repeated negations are significant. Negation is a powerful operation for Freud, who saw it as a potent generator of ambiguity. He argued that it often signified the positive form visible under the negated surface form.

One problem with this joke is not that the manager did not understand it, but that she understood it too well. She crashed through the buffers Helen had inserted to make this a joke rather than an insult. But jokes always take this risk. The forbidden content has to be seen, or people will not get it, but not seen, or people will be offended. This joke went wrong partly because the two people framed it differently. Office relationships are structured by dimensions of power and solidarity. Managers exercise power, but only up to a point. They need also to maintain solidarity. This may even enhance their power. Obama traded power for solidarity without losing power. Given that this was an office party, Helen could have expected fewer assertions of power. This could have been a successful joke, a complex, subtle, socially competent mix of insult and goodwill towards her colleagues.

Helen's joke was only a failure after the manager used her authority to declare it one. In this respect, it was the manager who made the mistake, misinterpreting a joke by resurrecting a deep structure she should have ignored. Where the US president used jokes to relieve tensions, this manager turned a joke that did just that into an offence. In the process she did not enhance her power. Her assertion of power against Helen weakened her own status, isolating her.

Jokes are excellent objects for social semiotic analysis precisely because there is no objective guide as to what is a good or bad joke. Their content reflects complexities of relationships in the situation. Here, differences of power are crucial.

This analysis is a 'thick description' of a minor incident whose implications reverberate higher in the system. There are many possible uses of this analysis. The incident illuminates configurations of power and solidarity in Helen's workplace whose toxicity she already knew, but not in such depth.

This section describes everyday social semiotic advice for Helen to use or not as she liked. I emphasize two points. *Normal social interaction is characterized by shifting relations of power and solidarity, which frame social semiotic analysis of every instance, small or large.* In this situation, *meanings are routinely shifted, changed, concealed or distorted, seen differently or denied by all participants.*

> There is a rich field of sociological study of ambiguities provoked by different attitudes to organizations. For example, Pauksztat et al. (2011) surveyed 146 non-managerial employees of an organization and found that 'loyalty' empowered some and inhibited others from expressing the dissent that organizations need. A 'thick description' of Helen's small office could generate rich hypotheses about contradictory outcomes where dysfunctional styles of management cannot balance power and solidarity skilfully.

Big research

Thus far I have talked mainly about small-scale investigations within the reach of individuals armed only with ideals, semiotic skills and a computer. But social semiotics is multiscalar and needs to confront the opportunities and risks of big research.

Science and technology research has multi-million dollar budgets. Until recently this has not been an option for humanities and social science researchers. Nowotny et al. (2001) proposed a new, more inclusive research model they call 'Mode 2'. Mode 1 research was based in disciplinary structures housed in universities. Mode 2 research responds to the increasingly complex problems of modern society. It is collaborative and interdisciplinary, orientated to solving real-world problems using digital technologies.

Should humanities and social science researchers explore this option? If so, could social semiotics be of use?

In what follows I report on my personal attempt to work with this model. In 2010 I became part of a successful bid process for a proposal for a Cooperative Research Centre (CRC) in Australia: $27m over five years, with over seventy partners, universities, government bodies, NGOs and industry bodies in the areas of health and digital technologies. Our project, inspired by an organization called Inspire, addressed the endemic problem of youth mental health and suicide rates, looking for solutions in digital technologies and young people's use of them.

Partners in the mental health and youth sectors were convinced that the current system of health care for young people was not reaching or connecting with them. Its top-down system needed energy and initiative from below, from young people using digital technologies in empowering ways. The CRC was explicitly framed as a radical intervention. *Being big helped give its interventions impact.*

Collaborative social semiotics

In this section I use social semiotics as an ad hoc interdisciplinary collaborative practice, attaching feedback loops to research conceived and driven by others, *to sketch a role for social semiotic disciplines in big research.* I organize these interventions through a hermeneutic spiral.

1 *Theory* I start my multiscalar spiral from outside the project, *exploring big meanings in complex forms: theory.* I begin with a familiar place, sociological classics, in this case Durkheim's *Suicide* (1952). *Social semiotics reads theory as data,* as source of key meanings. 'Reading theory' is a key social semiotic strategy.

Durkheim's research object was big – suicide across Europe and the USA. Beyond that he had an even bigger object: 'the causes of the contemporary maladjustment being undergone by European societies' (1952: 47). He sought to uncover what he termed 'social fact', a 'collective reality' (1952: 48) – a very large, complex multiscalar entity that he believed became visible only through sociological research, but which determined individual realities. Durkheim's research object was big, but his research was not so big by modern standards of big research. *Big meanings and big research are separate qualities.*

I cannot expect most of my CRC partners to read Durkheim's book. It is my task as a team member to mediate it in this interdisciplinary project, as they too mediate what they know. *In Big Research no one knows everything; everyone knows something.*

2 *Social semiotics and sociological method* I read Durkheim with a double gaze: as a sociology classic, and as if he was a classic of social semiotics. As a proto-semiotician he took suicide as a primary signifier, a motivated sign of dysfunctional societies which produced them. He then used statistics as signifiers of suicide. Although statistics were his main data, Durkheim had an exemplary

distrust of mere numbers. He treated them as statements, signs needing interpretation, not raw facts. More radical semiotically, he proposed that the same signifier, suicide, could have four different, contradictory meanings, which sociological investigation could disambiguate.

Durkheim proposed four types of suicide: egoistic, anomic, altruistic and fatalistic. Egoistic suicide proceeded from lack of social integration, in societies that lacked means of integration. Anomic suicide proceeded from lack of social control, in societies that lacked controls. Altruistic suicide proceeded from excessive social integration, while fatalistic suicide was associated with excess of control.

Durkheim defined egoistic suicide:

> 2.8 If we agree to call this state egoism, in which the individual ego asserts itself to excess in the face of the social ego and at its expense, we may call egoistic the special type of suicide springing from excessive individualism. (Durkheim 1952: 209)

CDA/social semiotic analysis uncovers local social meanings in this text. 'If we agree' constructs a community of readers. They ostensibly have power to agree or not, but Durkheim immediately goes on to take their agreement for granted. He constructs imaginary solidarity to assert imaginary power. His terms introduce powerful value judgements. 'Egoistic' (French *egoistique*) carries heavy negative judgement, as do repetitions of 'excess(ive)'.

But Durkheim's basic model, his underlying analogue model or meaning, is more complex and contradictory. In spite of his surface emphasis on integration and order, two of his categories reflect the damaging effects of excessive integration and control.

Durkheim used two modes of research, which today might be called 'qual' and 'quant', combining them in ways which *foreshadow the now fashionable category 'mixed methods'*. In the process he produced *multimodal texts, combining words, numbers and maps*. He used literary texts to illustrate his types, to build a rich picture of them as complex analogue meanings. Durkheim did not mark his use of qualitative research, but it played a major role. His practice was richer than his theory, as social semiotics can point out.

3 *Project design* Good research needs an angle on its big meanings, to inflect or transform them. The next loop of my hermeneutic spiral reaches the CRC project aims. Without using Durkheim's terms, egoism and anomie, the CRC reversed their emotional charge. They

gave positive value to young people's typical behaviour. Young people are usually condemned as much today as in Durkheim as 'egoistic'. But the CRC invoked a widely blamed cause – young people's love of new technologies – as a site for solutions.

The juxtaposition with Durkheim brings out how revolutionary this project is. If it succeeds it will find a solution in what is usually seen as the problem. It uses the power of digital technologies, again often seen as a problem, to make the revolution thinkable. By *connecting the project's practical aims with these big meanings, its outcomes become more significant.*

4 *Individual research* The CRC programme consisted of many interconnected projects, not a single massive experiment with consolidated data. *Mode 2 research uses a dispersed strategy linking many projects.*

The next stage of my spiral brings a semiotic perspective to the level of individual projects. Two CRC partners, Mission Australia and the Black Dog Institute, commissioned and published a survey, the *Youth Mental Health Report* (Ivancic et al. 2014), which surveyed 14,461 young people and applied a psychological test, Kessler 6, which correlates behaviours with diagnoses. On this basis they divided the cohort into two. One cohort had 'probable serious mental illness', the other not. The authors added 'probable' to signify caution. Kessler 6 is supported by both the Australian Bureau of Statistics and the World Health Organization. That authority is a conventional sign which gives them legitimacy. This is all good informal semiotics.

The authors' main claim has *the standard format for sociological reports, which is multimodal (words and numbers):*

2.9 Just over one fifth (21.2%) of young people aged 15–19 who responded to the survey met the criteria for having a probable serious mental illness. (Ivancic et al. 2014: 6)

The report lists twelve 'issues' (i.e., meanings) and gives the proportions of those whose meanings they are. For example, 61.6 per cent of those with 'probable mental illness' say they are 'concerned/very concerned' about 'school or study problems', against only 31.3 per cent of those with no probable mental illness. The measures are crude, but the social semiotic picture, the fuzzy analogue meaning, is rich and productive.

Table 2.1 rates answers to questions about how comfortable young people are in seeking help from different sources. The final column I

Table 2.1   Sources of help and mental illness

Source of help	Probable mental illness %	No probable mental illness %	Durkheim type
Friend(s)	13.2	4.5	± egoistic
Internet	15.7	10.9	± egoistic
Parent	32.8	10.3	± anomic
School counsellor	51.9	38.3	± anomic

Source: Adapted from Ivancic et al. (2014: 10)

have added classifies these as signifiers of Durkheim's categories. These figures suggest this cohort is more likely to be anomic than egoistic, in Durkheim's terms, and more strongly so for those with 'probable' mental illness. What social semiotics adds to good basic sociological research is this conceptual linking role. Since these meanings are connected with likely behaviours, *this reading of these figures connects meanings and actions in a single complex whole.* It links individuals and social forces across distorting divisions between macro- and micro-analysis. It illustrates the general point *that social semiotics and standard quantitative sociology are compatible and complementary.*

Big meanings, close readings

In this final section I develop an interdisciplinary thought experiment, related to big research but less closely. *There is a fuzzy continuum of relationships between more and less free-standing semiotic research. Research groups can be too tightly as well as too weakly organized.* To illustrate, I use a hermeneutic spiral to analyse the famous first line of Hamlet's soliloquy:

2.10 * To be or not to be, that is the question. (Shakespeare 1963: 93)

CDA's object of analysis combines language, meaning and society, texts produced in interactions in social contexts. Hamlet's words can be interpreted in relation to three contexts. In the play they are spoken by Hamlet, prince of a dysfunctional state, medieval Denmark, as he contemplates suicide. They occur in a play, a soliloquy before an audience who lived in dysfunctional Elizabethan England. I read them in dysfunctional twenty-first-century Australia. This is diachronic analysis, with problems of connections and incommensurability across turbulent stretches of time.

Hamlet's language here is anomalous. I draw on my intuitions about normal English. Adjusting for differences in time and genre, the sentence seems so odd I give it an asterisk. It is ungrammatical (lacking a main verb, using auxiliaries as substantive verbs). It is also problematic socially. Like Anders Breivik, this man is talking to himself.

Soliloquies were a dramatic convention of the time. But conventions still have social meaning. In this play the disturbed usurper king Claudius speaks to himself once. Mad Ophelia, a female suicide, talks and sings to herself. Only Hamlet has regular soliloquies. In a Spitzerian reading, multiple forms of a similar aberration, distributed between different characters and levels, add up to a single complex sign, of Hamlet's, Shakespeare's, a sixteenth-century English crisis. Or, as some claim, a European crisis of modernity, still unfolding in the twenty-first century.

Paraphrase helps to show how aberrant the sentence is:

2.11a The (my) question is whether I should continue to live or not.

Or to push it further into clarity, though away from what he says:

2.11b I ask myself whether I will kill myself (or someone else – e.g., Claudius his uncle, whose murder is also on his mind) or not.

These paraphrases identify the acute problems of this text. They show Hamlet's inability to ask a proper question. He gives two alternatives, without words or intonation to mark that this is a question. Then he states that it is a question. 'Question' could have meant 'topic for debate'. Even so it is still strange usage.

Spitzer's method looks for something common to a set of anomalies. In this case, Hamlet eliminates 'I', the pronoun which carries his self-identity. Removing 'I' is an iconic sign, reflecting in language what suicides do in reality. He collapses the two key terms of normal social interaction, 'I' and 'you'. He also distances words from what they are about, especially the key words 'life' and 'death', 'kill' and 'live'. He cannot talk about what his decision means, much less what his choice would be.

In Durkheim's terms, Hamlet is an egoistic suicide, though there are elements of anomie too, in the clash between his overdeveloped conscience and the moral flux of Denmark. I am interested in Shakespeare's implicit theory of suicidal mentalities. He embeds this in a richer set of mechanisms of language and meaning, from which sociologists and psychologists could still learn much. *His complex analogue meaning helps explain a common process found at many levels, at many times.*

To connect more directly with my CRC colleagues, I look at contemporary instances of youth suicide. On 30 January 2008, a seventeen-year-old Australian schoolgirl, Hannah Modra, killed herself. Eight months later a TV programme, 'The girl least likely', was broadcast about the tragedy (ABC 2008). Most participants were friends and family, who expressed surprise and shock at what had happened, interspersed with extracts from Hannah's diary, read in voice-over. Here is her final entry:

2.12 Fainted at school today, at the front of the whole assembly. Most people managed to finish all their homework. I feel like I can't do anything.

This seems a simple text, but in the context that is the first aberration. The first challenge of Hannah's case was that no one saw it coming. Were there signs that everyone missed?

CDA uses context as a starting point for analysis. Here there are two contexts, Hannah's situation writing alone in her room and the context for the incident. The incident was highly embarrassing, but Hannah mentions no feelings of shame or any other feelings that will lead her to kill herself in a few hours. She uses the word 'feel', but this is more about what she thinks, not what she feels, and what she 'feels' is the absence of action. A diary is in ways a real-life soliloquy. One social meaning of her writing is that, like Hamlet, Hannah cannot tell even her private self what she truly thinks and feels.

Looking at the language of the text as carrier of social meaning, two small signs repay attention. The first sentence lacks 'I', like Hamlet's. Hannah's syntax is bare – three sentences strung together with no connectors. Her text lacks what Halliday (1985) called cohesion, elements that hold it together. Her perceptions do not cohere. These two qualities are so normal in diaries they may seem insignificant, but for social semiotics *signs are significant even when they are common.*

'Big research' is often associated with science and technology research, where huge international teams with vast budgets address problems so large and complex as to need that support. Humanities and social sciences research equally 'big meanings' which need smaller but still heterogeneous, well-financed teams. *But bigger research is not always better. It produces new wholes which, like all social groups and bodies of meaning, can be too tightly or too weakly bonded, incoherent or oppressively unified*. Social semiotics exists to tell the difference.

Suicide is a big theme. Durkheim's classic study was big research in its time. There is scope today for different kinds of research, big and small, motivated by big meanings, in which social semiotics can play a part at every stage and level. A deep analysis using close reading of a multimodal corpus may produce insights that we urgently need, analysing only a few Hannahs, and perhaps one Hamlet.

PART II

From Linguistics to Semiotics

3
Words

I have been in love with words for longer than I can remember. I was always multimodal, but speech became my primary challenge as a semiotic animal, words my focus. I have produced and interpreted so many words they could have lost their capacity to amaze and enlighten me. Why should social semioticians still attend to words?

But words are surprisingly marginalized in modern linguistics. Alan Cruse diagnosed a crucial gap between attitudes of 'the layman' (2004: 81), who sees words as the primary bearers of meaning, and linguists, in whose 'more formally oriented accounts word meanings are left largely unanalysed, or reduced to mere skeletons of their true selves' (2004: 85). In this chapter I argue that words are vital in more complex ways than most people realize.

Literary studies values words highly, even if only in literary texts. T. S. Eliot (1963: 194) wrote that words

3.1 Slip, slide, perish,
Decay with imprecision, will not stay in place.

Words for Eliot are not the fixed marks on white paper of printed texts but unstable unions of signifiers – written words and sounds they refer to – and signifieds, shifting meanings in his mind and his community of readers. In semiotics Saussure analysed diachrony similarly. Signifiers and signifieds drift apart inexorably, driven by forces so irrational Saussure despaired of understanding them. Eliot, a Nobel Prizewinning poet, understood basic semiotics, syntagms, paradigms and diachrony.

In this chapter I examine words in a social semiotic framework, bringing out their complicating properties most shared with other semiotic modes. Saussure saw linguistic signs as only conventional. But verbal language uses all kinds of sign – iconic, indexical, analogue and digital – conventionalized to different degrees. Words are multiscalar objects in multiscalar social and semiotic structures. They function in multimodal settings, alongside and interacting with other kinds of sign. *Analysis of words is richer and more illuminating because they are so complex and multidimensional.*

Words as complex signs

Analysis of words is usually kept apart from general semiotic theories. In this chapter I take the opposite approach. I examine words to make general points applying to all kinds of sign. I use basic semiotic categories to show how words work to carry meaning, both in everyday contexts and in more extreme conditions. When they are no longer treated as a special semiotic case, as they are in linguistics, *the many roles words play in language, meaning and society can be recognized, analysed and celebrated.*

Syntagmatic forms in language and reality

Words, like all signs, are framed by the intersection of syntagmatic and paradigmatic planes, a basic fact for analysing their meanings. Words normally appear in utterances, spoken or written language of different scales, inflecting aspects of reality in social contexts which shape their meanings and effects. They are always syntagmatic forms embedded in other syntagmatic forms, analogue forms interacting with related forms in reality. I illustrate how words take part in this basic semiotic process by looking at an article by Guy Rundle, US correspondent for the Australian online news source Crikey.com.

Rundle was trying to capture what was happening in the 'American mind' during the 2008 presidential election. His first posting began with a sketch of his immediate context, to communicate 'where America's at', as he put it:

> 3.2 Across the featureless boulevard is the sprawling shopping centre – identikit buildings of identikit chains in low-rise buildings in a half-hearted pseudo-Southern style. Alienated isn't in it – the place makes Jeffrey Smart look like Grandma Moses. (Rundle 2008:1)

Good journalists are good semioticians, as are good historians, anthropologists and advertisers. *Social semiotics should help people to be better writers, as well as better readers.* Rundle's text has serial multi-modality, translating his semiotic reading of 'America' from visual to verbal form. As he scans his environment, responding to many signs and meanings, he selects out a seemingly simple picture, an analogue form composed around two main features, the road and the shopping centre, and turns each feature into an indexical sign. The road signifies a rootless mentality, people always going somewhere else. The shopping centre signifies community or its lack in America. Both meanings are conventional as well as indexical. Rundle is reproducing a stereotype of America.

These two non-verbal signs, their relationships and implications, organize the meanings of Rundle's verbal text, what it signifies, as a key stage in the process of generating the broader meanings of the article. Yet *there is no simple one-to-one relationship between the verbal text and the signs it constructs and reflects.* Each of the two visual signs and their referents corresponds to a word ('boulevard', 'shopping centre'), but the verbal text inserts them into a syntagmatic flow with many words that modify their meaning. *One meaning is expressed through many words: each word has many meanings.* Meanings at each level consist of signifiers (in this case, words and the corresponding visual sign) and signifieds (in this case, a highly selected picture of reality), each forming distinct but related wholes. Readers interpret Rundle's text and meaning by relating these structures in a complex, analogue process.

I look more closely at Rundle's text. The first sentence up to 'shopping centre' is a syntagmatic form which represents the scene in front of him. In this respect it is an analogue sign. The position of words in this syntagm is a multimodal signifier, a further analogue sign which carries analogue meanings, which fine-tune Rundle's meaning. The order departs from what is expected, deferring the subject (the shopping centre). But the whole can be understood as an indexical sign, signifying his perception: first the road closest to him, then the shopping centre. In this way, *the meaning of the words is overlaid by the meaning of the order.*

Rundle weaves together social and referential, syntagmatic and paradigmatic meanings. He does this within each word and by juxtaposing words which distribute these kinds of meaning. Meaning is not a thing which words have. It is the product of many trajectories which pass through words and texts, individual and connected signs in many semiotic modes. *Yet words as concrete signs are key sites for understanding this complex, open-ended process.*

Paradigms as meaning

Paradigmatic structures were briefly described in chapter 1. Here I bring out more ways they operate to enrich meaning and its analysis. As Halliday said, meaning is choice, but that choice is built on shifting sand. Choice is an indexical sign as to who is doing the choosing. It also depends on the terms of the choice, as an operation on paradigmatic structures which inflect relevant reality in their terms.

This simple principle is complex to apply in practice. Some paradigmatic sets are small, closed and well known, as is the case with many paradigms in grammar. But most paradigmatic sets are open, provisional, not ordered or shared by everyone, even in a group. Saussure's picture is more helpful, with many 'associative' planes intersecting with every syntagmatic element, every word.

For those who want meanings to be certain and shared by everyone in a group this is inconvenient. Paradigmatic meanings are not like this. They are inferred, not fixed. But they are too important to leave out of analysis and are sufficiently guided by rules to provide a reasonable, probabilistic basis for judgement and action.

For instance, 'boulevard' is a kind of road. I interpret it in a small paradigmatic set of roads. Boulevards are large compared to streets or roads, on the same scale as avenues, and smaller than autobahns. This semiotic fact can be translated into statements about meaning in an everyday sense. 'Boulevard' means a road which is grander than a street. But 'boulevard' is intersected by other paradigms which inflect its meaning. For instance, it comes from French. This fact is known by many users and understood as part of its social meaning, implying dignity and style. Is this paradigm relevant and, if so, how do we know? In this case, this meaning seems to be cancelled by 'featureless'. But that context is not decisive. The combination of fancy word and banal object here could be intended to convey this contradiction. I guess it is part of Rundle's meaning. Others might disagree.

Paradigmatic structures are crucial to the larger meanings and purposes of this text, yet not always presented directly in words. At some points Rundle says in words he is trying to communicate 'where America's at', but mostly not. Yet I have evidence to suppose that his primary meaning is this paradigmatic set, 'America' versus 'Australia'.

Australian/American forms a two-term paradigmatic structure. This can be seen in Rundle's reference to Jeffrey Smart and Grandma Moses. One is Australian, the other American, but Rundle does not mention this. He is an Australian reporter writing from America for an Australian audience about an American scene. The text was written and uploaded in the USA, for immediate consumption in Australia. The technology creates a virtual space in which there seems no difference between the USA and Australia, yet the paradigmatic structures also imply the opposite: that the unique, lived experience of America is incomprehensibly different. You must be there, living it, to understand it. Even so it will not make sense. A play of paradigmatic meanings drives the spatial paradox of the text. America is incomprehensibly different, yet this reporter can make it familiar.

Rundle communicates all this through a dance of paradigmatic categories triggered by his words, moving expertly between verbal and visual sign systems. *Words convey meaning not only in the words themselves but in the structures that surround them, paradigmatic and syntagmatic.* Rundle's meanings slip and slide, as Eliot said, but this is not a problem. It is how words work.

Words in speech and writing

Speakers of English typically suppose that they know what a 'word' is and how big it is. They assume it is the same thing in both speech and writing, as though there were no difference in these two modes. But words take different forms in spoken and written codes. To become aware of these differences and how they are unconsciously overcome in practice reveals many things about how words and language work.

An Australian satirist, Alistair Morrison, illuminated these issues in his mock dictionary of Australian English *Let Stalk Strine* (Let'/s talk /Australian), written under the pen-name 'Afferbeck Lauder' (Alphabetical Order). Typical entries were:

3.3 'Gloria Soame' (gloriou/s home); 'Emma Chisit' (How-mu/ch-is-it); 'Laura Norder' (Law-a/nd-order) (Morrison 1965)

Morrison's satirical strategy is a Shklovskyan 'making strange', like my imagined Pleiadeans in chapter 2. His satire relies on a basic feature in language use, which Halliday (1985) calls *construal*. Chomsky (1968) proposed 'poverty of stimulus' (POS) as a defining feature of language acquisition: children build a remarkably coherent shared grammar from exposure to imperfect data. The same quality, highly active sense-making or construal, can be seen in the normal recognition of word boundaries. Speakers 'slip, slide' words into each other, but listeners usually guess correctly where the boundaries should be.

Writers and readers have this problem solved for them in print. Blank text and other markers identify word, phrase and sentence boundaries as part of the meaning of utterances. They do this so effortlessly they do not notice the differences between speech and writing. Humans as semiotic animals continually make and construe meanings from imperfect materials, often construing so well they do not notice how powerful their construals are. Morrison's trick is reverse construal. He refuses to make sense of spoken language, inviting his readers to make the wrong sense of its written form. Part of his satire comes from the social meaning of the clash between written and spoken forms, in which the spoken forms of his fellow Australians are made to seem incomprehensible by their written forms. The main device is simple: insert breaks in words, remove breaks where they are expected. It is salutary how much this disrupts the sense of the words and phrases. Knowing these breaks is part of comprehension.

Morrison exaggerates the differences between words in spoken and written language, but *the differences are real and important.* Paradoxically, his parody implies the opposite of what is the semiotic case: *Written language as a code is severely impoverished compared to speech.*

Syntagmatic bonds

Morrison's main target is clichés, common phrases he uses to signify Australian culture. Clichés are a misunderstood aspect of English and other languages. These are short syntagmatic strings whose elements go together so commonly that they function in some ways like single words. Morrison implies a common judgement on clichés – that they are indexical signs of inferior thinkers. They are often criticized as poor writing. However, this phenomenon signals a general property of all sign systems. *Syntagmatic forms are built up of bonds and separations of varying strength.*

For instance, the parts of compound nouns such as 'low-rise' go together without being judged as a 'cliché'. Spoken language can subtly signify this kind of affinity, but writing is less flexible. Affinity can sometimes be signified in spelling, with dashes indicating partial fusion, or words actually joined, as in 'featureless'. Spoken language does this far more expressively. In this respect as in many others, speech has resources that are not recognized by masters of the written code like Morrison.

Morrison's satire reveals much about how structures like this work. For instance, he intuits that 'glorious home' and 'law and order' go together. Linguists call this 'collocational affinity'. These can then be counted, with numbers that themselves have meaning.

In my Google count of these phrases, 'glorious home' had 312,000 hits, but 'law and order' 38,200,000. The Google count is a crude measure. Here I use it only to support intuitions like Morrison's and mine. It is part of his knowledge of English that they go together. They have affinity. They carry potent social and referential meanings, in similar ways as do single words.

These numbers are an indexical sign of the effects of conventionalization on their form and function. This conventionalization affects meaning, social and referential, and the relations between the two. When the two words 'glorious home' are fused together it weakens the referential meanings of both 'glorious' and 'home'. Conversely, the social link between this kind of speaker and the kind of house she likes is foregrounded. This also happens with 'law and order'.

This leads to a contradictory effect of meaning. As words are endlessly repeated in different contexts, their referential meaning becomes unmanageably complex. They become fuzzy, full of contradictions, and their referential meaning becomes less salient. They become too complex for some, reassuringly simple for others, who feel they do not need to understand the referential meaning. *Large, fused syntagms like clichés can have powerful and contradictory effects in discourse.*

This analysis illustrates five general propositions for social semiotics:

1 *Signs (words and images and their parts) are linked with bonds of varying force, from separate words to fused clichés, ranged along a fuzzy continuum.*
2 *These bonds and their strength are recognized by producers and receivers of signs as part of their knowledge of the language, part of its meaning resources.*
3 *The greater the affinity as a syntagmatic quality of the elements, the more likely these are to form a whole whose meaning is different from the sum of the parts and overrides their referential force.*
4 *Processes of conventionalization act on these larger structures to weaken referential meanings and strengthen social meanings.*
5 *Features of codes condition individual meanings and are also meanings in their own right, with implications for understanding social contexts and forces.*

Words and meanings

Analysing words in texts

This book aims to contribute to analytic capacities. In this section I show how analysing words weaves into holistic analysis that draws on many levels and codes, using an example long enough to illustrate analytic methods in complex real-life practice. I published an analysis of this piece in context (Hodge 2011), in research on the theme of climate change in museums. The text comes from a blog by an Australian journalist, Andrew Bolt, a well-known Australian 'climate change sceptic/denier'.

Bolt was commenting on a new exhibition on climate change mounted by the Australian Museum in Sydney. His blog included text from the museum's online description of the exhibition:

> 3.4 [It] takes you on a surprising trip through two possible scenarios: one where nothing has been done to combat climate change and the other showing how nations, communities and individuals can take positive action to help save the planet . . .

Bolt embedded this in a paratactic structure consisting of his own commentary:

> 3.5 Note
> • The exhibition's utter certainty that the world is warming, and its failure to concede there's a debate . . .
> Frauds. What is this doing in a museum? Witness the decline of science. (Bolt, 4 May 2009, quoted in Hodge 2011: 112)

I make two methodological points:

1 *Words function and have meaning only in contexts, which act as a whole to alter the meanings of their parts.* When inserted into Bolt's framework, supported by his community, the museum's pedagogic invitation to young visitors is made to seem like pathetic propaganda. The phrase 'save the planet' is emptied of the serious meaning it has for the museum, to become the cliché Bolt's community sees it as.
2 *Words, simple and complex, may correspond to complex syntagmatic structures of meaning more equivalent to a sentence than to another word.*

In this instance Bolt writes:

3.5 . . . its failure to concede there's a debate . . .

Each content word is a complex statement which incorporates contentious claims. The best way to represent the meaning of 'failure' is as a sentence of the form:

3.6 'X has tried to do something and not succeeded.'

Similarly, 'concede' corresponds to a sentence like:

3.7 'X recognizes that Y is right or prevails on this matter.'

Museum staff would not agree to any of these statements. Conveying these meanings as words rather than as a series of sentences has the effect of making them more difficult to recognize and contest, especially when, as in this case, they are strung together in a single sentence. This is the semantic equivalent of cluster-bombing. Such words are simple, hard to oppose, and cause collateral damage.

This is often a highly effective tactic. My analysis exposes the trick, the 'cues', as Fairclough (1992) calls them. Yet at the same time the analysis brings out what Fairclough calls 'traces' of processes of making meaning that this author and his group habitually follow, the mental processes and assumptions of 'climate change deniers'.

It is often impossible to decide how deliberate the tactic is by analysing isolated texts. That problem shows only that here, as usual, social semiotics has to go outside given texts to find other data in social and material reality.

Counting words

As I argued in chapter 1, big meanings and the words that carry them are important sites for analysing social meaning, where social issues and meanings collide with semiotic forms. The Bolt text deals with one of the biggest of meanings, climate change/global warming. In this section I suggest ways to analyse the play of words and meanings, large and small, in texts such as this, in debates of this kind. In this process analysis can make good use of the fact that words are concrete and identifiable and can be counted.

One writer on climate change, Mike Hulme (2009), called it a 'wicked problem'. By this he meant it was so complex and shifting that people cannot agree on even how to define it. It is 'wicked' because some attempted solutions make the problem worse. The

Table 3.1 Word counts in Bolt's text

Term	Count	Combined count
Museum	3	6: Museum + exhibition
Exhibition	3	
(Global) warming	3	5: Global warming + climate change
Climate change	2	
Ice	3	
Warm-	3	
Glob-	1	3: Glob- + planet + world
Planet	1	
World	1	

condition of 'wickedness' of problems is inseparable from problems of meaning in far-from-equilibrium conditions.

The Bolt text has an identifiable topic, represented by a small set of content words which bring into the text the issues and parts of reality that drive the communication. *Words and meanings do not always have a one-to-one relationship, but there is usually a significant correspondence which makes content words a convenient starting point for analysis.* Identifying them is usually easy. Most readers would get the general meaning that this text is about 'climate change' and 'museums'. This is confirmed by a word count of content words, shown in rudimentary form in table 3.1, which throws up some suggestive patterns to follow further. First, the text has a double focus, a double object in dispute, museums and climate change, as well as polarized participants. The syntagm formed by the combination of these potent terms, not one or other on its own, is the complex issue.

I have combined these words in a single table, but it is important to see who says what. The museum talks of 'climate change', but Bolt talks of '(global) warming'. It is analytically important not to assume these words mean much the same thing. Each word has complex meanings, constructing the world and the problem in different ways. For instance, each is a complex syntagm, formed out of different elements that are combined in new wholes, in which component elements acquire different meanings and different relationships to reality. Each corresponds to two sentences, each having a different form and meaning. 'Climate change' could come from a transitive sentence, '[X] is changing the climate', where [X] could be either humans or other agents. Or it could come from an intransitive sentence: 'Climate changes' (with no specified agency).

There is similar ambiguity about 'global warming'. Either this is transitive, in which some force, humans or natural, is making the globe warmer, or it is intransitive. The globe is getting warmer, with no one or nothing specifically responsible.

Google figures show the different popularity of these terms. 'Climate change' had 93,000,000 hits, 'global warming' 70,000,000. Both numbers are huge – larger than 'law and order' (38,200,000). 'Climate change' is more popular, but not on a different scale. This difference can be given further social meaning by looking at Bolt versus the museum. The sceptic/denier consistently prefers the less popular 'global warming'.

The concept of 'frame analysis' as developed in cognitive linguistics has been useful for analysing big meanings in words and texts like this. Charles Fillmore (2003) used the term 'frame' for complex, extensive analogue meanings of individual words. For George Lakoff, 'frames' are ideologically charged schemata organized by macro-frames, often themselves organized as models of the world. These are realized ultimately through choices of words and the metaphors they express.

From a social semiotic perspective, this theory suggests a systematic analysis of political and everyday discourse which follows multiscalar pathways, from specific words and images down to deep complex and contradictory analogue forms of that society. Lakoff (2004) deployed this model on political discourse, particularly American Republicans versus Democrats, and showed that Republicans framed issues in ways that made their solutions seem more plausible. He wanted Democrats to fight back, in a battle of frames.

Lakoff's approach needs to recognize the complicating presence of contradiction. For instance, Bolt was one-sided, yet he invoked a 'debate' frame. The museum, in contrast, adopted the frame of educators, concerned to 'inform' and 'surprise'. Yet it embedded one of its scenarios in a war metaphor/frame: no one 'combats' climate change. In its other scenario the museum had a different frame: people 'tak[ing] positive action to help save the planet'.

This analysis brings out contradictions in both combatants and also suggests why they had different effects. The museum undercut its commitment to positive social action, whereas Bolt pretended to be engaged in debate to cover the fact that he was unscrupulous in argument. In both cases, some words misrepresent the underlying frames. 'Frames' are analytically useful, but with them, as with all text-based forms of analysis, we need to be aware of *the continual tension between signs and realities, reflecting and constructing competing versions of the world.*

Below the word

Atoms of meaning

The US linguist George Zipf is one of a small number of linguists who have influenced Nobel prize calibre scientists. 'Zipf's law' was adapted by the Nobel Prizewinner Murray Gell-Mann and the chaos theorist Benoit Mandelbrot, to name but two. Yet Zipf's work went largely unnoticed in linguistics. In this section I suggest why this work is potentially so important for social semiotics, in a study of language, meaning and society adapted to the world of complexity.

Zipf (1949) worked in comparative linguistics in the 1930s, using large corpuses forty years before that was fashionable. When he counted words in his large bodies of text, which included Chinese as well as European languages, he found a pattern that surprised him. When words were ranked in order from most to least frequently used, the most frequent were much more common than the next most frequent, with a regular curve down to common words. So 'the' is the most common word in English corpuses (roughly 7 per cent). 'Of', the next most frequent, occurred far less often, with a word count of around 3.7 per cent.

The resulting graph began steeply, with a long, flat tail following an exponentially decreasing curve – hence the name 'power law' for curves of this kind. Zipf found the same pattern with rank and size of cities. Others found power laws in many other places. The internet, for example, is full of power-law phenomena, with power-law links between the rank of websites and numbers of links or hits (Adamic and Huberman 2000: 2115). Power-law distributions can be found in many semiotic modes, visual and behavioural. In this section I explore one implication for analysing verbal language. Zipf's law threw a spotlight on some well-known facts about verbal language which had nonetheless been relatively ignored, because prevailing models of the time could not make sense of them. *Frequency is an important clue into how signs have meaning.*

Zipf's law brings to our attention a remarkable phenomenon in verbal language. Words that are frequently used are likely to lose markers of structure, to seem more simple. Yet at the same time *their multiple uses are likely to leave traces in multiple meanings.* 'Climate change', for instance, remains a compound made up of two distinguishable words. However, the pressure of multiple uses still drives the two words closer together, a signifier many orders less complex than what it signifies.

This effect can be seen more clearly in the structure of the vocabulary of languages. Linguists generally make a division between two major classes of word. One kind is called 'content' words and supplies the content of most utterances, as nouns, verbs, adjectives and adverbs. These are analogue signs, providing pictures of the reality being talked about. They are often called an open class. There are many of them, and new ones are relatively easy to add. But even the most common is usually not common in a given text. The other kind of word is thrown into sharper relief by Zipf's figures. They include parts of speech pronouns and articles, such as 'the', and are often called 'grammar' or 'function' words. They are described as a closed class, because such words change much more slowly, and are typically short and unobtrusive, yet, as Zipf showed, they are usually the most common words in most texts. In the Bolt text, for instance, there are thirteen instances of 'the'.

The problem of balance between content and function words becomes even more acute if we add what linguists call 'bound morphemes' to the list of grammatical/function words. 'Morpheme' refers to units of meaning in verbal language, but these can be 'free' (able to stand alone, e.g., 'the') or bound, always attached to another morpheme (e.g., the -s/-es which pluralizes singular verbs). Like clichés, bound morphemes are highly cohesive.

Punctuation markers could be included here, signifiers in the written code which are also 'function' words. There are twenty-eight punctuation marks in the Bolt text: eleven commas and six full stops, with the others following a power-law distribution. These are not usually seen as words or signs, but they carry significant meaning. For instance, Bolt has twenty-eight punctuation marks in his 109 words, the museum only five in fifty-five words, less than half on average. Bolt has many more commas (eleven to two) and full stops (six to one), signifying how he breaks his text up into small units, paratactic compared to the museum text.

In the Bolt text there are nine instances of -s for singular verbs, nine -ing, seven -s for plural nouns and four 'this', before any content words appear. I show this in graphic form in figure 3.1 to demonstrate the outlines of the power-law curve, though there are too few examples for this to work. In this list I mingle words on different scales (simple and compound words) with collocations at

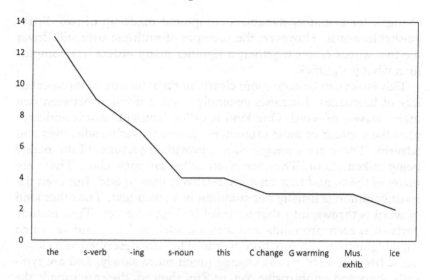

Figure 3.1 Word count in Bolt's text

one level and a series of smaller units, morphemes and bound morphemes. To this I add signs which are not usually seen as words, such as commas, etc. This list challenges common ideas of what a word is, in a multiscalar system of units of meaning in the written code. In this system *words have a fuzzy scope, beginning with signs below what would be normally seen as words and continuing above that level.*

From there follow some implications for theory and analysis of words as verbal signs:

1 *Words should be analysed in syntagmatic contexts, but they can also be analysed as syntagmatic forms in themselves.*
2 *Syntagms above the word still sometimes behave like words and can be analysed accordingly, and so also structures below the word.*
3 *When analysed in themselves, words still combine social and referential meanings, like all signs, visual and verbal.*

In the history of science, some of the greatest advances have come from the discovery and exploration of small-scale phenomena, hard to see or invisible to unassisted human perception, which have proved to have decisive effects on phenomena at larger scales: atoms and sub-atomic particles in physics, microbes and genes in biology, micro-chips and nanotechnology in computer science. Similarly, the study of 'atoms of meaning' is still in its infancy, an exciting site for linguistic and social semiotic research.

Function words

The way meaning happens in the two classes of word, 'content' and 'function' words, has useful parallels to two of Peirce's signs, iconic (analogue) and indexical. In many understandings of meaning, iconic signs are easier to understand as meanings, but functional signs play an indispensable role. Since they are usually small and often bound morphemes, they are easier to ignore. 'Function' words are like nails or mortar. Without functional signs meanings collapse on themselves and disconnect from the world.

Peirce's 'indexical' comes from Greek, *deik-*, 'to point or show'. The *deik-* family of meanings includes another key term for social semiotics, *deixis* (adjective *deictic*), concerned with pointing. The word *deixis* was introduced into linguistics by the great German psychologist Karl Bühler (2011), for whom it had a generic sense, any aspect of language which located a referent in the fundamental physical dimensions of space and time.

Bühler's career was disrupted by the Nazis. His linguistic work was not translated into English until 1990 and has not had the influence in English it deserves. It still provides a coherent framework for thinking about the full range of 'function' words and morphemes in English and other languages. As the US discourse analyst James Paul Gee wrote: 'Deictics tie speech and writing to context' (2010: 9). Aspects of deixis are also important in other semiotic modes (see theories of perspective in art, the gaze in cinema, Mulvey 2009; and Kress and van Leeuwen 2006 on 'reading images').

'Deixis' is not greatly used in linguistics, and indeed has a confusing array of meanings in different schools. For some its meaning is restricted to a few function words involved in pointing, in space (this and that) and time (now and then). 'The' is usually but not always included as a deictic. Personal pronouns (I and you) are often seen as deictic. Tense is often seen as deictic, since these meanings, often attached to verbs as free morphemes (e.g., will) or bound morphemes (-ed, -ing), locate actions in time.

Horst Ruthrof (2015) introduced a semiotic dimension to the concept by distinguishing explicit deixis, marked in verbal language, from implicit deixis, carried by a broad range of other semiotic resources. I use the term in the broadest semiotic sense to include the number system.

To illustrate deixis in verbal language I focus on 'the' in the two texts, by Bolt and the museum, which make up his blog.

3.8 The Australian Museum in Sydney has an interactive exhibition. (Bolt)

'The' here ties this text to its context, the basic function of deixis according to Gee (2010). It also binds together the other elements of the phrase, [Australian] [Museum] [in Sydney], all of which have a deictic function. The single word 'the' ties the discourse together and ties the discourse to its context. This is what Halliday and Hasan (1976) call 'cohesion'. The function of this may not seem obvious. However, in this case, Bolt wrote his blog in Melbourne about an exhibition in Sydney which he had not seen. In fact his blog was posted hours before the exhibition opened. Most of his blogger fans lived in other parts of Australia, too.

Bolt is condemning an exhibition he has not seen and has no intention of seeing. Yet he also wants to be persuasive, to give the impression that the reality he is talking about is clear and beyond doubt. His use of 'the' plays a role in creating this effect. Each use of 'the' in this as in every text plays some part in the form of meaning. This fact is especially important for social semiotics. Otherwise this class of signs is likely to be ignored as irrelevant to the meanings constructed in the given case.

Such words also carry meanings as patterns. For instance, of thirteen uses of 'the' in the blog, Bolt contributed ten of 107 words: 9.3 per cent. The museum text had three of fifty-one words, 5.6 per cent. The total number of words is so small that these numbers are not statistically significant. However, statistical significance is only one way counting carries meaning. This is a fact about the two texts from the two authors, irrespective of whether it is true of their respective writings more generally. It is a perceptible meaning, not an inference about a population, as would be the case with statistical analysis.

The difference between Bolt and the museum is marked. Bolt has a heavy use of 'the', the museum a light use. The difference carries subtle but detectable social and referential meanings and effects. In Bolt's case this feature contradicts the basis of his claimed position as climate change sceptic. His position is that he doubts that climate change is happening. Yet this position comes across not as doubt but as certainty (that his opponents are wrong and lack credibility, etc.). He uses deixis to bind himself and his audience to a concrete object, this particular exhibition. Its reality allows him to seem equally certain and right about climate change. The museum's low use of this form of deixis signals the opposite. Its text is not tied so closely to a reality, either the exhibition or climate change itself. Instead of Bolt's short sentences, each one tied explicitly to reality, the museum weaves a longer, more complex sentence less strongly tied to its two contexts. This left it vulnerable to Bolt's attack.

'The' is complex and fuzzy, like all high-frequency words in power-law curves. As a deictic it points to many different things. In the phrase 'the museum of myths', 'the' points forward in the text, promising to define this new class of museum, not yet identified. In 'the Australian Museum in Sydney' it acts to make the whole phrase deictic, locating the museum as well as identifying it. The single word 'the' points in four directions, often more than one in any given case. That means it has at least four meanings. In fact it has more. It is highly fuzzy. This is a quality of all these words. This fuzziness is one of the qualities that has made people suppose they have no meaning. In practice they have too many.

Personal names are also part of the deictic system. In the Bolt text there are five names: Andrew Bolt, the Australian Museum, Sydney, Antarctic and Arctic. Acts of naming bring in segments of reality which are full of analogue meanings. Bolt is a popular journalist, for instance, associated with hostility to left-wing causes.

These are analogue meanings like those carried by words, yet they are located in the reality to which they refer, not fixed in words. Yet this is a difference of degree, not kind. Personal names, like content words, have meanings shaped by digital signs (paradigmatic structures that distinguish Bolt from climate change proponents such as Lord Stern).

In this discussion I have shown different kinds and scales of linguistic signs which have different functions and effects. Being aware of these differences means a greater range of analyses of words opens up. Yet these differences typically combine to construct relations between realities and referents inside and outside texts, in the continual dialectic between language, meaning and society that constitutes social semiosis.

Analytic tools

Dictionaries

Dictionaries are important tools and resources for using any language. The rest of this chapter will show how they can be best used, how to supplement or correct them, and what information and understanding about words they should ideally contain.

Dictionaries have a place in a continuum of reference tools for words. These include the encyclopedia, which organizes reality under thematic categories represented by words. Eco (2014) distinguished between dictionaries and encyclopedias as fundamentally different ways of organizing knowledge. Dictionaries are at one end of a continuum, organized according to the form of words as signifiers, not their meanings. This simple digital system was invented millennia before the first computer. All words beginning with 'a' are stored first, followed by words beginning with 'b'. All words beginning with 'a' are then ordered by their second letter, and then their third, and so on.

Two prerequisites were needed for this beautiful machine to work. One was a fixed agreed order for the letters, so that they act like numbers. This has not been done for any other semiotic sign, which makes this tool unique for linguistic signs. The other is an agreed translation of the sounds of the language into letters. This second has taken a great amount of time and effort. It privileges spoken over written language for lexicographers.

In these and other ways, dictionaries are not like whatever the form is that speakers of a language use to store their inventory of words. Some linguists use another word for dictionaries, 'lexicon', from Greek *lexis*, a word or phrase, to refer to the inner dictionary or repository people use in practice. Even though 'lexicon' means much the same as 'dictionary', I prefer to keep it for the inner storehouse. Cognitive psychology still lacks an agreed description of what this device looks like, but a cognitively realist social semiotics cannot assume this 'inner lexicon' is structured like a dictionary. It is more likely to be structured as a network, as in connectionist models. It probably includes analogue and digital structures and patterns.

In the following sections I look at aspects of words and language that may be found, to some extent, in some dictionaries, and which are so important that dictionaries can be used as a starting point for citizen researchers to follow them up. My practical aim is to help readers to better track meanings they encounter or want to use. Sometimes that involves critical use of existing tools. Often it means empowering readers to draw on their own knowledge of the language they are dealing with *and develop strategies for using their inner lexicons more critically and creatively.*

Words in time

Raymond Williams, a founding father of modern cultural studies, emphasized two strands of thought: the importance of history and the study of words. His *Keywords* (1976) showed the value of a consciousness of the history of words for innovative social analysis, something most of his followers do not yet appreciate. He described the sense of revelation he felt 'when the most basic concepts – the concepts, as it is said, from which we begin – are suddenly seen to be not concepts but problems, not analytic problems either but historical movements that are still unresolved' (Williams 1977: 11). I emphasize here the transformative effect he attributes to what to many seems a dry, abstract scholarly pursuit. As a result of this work, key concepts have more meaning, and they mean in a different way. The effect Williams found for history and cultural studies applies to all fields. *The social historical study of key words transforms the conceptual possibilities of every field of thought.*

I use a social-historical framework for analysing lexical sets in dictionaries. Single major words are usually listed with a core or main meaning and subsidiary or 'derived' meanings. Often the core meaning is a 'literal' sense of the word, a concrete form of its meaning, with derived meanings, applications or metaphors of the meaning. I understand these as transformations, *contemporary traces of transformations carried out by historical agents, whose actions are usually still recoverable as meanings.*

There is a similar pattern in the related words in a larger set, reported in major dictionaries, linked by similarities of form and meaning which have historical origins. This set is usually treated as part of the knowledge of the language, even though most actual speakers do not know all of them.

Then there is a larger, more heterogeneous set of words derived over a much longer time from much earlier originals. These include many instances of which contemporary speakers are not conscious. This hyper-set is known only to scholars. Most linguists suppose that some histories of words are in some way part of knowledge of the language, but not the scholarly roots. I suggest that the boundary between the two kinds is more fuzzy and permeable than linguists think. These are patterns, and the human mind has a remarkable capacity to detect patterns. Williams reports a 'sudden' revelation as part of his personal experience, liberating and enabling. I have felt the same.

Some modern dictionaries give some history of words, but most shorter dictionaries do not, and historical roots and etymologies are almost absent. This is a pity for social semiotics and CDA. In this book thus far I have given etymologies without justifying or explaining my version of the practice. In this section I do so.

The great age for etymology was the nineteenth century. The dominant form of linguistics then was comparative philology, founded by Sir William Jones. This provided a framework for many erudite multilingual scholars, including Saussure, to accumulate an exceptional stock of knowledge about European languages, encoded in magnificent dictionaries. For many reasons, there was a decline from this high point. This work was neglected, dismissed as a minor, obsolete form of research. 'Etymology' came to signify trivial, old-fashioned or speculative scholarship. But the work that was done can still be accessed with only a small effort. *Etymology is a powerful resource for everyone dealing with words*. It is especially powerful within a social semiotic framework.

In addition to the *OED*, I recommend the work of Eric Partridge (1966), which incorporates more than a century of etymological scholarship. I commonly consult Lewis and Short ([1879] 1922) for Latin and Liddell and Scott (1849) for Greek, both monuments of nineteenth-century scholarship which have not been superseded, though they are not user-friendly for English speakers.

Etymology comes from Greek *etymon*, 'true' + *logos*, 'word'. This flags a potential danger in etymological enquiries, satirized by Plato in *Cratylus* (1892). Greeks in Plato's day pursued words back into the mists of time and never found the 'true' word. Instead, they invented convenient histories. In the twenty-first century we inherit better scholarship than the Greeks had, but the problem remains. What 'truth' is conveyed in these histories, and what is its use for analysis?

A short history of 'globalization'

I illustrate with 'globalization'. This word is so big and variously defined that it can be seen as a 'wicked' word for a 'wicked' problem. It has become a defining word for business, defined here in a management textbook:

3.9 Globalisation was initially conceptualised as the worldwide process of economic and industrial restructuring ... Today, globalisation is also seen to include the process of continuous change to gain competitive advantage. (Davidson and Griffin 2003:146)

In this version of world history, offered to would-be future managers of the globe, 'globalisation' first appeared in the 1970s, the distinctive product of world capitalism. However, the meaning and root was already present in Marx and Engels in 1847:

> 3.10 The need of a constantly expanding market for its products chases the bourgeoisie over the whole surface of the globe. (Marx and Engels 1970: 38–9)

As we see from this example, definition is not a neutral semiotic act. It is part of a strategy to control meanings through words and people and histories through those meanings. *Battles over definitions can be part of a broader struggle over social processes of meaning, in which historical analysis can be a weapon.*

In the case of 'globalization', neo-liberal appropriations of the word were so convincing to activists that, until recently, many defined themselves as 'anti-globalization', as though the word referred only to neo-liberal economic practices. Opponents to capitalist forms of globalization have reclaimed the word and now talk of 'alter-globalization'.

The first step in analysing 'globalization' breaks it down into component morphemes: glob+al+iz+at+ion, traces of four transformations. Underpinning this string is a single Latin word, *globus*, referring to any spherical object of any size, from a ball of dough to a planet to a representation of Earth. This range complicates the search for a single metaphorical basis for the word. Further layers of meaning emerge when we look behind the Latin root. In what follows, all glosses come from Partridge (1966), Lewis and Short (1922) and Liddell and Scott (1849). None of them is contentious.

Globus probably came from an important, highly generative Indo-European root, **kwel-*, which meant 'circular movement'. Through **kwel-*, '*globus*' is related to a range of words that superficially may not seem related. 'Wheel' is a cognate word, from Old English *hweol*. So is 'pole', akin to Greek *polos*, which refers both to what wheels turn around and what Earth itself revolves around. Another cognate Latin word is *col-*, 'to plough' (initially a movement around a field), 'to worship', connected by an ideologically motivated extension to '*colonia*'. It also led to *cultura*, products of the different senses of *col-*, and thence 'culture' in all the many senses of that complex word discussed by Williams (1976).

*Kwel- was important and generative because it was embedded in basic religious and cosmological ideas. Circles and circular motion

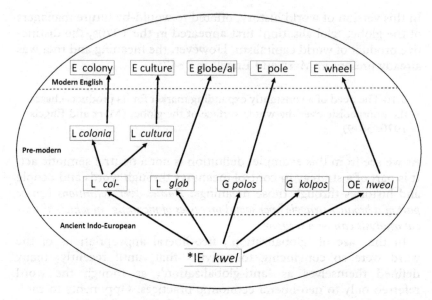

Figure 3.2   Semantic network – *kwel*/global

had potent metaphysical meanings, so much so that we could rea-
sonably include religious ideas in **kwel-* which appear in many of its
descendants. '*Globus*' itself is most closely akin to Greek *kolpos*, 'an
enclosing space', 'a woman's breast or womb'.

As one strategy I set up this set of words as 'semantic networks' as these are studied in cognitive science (e.g., Steyvers and
Tenenbaum 2005). These are usually studied across large vocabulary sets in common use. I adapt this model here to examine a small
set operating across deep time. The word 'globalization' is often
seen as so new as to need almost a new language. It is salutary to
recognize that the terms used today to grasp it have roots in the
depths of pre-modernity, when semi-nomadic Indo-Europeans
roamed across vast tracts of Europe and Asia. Figure 3.2 represents
time as a series of layers, yet the image exists in a single space and
time, in which physical space and time are collapsed. Eight thousand years can be seen in a single instant, across five continents. Yet
different networks have a different kind of reality and explain different phenomena. Analysis in these terms does not suppose the past
is really the same as the present. There are clear discontinuities, less
fuzzy boundaries.

Focusing only on the root *glob*, as it underpins different uses and
meanings of 'glob-al', I suggest that some shades of meaning of the

Latin continue to be detectable in modern inflections. Marx's 'globe' is not just the various countries, developed and underdeveloped; it has a strong sense of its unity as perceptible. This sense also underlies Robertson's invention of 'globality' (1992), a positive sense of the planet as a whole that he sees as a new product of globalization.

The Australian Museum opted for the term 'climate change' rather than 'global warming', preferred by climate change denier Bolt. This analysis of 'global' suggests that the museum and the climate change movement generally may be making a tactical mistake. The potent positive 'global' should not be left to its enemies.

Steyvers and Tennebaum (2005) claim that the form of semantic network they discover has the form of a 'small world' in the sense used by Duncan Watts (1999). It is bound together into an integrated system by networks linking nodes. Some nodes are more important than others, with a power-law distribution. *'Small world' systems are integrated by a small number of big nodes, as are Big Words in social semiotics.*

Visual signs as words

The same approach can be used with visual iconography, where some formal images behave in similar ways to words. For instance, the insignia of the United Nations, designed after the Second World War in 1947, draws on an iconographic tradition going back to ancient Greece and Rome 2000 years earlier. The visual tradition, in a different semiotic mode, has many similarities across a comparable depth in time. At the centre is a concentric globe, in which component countries are distorted as they fit into the unity of the planet. This image is encircled by two intertwined olive branches, icons of peace for Greeks. These iconographers needed to go back so far in time in order to have a symbol that unifies so large a global space. It also

Figure 3.3 The UN insignia

carries traces of that history. Inadvertently, it views the globe from above the north pole, from the point of view of what was later called the 'global north', for whom the 'global south' hardly existed.

I use these semantic networks over deep time, as Williams proposed, *to restore and extend contemporary control over words and meanings*. Connections in semantic networks are virtual, but they can be made actual. *Semantic networks based on scholarship identify navigation links to build on and use by everyone engaged in battles over big words and their meanings.*

Beyond reason

Affectual meanings

All words have social and affectual meanings, which form part of the package of meanings of the words in contexts. In some contexts those social and affectual meanings are mobilized more than others or have different, sometimes even opposite, effects for different participants. Most dictionaries give minimal support to judgements and intuitions about affectual meanings, yet they are so pervasive and influential in effects of meaning that social semiotics must include them.

In semantics, this class of meanings is often lumped together under the category of 'connotations', contrasted with 'denotation' – i.e., what the word refers to. This binary pair is so open and vague that many linguists find it unusable. But, from a fuzzy perspective, vagueness is good if used well.

Affectual meanings are not consistently included in dictionaries, and they are more variable between different people and groups. In spite of these difficulties, fuzzy, approximate ways of including this dimension are part of language-users' inner lexicon. These meanings are social and public, with social and public effects. One set of words is generally recognized but kept separate from normal vocabulary: swear words, taboo words, rude or profane words. These are found mostly in talk rather than in writing, in informal rather than formal contexts, and used by low- rather than high-status speakers. Affect is a systemic part of language, a paradigmatic set that affects the meaning of all words.

Psychologists have contributed more to this area than linguists. To suggest how to incorporate this dimension into social semiotics, I draw on a brief dictionary of affects developed and tested by two US psychologists, Margaret Bradley and Peter Lang (1999). They tested a sample of 600 words on a group of psychology students, roughly

Table 3.2 Ten affectual meanings

Word	Happy BH	Happy B/L	Aroused BH	Aroused B/L	Dominance BH	Dominance B/L	Frequ B/L
Car	6.5	7.73	6	6.24	7	6.98	274
Child	8	7.08	6	5.55	7	5.10	213
Failure	1	1.7	7	4.95	2	2.45	89
Fraud	2	2.67	7	5.75	2	3.58	8
Museum	5	5.54	4	3.6	5	5.32	32
Perfection	8	7.25	6	5.95	6	6.71	11
Surprised	6	7.47	7	7.47	6	6.11	58
Travel	7	7.10	6	6.21	7	6.31	61
Warmth	6	7.41	3	3.73	4	5.61	28
World	5	6.50	5	5.32	4	5.20	787

Source: Adapted from Bradley and Lang (1999)

half women, half men, testing three dimensions of affect: positivity (happy–sad), intensity (arousing–calming) and what they call 'dominance', their sense of power in relations to the object.

I illustrate how this approach can be integrated into social semiotics by looking again at the Bolt text. I selected ten words from the Bolt text which also appeared in their list. I then carried out their test, assigning the words their affectual meanings in a scale from 1 to 9, without knowing the values they assigned to them. I then compared my ratings with theirs. The results are given in table 3.2. I was surprised to find that all my thirty judgements fell within one standard deviation of theirs. This suggests that affectual meanings are relatively stable, part of the inner knowledge of the language. The two methods of accessing this set of meanings, by psychological questionnaire or using intuitions, are complementary.

Each of Bradley and Lang's three dimensions is a complex meaning which needs to be interpreted before we can see what these figures imply. The first, happy–sad, indicates positive affect, which also signifies a solidarity relationship. With 'child', for instance, Bolt created a social/affectual syntagm with strongly positive links to children. So did the museum display. The potent affects around 'child' as word and meaning are sites of struggle.

The third category, 'dominance', is an interesting dimension, since it connects with the major set of social meanings around power. My response departed from that of Bradley and Lang here. For me, the affectual meaning of 'child' generated more sense of my power than it did for their subjects. In this list, the highest rating item under this dimension was 'car', which was also the greatest source of pleasure.

We can use fuzzy forms of these judgements (imprecise three-term categories) to map the affective geometry of the two sets of statements, Bolt's and the museum's, in *a battle for affects which translate closely into social meanings*. Each mobilizes responses on their side by their choice of words with affectual meanings.

However, in this, as generally with social meanings, *meanings vary with different social categories*. Bradley and Lang tested their terms with women and men and found variation across gender. With 'child', for instance, the positive affect for women was 8.00, against only 6.15 for men. Conversely, men had a stronger feeling of dominance in relation to 'child' than women did: 5.35 to 4.85. With their sample size none of these figures was statistically significant, but the general implication holds. *Different social agents have different responses, different social and affectual meanings, in relation to significant items of vocabulary associated with different classifications of the social world.* For strategic semiotic analysis, these differences are often traces of the assumptions of senders, *a site for analysing where their strategies of persuasion may be ineffective or counter-productive.*

Far-from-equilibrium signs

The affectual dimension of meaning has been hard to integrate into rational forms of analysis, in political as well as linguistic theory. These problems are worse for analysts when meanings shift into far-from-equilibrium conditions where non-linear logic prevails.

The following text came through my email to advertise a video produced by a feminist collective (*colectivo mujer*). It began:

3.11 La marcha de las putas (The SlutWalk)
Is SlutWalk feminista?

The email gave a brief history of the SlutWalk protest marches, which began in Toronto, Canada, and became a global movement of rallies across the world, including in many Latin American countries. Activists report the trigger as being the words of a police officer, speaking on crime prevention at a safety forum. He said: 'women should avoid dressing like sluts in order not to be victimized.'

The authors of the video invited their audience to reflect: 'Are SlutWalks simply the pornification of protest? Or are they reflective of successful feminist action?' These are very good questions. Can activists transform key words like 'slut' that have been loaded with social and affectual meanings, used as instruments of control? SlutWalk is an experiment that asks what happens when the dominant forms of language are used in a strategy of resistance.

'Slut' does not appear in the Bradley–Lang list, but the related 'whore' does. Their subjects showed clear differences between men and women. The word rated 3.92 against 'happy' for men but only 1.61 for women. This difference was statistically significant for their sample. For arousal, it rated 6.58 for men against 5.54 for women, and, for 'dominance', it rated 5.83 for men and 4.10 for women. Putting these figures together, it is clear that men and women give different social and affectual meanings to 'whore'.

The effect of 'slut' may be due to more than the power of these associations. Saussure influentially defined linguistic signs as arbitrary, by which he meant in particular that their sounds have no relation to their meaning or referent. Others have queried this doctrine. Kress and van Leeuwen (2001) found that many aspects of written texts are 'motivated' signs. 'Slut' raises another class of exception to Saussure's doctrine.

The word 'slut' in print does not seem to resemble women in any way, but the way it can be pronounced can be significant. The soft sound of 'sl' followed by a short vowel and an explosive 't' can express violent rejection. Especially as spoken by aggressive men, it is an indexical sign, not of women but of men's attitude. The same is true of *puta*, the Spanish equivalent. I have heard this word from men many times in Mexican streets, hitting women targets almost like a physical blow. Part of this force in Spanish comes from the initial 'pu', able to project sound like spit. Men usually shout it – another indexical sign of rejection and violence.

This meaning is not inherent in the sound or written form of the words. Nor does it represent the meaning of its women targets. The physiological conditions of producing the sound become more prominent, not so subordinated to the neutralizing effect of the words and sentences in which they appear. The boundaries between sounds and meanings, signifiers and signifieds collapse in these far-from-equilibrium conditions.

The example of 'slut' in 'SlutWalk' shows the potential instability of this term around a fissure line which exists between judgements of men and women but is controlled in normal usage. Writing plays an interesting role in the resistance. 'SlutWalk' being made into a single word fuses the emotive word in a single structure, which helps neutralize the meanings of its two components. At the same time it blocks the reversion of 'slut' to its visceral primal meaning. But only empirical social analysis can show whether this subtle tactic survived the brutality of gender warfare.

The SlutWalk campaign is a research project into the dynamic processes of language and social meaning. The experiment so far shows that these meanings can be inverted if enough people mobilize their social power as agents of meaning. It shows that some fissures revealed by an instrument like Bradley and Lang's may be a site for transformation. It also shows that that process of inversion is itself open to inversion in these conditions.

That outcome is one reason why it is so interesting. Research instruments like that of Bradley and Lang attempt to establish a common base line, applicable in normal conditions to most people. *But social semiotics also needs to know how these 'normal conditions' unfold in far-from-equilibrium states, where small changes may become visible butterfly effects that may lead to new versions of 'normal'* – new words and meanings associated with new social relationships.

This example brings out a paradox that runs throughout this chapter. Words are so common, small, complex and unstable that they should not have any observable effects on societies or individuals. Yet sometimes they have remarkable effects, leading into deep processes of society and thought. It is social semiotics' task to see why and when, in a usable form.

4

Grammar

For most linguists grammar is the supreme object of their study, the mystery at the heart of language that linguistics exists to explain. Yet outside linguistics this fascination has proved hard to communicate. For non-linguists, 'grammar' often seems difficult, obscure, pedantic and irrelevant. In this chapter I hope to show that that's a pity.

Within linguistics, grammar has been divisive. The dominant modern linguistic theory is Chomsky's transformational/generative grammar. Halliday's alternative tradition is carried by his systemic-functional grammar (1985). The 1980s 'linguistics wars' (Harris 1993) were fought mainly over competing models of grammar, Chomsky's 'extended standard' theory versus models developed by his former followers – for example, George Lakoff (1968), Charles Fillmore (2003) and James McCauley (1976).

This conflict motivated me to write this book. What can non-linguists think if they see linguists fighting to the death over what grammar is? I have come to think there is far more in common between Chomsky and Halliday than what is different. Differences exist and can be productive, but what these two share is a stronger basis for a future linguistics and social semiotics.

In this spirit I extend grammar to illuminate social meanings and issues. I integrate grammar into 'reading as analysis' (Carbó 2001) with *deep reading* as key to interpretation. I use *multimodal grammar,* as in Kress and van Leeuwen's visual grammar: 'the way in which depicted elements – people, places and things – combine in visual "statements"' (2006: 1). I use *grammar for social and cultural analysis,* as in Bonfil's theories (1987) described by Coronado: 'The cultural matrix is the "grammar" of cultures from which forms emerge and are structured, in which their meanings are realised' (2014: 142; my translation).

Grammar and origins

Grammar is what it is because of the history that leads into the present. But to have a dynamic grasp of that history we need to understand why it was so and what choices were made then which we would not make now. I use the strategy of counter-history to ask: What minimal differences in the past might have led to different outcomes in the present?

Chomsky and Halliday

I begin this story in the 1950s, when Chomsky and Halliday, founders of two alternative schools today, published their first works. My personal quest, to reconcile my twin linguistic fathers, is a means to an end, a better, stronger, more comprehensive social semiotic theory. I resolve some divisive problems in linguistics in that framework. How is grammar related to meaning and political struggle? How can it illuminate social processes of meaning?

Halliday and Chomsky both became linguists in the 1950s. Halliday (born in 1925) was a British war-time counter-intelligence officer in China, where he learned and later researched Chinese. When he returned to Britain and completed his doctorate he was refused an academic job because he refused to sign a statement saying he would not join the Communist Party.

Chomsky was born 1928 in New York to Jewish parents. Before studying linguistics he developed lifelong left-wing commitments. Having gained fame as a linguist, he became an equally famous critic of US policy. Yet he mainly disconnected his linguistics from his politics. Halliday likewise never published linguistic critiques of political texts.

The relations between individual biographies and broader contexts are complex and unpredictable. So are the relations between specific ideas and the Zeitgeist, the spirit of the time. I particularly want to identify factors that may have led to the long split between linguistics and political engagement. Both founding fathers were formidable theorists, men of great integrity, committed to the left. Why this gap? Was there something about their ideas on grammar that blocked these connections?

The immediate context for Chomsky's revolutionary linguistic theory was 1950s America. I take McCarthyism as a signature phenomenon of this context and source of materials for analysis. In 1950, the Republican Senator Joe McCarthy gave a major speech which claimed a vast communist conspiracy among US government officials. His claims provoked widespread paranoia and a series of witch-hunts of left-wing intellectuals. This must have impacted on Chomsky as a graduate student in linguistics, as his close circle included many who would have been threatened by McCarthyism. Halliday has said that this episode had its effects in Cold War Britain (Bilal 2013).

McCarthyism was constituted in texts and in explosive discursive, semiosic processes that carried the effects very far, very quickly. In this chapter I am especially interested in a specific counter-history. What challenges could McCarthyism have provided for Chomsky's and Halliday's emerging ideas of grammar for politically engaged, critical linguistics? Semiosic contexts inflect meanings and are themselves meanings. McCarthy's strategy included waving a list in the Senate which he claimed contained 205 names of proven communists in public office, which he would not reveal. Waving the list was a multimodal signifier supporting his spoken words. This semiosic situation contains multiple splits. McCarthy's speech is a surface text split from its real meaning, supposedly known to the speaker but not the audience. The speaker demands absolute trust from his hearers at the same time as he excludes them. We do not need a theory of schizophrenia to see this as a way to provoke paranoia.

I quote a passage from the famous speech which launched McCarthyism:

4.1 Today we are engaged in a final, all-out battle between communistic atheism and Christianity. And, ladies and gentlemen, the chips are down . . . They are truly down.

What kind of grammar could help analyse this text, and this threat? And how could we get to it from Chomsky's and Halliday's theories of grammar?

What is grammar?

The relevant history of this moment covers more than sixty years. Neither Chomsky nor Halliday supposed they were inventing the concept. Likewise, in developing broader concepts of grammar for social semiotics, I still build on linguistics and traditional ideas of grammar.

I begin with a long history, from etymology. 'Grammar' comes from Greek *grammatike*, from *graph-*, 'to carve or write', hence what is carved or written, pictures or letters. It already had multimodal origins.

'Grammar' came from signifying systems which connect with visual systems, not speech. Derrida (1976) used 'grammatology' in this sense to describe a semiotics of writing. 'Word', in contrast, came from Indo-European **weirdh*, 'what is spoken'. Latin *verbum*, both 'word' and 'verb', comes from the same root. The twists and turns of history left contradictory traces in grammar's meanings which contribute to its meaning potential today. Over millennia, 'grammar' migrated to refer to signifieds not signifiers, codes not contents, deep patterns in speech as well as writing. It still includes both parts of all these oppositions, to some degree. The underlying root, 'carve', is still detectable: what is grooved, following lines laid down by repetition. Repetitive learning, 'drills', is still part of the meaning of grammar, though not connected consciously to the core meaning. In this sense it has similar meanings to Bourdieu's *habitus*, dispositions ingrained in individuals by continuous actions (1972). Grammar is a kind of *habitus* of language, *habitus* like a grammar of practice.

The etymology raises issues for social semiotics about the scope of grammar. How wide does it go? From writing to speech and beyond? To all signifying systems in all media? Including electronic? Including behaviour? How long does it take for elements to be deeply grooved, hard to shift? As usual with remote etymologies, everyday users are not conscious of these meanings. Yet, as Williams (1977) argued, they can be actively grasped in the present and used to transform the understanding of a field of meanings. They can trigger counter-histories based on what happened in the past, still detectable in the present.

'Grammar' as understood in linguistics is narrower in scope. To illustrate, I use the *Oxford Dictionary of English Grammar* (*ODEG*; Chalker and Weiner 1994: 177). Their account of 'grammar' would have applied equally to Chomsky and Halliday and their contemporaries. *ODEG* lists four main meanings of 'grammar'. First is 'The entire system of a language, including its syntax, morphology, semantics and phonology'. The second limits grammar to structural rules, syntax and 'possibly morphology', but excludes semantics and phonology. The third is a 'book containing rules and examples of grammar'. The fourth is normative judgements on uses of these rules, as in 'bad grammar'. These four meanings co-exist alongside each other. They range in scope, from the comprehensive vision of meaning-1, the entire system of language, to meaning-4, the trivial pursuits of pedants. In between is the narrower study of syntax. There is a fault-line here, between a grand vision of grammar and a specific scope. *'Grammar' for linguists is a fuzzy term, with both a grander and a narrower scope.*

For Chomsky, 'a grammar of a language purports to be a description of the ideal speaker-hearer's intrinsic competence' (1965: 4). This is meaning-3, 'grammar' as a description. But what this grammar describes is meaning-1, 'the entire system of language'. In practice, Chomsky swung between the broad scope of meaning-1 and the structural rules and syntax of meaning-2. Halliday revealed similar ambiguity over the scope of 'grammar'. Sometimes his 'functional grammar' was a meaning-1 theory of language as a system. At other times he talked of a 'tristatal system: semantics, grammar, phonology' (1976: 39), where grammar is close to the narrower *ODEG* meaning-2.

As this analysis suggests, traditional linguists, including Halliday and Chomsky, share a fuzzy definition of grammar as both broad and narrow. This is not a problem, for them or for linguistics. The broader sense expresses grander aspirations and justifies their sense of the importance of grammar, while their analytic practice is mostly narrow. For me it represents an opportunity for transforming the study of grammar.

Halliday and Chomsky share many assumptions about grammar. In many features where they are often seen as opposed, they represent different or overlapping positions on some major continua. For instance, Halliday's grammar is called 'functional', opposed to Chomsky's structuralism. But Halliday was also a structuralist, schooled in the same structuralist classics, Saussure (1974) and Jakobson (1962). Conversely, Chomsky attacked functionalism, but his target was Skinner's behaviourism, not Halliday's functional grammar. Similarly, Halliday emphasized social over psychological facts of language. Again, this is a false dichotomy. Chomsky did not doubt that language is social, and Halliday knew well that it involves mental processes.

Halliday's term *'multidimensionality'* is useful for managing these and other false dichotomies: 'A form may be ordered in a language by its being placed in a number of dimensions' (1956: 172; see chapter 1). Multidimensionality appeared in his first published article and is a major premise for the architecture of social semiotics.

Halliday and Chomsky did position grammar differently. Where Chomsky saw grammar as a discrete system, Halliday proposed it as part of a single system, the 'lexico-grammar', in which 'the lexicon . . . is simply the most delicate grammar' (1978: 43). By 'delicate', Halliday meant degrees of detail in what he saw as a continuum (1976: 72). But he also saw a boundary between grammar and lexis (words): grammar is characterized by closed systems, lexis by open ones.

In this book I combine Chalker and Weiner's four meanings of 'grammar', with the etymological sense adding a fifth. *Grammar is a set of rules and patterns expressed in grooves of behaviour, underlying every mode of language, at every scale, from below the word to social and cultural levels.* This is not so much a definition as a semantic space in which to connect traditional ideas from linguistics with new possibilities for understanding and using 'grammar' for social analysis.

I illustrate with McCarthy's text. His sentences are grammatical but, 'reading' his grammar diagnostically (Carbó 2001), I note something odd about 'between communistic atheism and Christianity'. 'Communistic atheism' seems to imply other kinds of atheism, yet here McCarthy seems to equate communism and atheism. These are opposed to 'Christianity'. Unstated here is another binary category, un-American/American. In this classification system, separate categories collapse into each other. This dysfunctional classification system generates the paranoia McCarthy provoked.

This analysis seems to be about the use of words, yet it examines paradigmatic structures organizing those words, driven by a wish to use grammar to understand something about politics. In Halliday's terms, *it is 'delicate grammar'.*

The Chomskyan paradigm

Syntactic Structures

Chomsky's *Syntactic Structures*, published in 1957, still exhilarates me as it did when I first read it. Chomsky revised his model several times in later years. His disciples took it in different directions again. In spite and because of these disagreements, *Syntactic Structures* is still a good place to understand the Chomskyan paradigm and to use it to build a new model for linguistics and semiotics.

I begin with a statement by Chomsky from his epoch-making book:

4.2 Syntactic investigation of a given language has as its goal the construction of a grammar that can be viewed as a device of some sort for producing the sentences of the language under analysis. (Chomsky 1957: 11)

The central point in this definition is the idea of a grammar as a 'device', described here as 'producing' sentences and elsewhere in *Syntactic Structures* as 'generating' them. Chomsky prefaces this with the phrase 'can be viewed as', which casts doubt on the status of the term – whether it is really or only metaphorically a device.

The concept of 'device' comes in a surprising part of Chomsky's exposition. The book describes three models of language. The third, transformational, is so important I give it a whole section. The second, on phrase structure grammars, describes, critiques and develops the currently dominant linguistic model. But the first, a Markov state process model, as described by Shannon and Weaver (1949), comes from a deceased Russian mathematician, Andrey Markov, whom most linguists of Chomsky's time would not have read or thought important. Chomsky critiques this model and seems to dismiss it. But why include it in the first place?

Chomsky's interest in Markov showed how innovative he was. *Syntactic Structures* was published only nine years after Wiener's cybernetics (1948) proposed homologies across biology, society and machines. Gregory Bateson published his cybernetic analysis of schizophrenia in 1956 (1973). Erving Goffman (1959) used a version of game theory to analyse interactions in work I see as foundational for social semiotics. The 1950s saw Cold War paranoia and cyborg theories and practices emerge together in the Zeitgeist. Chomsky was at this leading edge.

Chomsky rejects a Markov process model for English, on the grounds that English has properties which cannot in principle be produced by Markov machines. He does not use semiotic terms, but the quality Markov's digital model cannot capture is the analogue forms and structures characteristic of language. Chomsky does not reject the idea of a machine. Instead he proposes a better one, which he models on the common linguistic practice of 'parsing' (from Latin *pars*, 'a part'), where syntagmatic strings are broken down into constituent parts. Chomsky proposes a machine which can do this.

I summarize some features of this machine as Chomsky describes it. Firstly it consists of a set of ordered rewrite rules, an algorithm. The idea of 'rewrite rules' was a powerful current idea in biology, as in Crick and Watson's Nobel Prize work of 1953 decoding DNA (Watson 1970).

Chomsky's rules are applied in strict order to produce or generate a sentence. The rules are also represented in a tree diagram that has become an icon for Chomsky's grammar. In semiotic terms, tree structures like double helixes are analogue forms, produced by digital processes: a transformation of digital into analogue form. Chomsky introduced a particular kind of rule to cope with what he saw as a defining quality of human language. Rules specify contexts of elements, which act as a kind of structural memory. The example he gives is the agreement between nouns and verbs, where singular nouns take singular verbs. Chomsky includes this rule in the basic set. Contextual rules act on whole strings like transformational rules do. Both kinds of rule similarly simplify the set of rules and intuitively account for connections that users make.

These rules are presented as $[\Sigma, F]$, where Σ refers to a set of initial strings and F a set of instructions. Because this formula is so abstract it could be easily adapted to include all three grammars Chomsky has described. Since its input includes words and its output is sentences, Chomsky's device integrates meaning and form. At one point (1957: 48) he compares it to a machine whose output was all possible chemical compounds. The excitement and risk of Chomsky's initial theory of devices is that *the device in itself is potentially general.* It could describe many grammars other than his preferred one.

A dialogic framework

Chomsky rejected the Markov model because, as he claimed, the grammar of human languages contradicts it. By the same reasoning we can legitimately ask that Chomsky's device be adequate to the social dimension of language, even though that was not his intention. I restate Halliday's social, functional premise: 'Language is as it is because of the functions it has evolved to serve in people's lives' (1976: 4). In this vein, I add Bakhtin's (1981) premise of the dialogic nature of language in social life as a touchstone of the adequacy of Chomsky's theory.

My aim is to integrate Chomsky's device into social semiotic analysis. I return to McCarthy's text (4.1): 'The chips are down. They are truly down.' These two sentences are closely related, linked by a version of what Chomsky (1957: 36) calls a conjunction transformation, which combines two separate sentences. In this case it turns 'the chips' into the pronoun 'they' and adds the emphatic 'truly'.

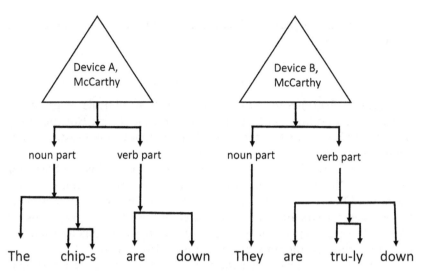

Figure 4.1 Dialogic trees

One sentence mirrors the other, with adjustments. These are normal forms in dialogue. However, here McCarthy generates both. It is a strange kind of dialogue, in which McCarthy replies to himself. Like Breivik's manifesto analysed in chapter 1, it looks like dialogue but is not.

In figure 4.1 I draw what is happening as a pair of tree diagrams, in which I represent the two sentences as the product of two Chomskyan devices, each corresponding to a McCarthy voice. Note that this is my interpretation of the relationships and processes which constitute McCarthy's sentence. It is an image to think with. Strictly it is a micro-grammar of a particular moment of a personal grammar. Yet it represents the tracks of how McCarthy thinks, his logic. These diagrams are generated by identical but separate devices, both located in McCarthy, following each other like successive turns in a dialogue. Applying Bakhtin's perspective, I see this as a dialogic form produced in monologic conditions.

Chomsky's original device is non-scalar, which simultaneously produces all sentences of a language and specific sentences produced from a limited vocabulary of words and forms. I treat it as a social semiotic fact on a micro-scale. It rapidly produces a hypotactic structure (tree diagram) but then adds a copy alongside it, in a paratactic structure. In this way I suggest we can connect Chomsky's *account of generative devices underlying actions and practices in language with particular instances,* as part of a social semiotic toolkit.

Syntax and meaning

In Carbó's (2001) form of critical linguistics, analysis of grammar and meaning go hand in hand in 'reading as analysis'. But the study of meaning has come to have a problematic place in linguistics, especially for its relationship to grammar.

Chomsky's work played a big part in creating this problem for linguistics. Yet he did not aim to exclude or ignore semantics and meaning. On the contrary, he made many attempts to include it in his theory. Eight years after the appearance of his revolutionary book he wrote: 'It is quite apparent that current theories of syntax and semantics are highly fragmentary and tentative' (1965: 148).

To explore this problem I look at a sentence produced and analysed by Chomsky in 1957, specifically intended to demonstrate the difference between syntax and meaning:

4.3 Colorless green ideas sleep furiously. (Chomsky 1957: 15)

Chomsky contrasted this with another sentence:

4.4 * Furiously sleep ideas green colorless.

In a later discussion, he proposed a comparable grammatical, meaningful sentence:

4.5 Revolutionary new ideas appear infrequently. (Chomsky 1965: 149)

These three sentences, all produced by Chomsky, form a continuum, from the non-sentence 4.4 to the fully meaningful 4.5. This creates an interesting ambiguity about the status of key sentence 4.3. It makes less sense than 4.5 but more sense than 4.4. What is this meaning, and how is it conveyed?

As I inspect these three sentences I try to hypothesize a pattern that makes sense of them – a device that can be plausibly attributed to the supposed author Chomsky. 4.5 seems straightforward, a normal output of Chomsky's normal device. 4.3 has many features that seem to reflect the operation of a phrase-structure machine as described by Chomsky, including a rule that gives the correct American spelling

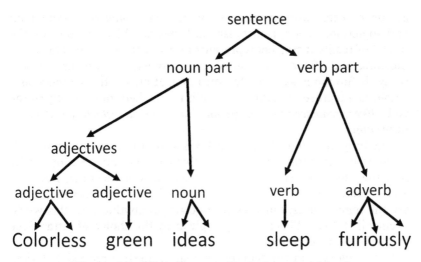

Figure 4.2   Tree diagram of 'colorless green ideas'

'colorless'. Given the many cues that seem to signal that this sentence is produced by a speaker or writer of English, I try to guess what is going on in it.

Sentence 4.4 is different. As Chomsky points out, it has many cues that this is a random string of words. Since the words are the same as those in 4.3, I guess that this is the product of a completely different device, one whose sole purpose is to produce random strings or to scramble existing strings. This is a Markov machine with zero probabilities, or a person acting like one. In this case I hypothesize that Chomsky has access to three devices (normal English, aberrant English and random generator).

I drill down into 4.3, and parse it. In figure 4.2 I have broken the sentence down into its immediate constituents, which I represent as a tree-structure diagram. For Chomsky this is the syntactic structure of the sentence. For me it is an analogue sign of how elements of meaning are related to each other in a semiotic whole. In 4.3, all three words, colorless, green and ideas, form a noun phrase which acts as a thing, which in this case sleeps. The action 'sleep' is modified by the adverb 'furiously'. Even though in this case it may be hard to build a clear picture of what the sentence refers to, it is a meaningful analysis of reality. It is a world in which there are things of different kinds, which act in different ways.

Halliday (1985) elaborated this basic model of a sentence. He built on traditional classifications of verbs into transitives, where subjects act on objects, and intransitives, which have only one participant and an action. 'Sleep' is intransitive. It has no object. As a result the model of reality it triggers represents non-linear causality. This is the meaning and effect of transitive and intransitive sentences respectively. It functions as an added meaning. It affects the sentence as a whole as a picture of reality, though it is attached most closely to the verb. *Every sentence type conveys an abstract picture which contributes to its meaning.*

The fully meaningful sentence 4.5 is also intransitive, even though its topic is 'revolutionary' ideas. In this case we can see more easily how the use of transitive versus intransitive adds meaning. Both 4.3 and 4.5 have the same analogue picture of the world, in which ideas are the main things, but they do not act on anything. In this world agency is diffuse. This meaning is given by the choice of intransitive forms for both sentences.

I see a pattern in the sentence which suggests a recursive device. 'Color + less' negates colour. This is then negated by the colour green. 'Colorless' implies a physical object, but 'ideas' are non-material. 'Sleep' is associated with tranquillity, not fury. Every element seems to contradict the previous one. I hypothesize a Markov device programmed accordingly, with low-probability transitions between successive elements. That would make it not the nonsense Chomsky claims, but a high-uncertainty, high-information statement.

I invoke Halliday to ask functional questions about this sentence. What functions might it have served? Chomsky stated that he used it as an example of a sentence that is grammatically correct but meaningless. Even if we accept that this was one intended function, according to the multidimensionality principle, many functions and meanings may co-exist.

This book is not the place for me to develop my own theory of grammar in any detail. It would *minimally include different devices, paratactic, hypotactic and transformational, on different scales in different semiotic modes, all uniting form and meaning, produced in social contexts by cognitive processes.* Its forms would evolve as functional in some contexts but could become dysfunctional in those or other contexts. It would not be a single coherent top-down system but an assemblage. Such a theory would resolve the problem of meaning created in the competing models, generative and interpretive semantics. No doubt, like all theories, it will have problems of its own.

The scope of grammar

Universals

Chomsky is associated with a doctrine of universals, with justification. He has been attacked for this aspect of his theory. Some of the ways he has expressed this idea left him open to criticisms. However, in this section I argue that all powerful theories run this risk. The answer is not to abandon this goal but to use it in more complex ways.

Halliday is often contrasted to Chomsky as a cautionary voice on universals. But Halliday's system-functional networks are potentially as universal as Chomsky's syntactic processes. Likewise, Whorf (1956) is associated with a doctrine of total relativism. However, he too noted regularities as well as differences across language.

This dispute is often framed as a war between irreconcilable positions with respective champions. I propose these as poles in a continuum, not fixed positions. Instead of 'universals', I look for 'relative universals', universals which are so only up to a certain point. Instead of being a contentious dogma, this idea guides particular research in a flexible, multiscalar social semiotics.

I illustrate with Chomsky's tree structures in *Syntactic Structures*. He illustrates these only with English, but linguists have found constituent structures in many languages, so they are likely to be more universal than in English. Yet they are not universal even in English. *They describe hypotactic structures, with branching structures heading downwards*, as captured in Chomsky's diagram. Yet *many syntagmatic structures in English are paratactic, with elements lying beside each other.* Universality can mean that they are usually one option, not necessarily the only option.

Halliday also has tree diagrams, though superficially they do not look like Chomsky's. Halliday maps paradigmatic, not syntagmatic structures. Neither Halliday nor Chomsky remark on this, but the fact that both these fundamental semiotic structures are framed in the same way makes tree structures seem more fundamental to semiotics of all kinds, likely to be present in most languages.

As illustrated in figure 4.3, Halliday's tree seems to be generated from left to right, equivalent to Chomsky's direction from top to bottom. The difference is superficial. Halliday's grammar is generative, too. Halliday has a richer notation system for his trees. His systems do not only branch out, they also come together. They cope with multidimensionality, the co-presence of different systems, and

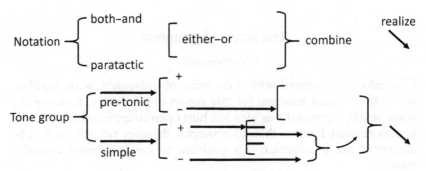

Figure 4.3 Halliday's system networks
Source: Based on Halliday (1976)

they link elements as well as split them. I propose for social semiotics *that all human languages and codes are likely to have tree structures in both syntagmatic and paradigmatic planes. They will also likely include paratactic structures.* These are both tracks or grooves along which semiotic processes may run, parts of the grammar.

Halliday's systems owe much to the classic structuralist analysis of phonological systems associated with Trubezkoy (1969) and Jakobson (1962). In this process, as described by Jakobson, sound systems always evolve through the same mechanisms, working with the same elements of human physiology, as Saussure outlined. Its product always had a tree shape, similar to Chomsky's trees.

Jakobson saw this process as universal, yet its product as always differentiated. The sounds of every language are distinct from one another, and *the function of this system is to produce this diversity.* The products of this device in different languages are systemically different, too, especially concentrated in some sounds which carry the accent. The Australian 'a' is not like 'a' in any other form of English (Fiske et al. 1987). But Jakobson's version of this device does not produce only differentiation. He proposed a pattern he called 'vocalic triangles' (Jakobson and Halle 1956). Oppositions (here between two different forms of open and closed sounds) also produced intermediate sounds which resolved the opposition. In figure 4.4 I use Hallidayan brackets to indicate this process.

Tree structures are found elsewhere in language. For instance, language families identified by comparative philology in Jones's tradition (Jones and Cannon 1993) have this typical form over a very long scale. The identification of these processes in language by linguistics pre-dated the discovery of similar genealogies of species

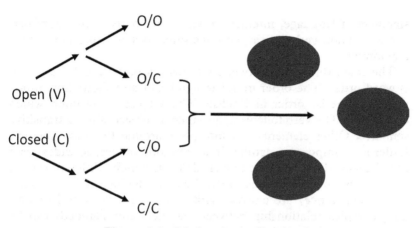

Figure 4.4 Jakobsen's vocalic triangle

in evolutionary theory. Is there a connection between biological and linguistic processes?

On an even more general, more 'universal' scale, *these tree diagrams resemble fractals, the self-similar forms produced over many scales in many very different phenomena,* according to Mandelbrot (1993).

Order and multimodality

'Grammar words' in English refer to a heterogeneous set of signs whose function is primarily to manage relations between elements within and between texts and the realities they refer to, with rules for their use which also carry meaning. Mainstream linguistics usually focuses mainly or exclusively on words or morphemes with this function. *Multimodal theory looks at all signs which have similar functions, with all semiotic resources.*

'Paralinguistic' systems are understood by most linguists as parallel systems operating alongside but outside verbal language, treated as outside the grammar. Only Halliday (1985) includes intonation patterns as part of the grammar. As he recognized, these patterns are analogue forms which affect meaning.

Writing has its own version of paralinguistic systems. Kress and van Leeuwen's study of multi-modality in print media (2001) showed the role played by composition and the order of elements, verbal and visual, on a page (see chapter 1). Word order is recognized as part of the grammar and the language, though usually marginalized. I look at how and what order means as part of the repertoire of signifiers of language, interacting with other parts of the grammar, verbal and non-verbal, as aspects of a single system which constitutes a grammar.

The main difference between Chomsky's sentences 4.3 and 4.4 is word order. The order in 4.3 is significant and shows how much work is done by order in English. The subject is the noun which comes first. The verb follows it, and then an object, if it is a transitive sentence. Other elements slot into place around this basic picture. Order is an important signifier in all semiotic modes, so widespread as to be a candidate relative universal. Yet it signifies different things, even within one code. Conversely, the main signifieds of order (e.g., power, coherence) are always signified by other signs and modes. This complex relationship between signifiers and signifieds can be seen as relatively universal.

In social codes, 'firstness' carries motivated social meanings, as Carbó (2004) showed in her study of Mexican parliamentary discourse. First speaker carries importance, but so does last speaker. The same principle underlies the system of turns in formal systems, as it does in other less formal settings, as 'conversation analysis' has shown (Sacks et al. 1974). Those who begin and end conversations both claim and exercise power. So do those who speak more, or speak louder. Order and size, however measured, are motivated signs.

English word order looks elemental to English speakers, an iconic image of reality itself. It is indeed an iconic image, but, as Whorf reminds us, it is an interpretation of reality, not a transparent reflection. Some linguists have investigated whether there is a universal pattern for subject–verb–object, a preferred or obligatory order, a potential linguistic universal.

The US linguist Joseph Greenberg (1963) investigated the order of subjects, verbs and objects (S,V,O) in a landmark study of world languages and found that 45 per cent were SOV languages, 36.6 per cent were SVO, and 18.3 per cent were VSO. No languages used the other three options. Other studies found a sprinkling of examples of the other three options but confirmed this basic picture. The figures illustrate Whorf's point, that analyses of reality that seem given by nature to speakers of a language may not be represented that way in other languages. Yet the figures also show a more general quality. In 81.6 per cent of the world's languages, according to Greenberg, the subject comes first. In the rest, the subject still comes before the object. Firstness is strongly associated with subject position. It is a fuzzy but motivated sign.

Halliday (1985) has a complementary analysis of firstness in

English. He associates it with information structure, organized around binary terms, Given–New. Many linguists do not call information structure part of 'syntax', but it is part of the syntagmatic plane. It is the source of syntagmatic patterns which may either overlap, reinforcing each other, or complement each other.

Word order in noun phrases is also significant as an indexical sign. Hodge and Kress (1993) argued that the order of words in noun phrases expresses the order of acts of classifications or attributions. Order functions as an indexical sign, which, like all signs, may or may not be true at the moment of utterance.

With McCarthy's phrase 'communistic atheism and Christianity' (3.1), for instance, the order of the elements is a subtle part of his meaning and carries significant traces (indexical signs) of his logic. 'Communistic' as an adjective must come before its noun in English, in which firstness in a noun phrase signifies that it is less important, dependent on its noun. So 'atheism' opposed to 'Christianity' is the major defining quality of the enemy, not 'communism'. Yet though both the order and its meaning are fixed, McCarthy is free to choose what he puts in the two positions. Here he could have said 'atheistic communism'. Likewise he could have had 'Christianity' first. By having 'communistic atheism' in the focal first position he makes it the marked term. *Order is a sign system with motivated but fuzzy meanings in all modes, including speech and writing, probably in all languages.*

Transformations

Transformations are fundamental for social semiotics, included in chapter 1. System and transformation combine as basic features of the theory. Both are relative universals whose scope goes far beyond language. Transformational analysis is a powerful tool in semiotics. There are few problems or texts where transformations are not crucial to social meanings and effects.

Transformations in linguistics

Chomsky played a complicating role in this story. *Syntactic Structures* (1957) proclaimed the importance of transformations. Chomsky there saw it as an essential part of grammar, the most elegant, economical way of arranging its structures and rules. At this stage he saw transformations as psychologically plausible, affecting meaning. He proposed the concept of 'deep structure' as a metaphor. I believe this can play a valuable role in social semiotics, to refer to a *dynamic, four-dimensional space, in which structures, processes and transformations have social and referential meaning.*

In later work (1995) Chomsky made transformations narrower in scope and less central, disconnected from meaning and cognitive processes. The changes weakened the explanatory value of his account of transformations, which in turn damaged the linguistics tradition based on his work. Chomsky deserves the greatest respect for his original theory and its inspirational effects. However, I believe his legacy is best preserved by returning to the *Syntactic Structures* model.

Chomsky's early theories were structuralist. His theory needed Halliday's functional framework to show how the same transformation can have many functions, and the same function can be realized by many transformations. It also needed a Hallidayan concern for paradigmatic as well as syntagmatic transformations, and an extension of semiotic modes.

Other strands of linguistics presented alternative models. Early Halliday (1956) included transformations by another name – 'inversions' – and he used the term 'grammatical metaphor' to analyse Chomskyan transformations. Coulson (2001), in the Lakoff tradition, talks of 'shifts and blends' in discourse. In psychotherapy, an interdisciplinary team from psychology and linguistics, Bandler and Grinder (1975) successfully used a realist version of Chomskyan transformations.

Yet Chomsky's eminence combined with contradictions in his theory to produce paradoxical effects. Because 'transformations' was part of the name of his theory, it was supposed that he must have a strong theory of transformations while leaving his followers without one. At the same time his opponents felt they could not use that term because it was part of his brand, even when they were actually talking about transformations.

Critical linguistics

In critical linguistics the social and psychological reality of transformations was central in tracking meaning in use (Kress and Hodge 1979; Trew 1979). Transformational analysis in this model offered a kind of X-ray into the minds of speakers and writers.

We used a list of common transformations in English as identified by Chomsky, all well recognized in English grammars. I applied the theory to the Chinese language (Hodge and Louie 1998) and found that, though Chinese has some different transformations in the grammar, the principles applied well. Transformations are a relative universal.

But in applying the theory to many examples I found I needed some distinctions. Transformations represent operations of minds, but not necessarily those of immediate producers. Pieces of language circulate over time, blurring or losing their connection with specific agents. *Transformations are social as well as individual, part of the grammar, as well as individual acts.* Transformational analysis follows deep grooves in the language which leave traces in the grammar. The habitual, social nature of grammar raises empirical questions about agency: Whose meanings?

I illustrate common functions of transformations in a newspaper editorial:

> 4.6 An investigation into the state of mental health in WA by the *Weekend West*'s Agenda team revealed a picture of fragmented, poorly-coordinated services and frustrated patients and families who were barely coping. (*West Australian*, 20 December 2011: 20)

In the phrase 'state of mental health', 'state' seems a nominalization of an adverb, 'how' (the system is). It could correspond to the transitive 'how professionals treat mentally unwell people' or to the intransitive 'how mentally unwell people cope (in life or under treatment)'. The interpretative process goes from a seemingly tidy surface sentence to a 'deeper' structure full of unclear, confused ideas. *Transformational analysis often reveals traces of meanings and thoughts, not always deliberate attempts to hide or mislead.*

Among the many possible transformations there is one that might be overlooked. These patients are not well. If they were they would not be patients. But, somewhere in this murky, capacious deep structure, 'unwell' has been transformed to its opposite, 'health'. This ideologically important transformation is not likely the work of the newspaper, which probably took the words of the government health service, which in turn follows the lead of international bodies such as the World Health Organization, which now avoids stigmatizing terms like 'insane'.

This transformation has social meanings. It transforms these objects of medical attention to signify a new concern for the feelings of the mentally ill, in keeping with a new ideological complex for representing disabilities. As indexical sign, the transformation comes from and hence also signifies the alliance between this editorial group and those who manage the discourses and practices of mental illness. But this relationship is not present in the text. *Analysing the social meaning of transformations always has to be supported by empirical research.*

In interpreting this text I guess the intervening transformational processes. Such guesses happen all the time in semiotic life to produce another class of indexical sign, based on estimated distances between surfaces and realities, in the world outside the text as within sets of text. *More layers of transformation signify lesser degrees of truth and reliability.*

Transformations as material practices

The transformations discussed above are primarily mental and linguistic acts, but, in a materialist multimodal semiotics, the theory must cover actions with similar functions and effects. Freud compared psychological repression with official censorship, where deletions of meaning occurred in the public gaze, not on Freud's couch. In critical linguistics, Tony Trew (1979) is especially associated with a materialist theory of transformations, seen as actual operations on actual texts.

I illustrate this form of transformational analysis with an example which involved Chomsky. In 2013, lengthy efforts by Frederick Maxwell to investigate the CIA relationship to Chomsky were met with a seemingly impenetrable response (Hudson 2013):

4.7 [CIA] We did not locate any records responsive to your request.

His endeavours were finally rewarded with the release of a letter from the director of the CIA to the director of the FBI. It seems innocuous, with only one phrase about Chomsky:

4.8 [CIA] . . . with the endorsement of Noam Chomsky.

Transformational analysis relies on assumptions and guesses about deep structure and the social relations of semiosis. The greater the reason to distrust producers of meanings, the more elaborate and unreliable the guesses. Distrust of the CIA is built into assumptions of its critics. But, without something more, distrust has nothing to work with.

Analysing 4.7 on its own, I see alternative deep structures: either 'there were no records' ➜ 'we did not locate records' or 'there were records but we destroyed them' ➜ 'we did not locate records'. By understanding this as a transformation, it raises a doubt about what happened and why the CIA used this form. If they had in fact destroyed records, this would be a serious act in terms of their charter. Without the letter, this doubt would have been right in fact but unproductive. In this case, a letter exists which mentions Chomsky, however briefly, '(these people) were endorsed by Noam Chomsky' ← 'Noam Chomsky endorsed (these people)'. Moreover, this phrase implies, is the trace of, an act of surveillance leading to this claim: 'X (the CIA director) knows that (Noam Chomsky endorsed these people)'.

The letter now exists, as proof that there were records, so we can combine the two analyses to show that there was surveillance of Chomsky, in spite of previous denials, and records of this, again denied. This letter exists, so it was not destroyed, but other records might have been destroyed as the analysis implies. If so, the CIA has inadvertently provided evidence of possible dubious or illegal activities.

This interpretation is a reconstruction, as is transformational analysis in general. Most of the proposed transformations, linguistic and material, are ad hoc, not part of the grammar, but the grooves of verbal transformations in the grammar help guide interpretation. That is the main lesson from this instance. Transformational analysis clarifies meanings and identifies shifts or absences which can only be confirmed by detailed empirical research. It can seem mere speculation if it is embedded in an autonomous linguistics or semiotics. But in tandem with relentless social investigation, itself a form of transformational analysis, it becomes a tool that can penetrate even a nut as tough as the CIA.

Towards a general theory of transformations

Chomsky wrote in 1957, four years after Watson and Crick announced their decoding of DNA. In Watson and Crick's model, information was stored in the genetic base and transcribed (Watson 1970). Chomsky's initial theory included rewrite rules, and in later versions they played an even greater role. However, the end of the twentieth century saw a new complementary emphasis on epigenetics, the decisive effects of contexts, 'epigenetic environments', on the expression of genes (Edelman 1988; Jablonka and Lamb 2005). Epigenetic research shows that the most elegant and plausible way of accounting for the diversity of genetic outputs is through a model with a similar architecture to early Chomsky's, with base rules, rewrite rules, analogue forms and transformational rules acting on base forms.

The structuralist model of phonology can be understood in these terms. A small number of basic generative principles, such as open–closed, voiced–unvoiced, interacts with the vocal apparatus as an epigenetic landscape. This produces not only different phonemes but also differences between phonemes across languages and dialects, and even expressive differences for individuals, what Barthes (1977) called 'the grain of the voice'.

It is plausible to suggest not only that transformations are relatively universal, but so too is the four-element architecture independently proposed in epigenetics and described by Chomsky in *Syntactic Structures*.

1 *Transformations are motivated changes introduced into structures or systems.*
2 *All kinds of structure, syntagmatic and paradigmatic, in all semiotic modes, can be transformed.*
3 *Transformational analysis uses cues to follow normal processes of inter-pretation, reconstructing hypothesized processes of generation in imag-ined 'deep structures'.*
4 *Transformational chains are understood as having direction, from later ('surface') to earlier ('deep') meanings. Deeper meanings are under-stood as closer to the 'truth', reality for producers of that meaning.*
5 *The social meaning of transformations is what they do to images of reality (analogue signs), on behalf of what hypothesized agents.*
6 *Transformational analysis projects real cognitive processes. However, grammar provides a storehouse of grooved transformations available for many users.*

Grammar and cultural analysis

For social semiotics a key aim is to develop methods of analysis which illuminate issues of culture and society. In this section I do this by examining the theme of gender and the role of grammar in it as devel-oped by the linguist Whorf.

Covert categories

Whorf's work on grammar was original and influential. Both Chomsky and Halliday absorbed or reacted to his work. Yet in some respects his ideas went beyond both. In a famous article he wrote:

4.9 One cannot study the behavioral compulsiveness of such material without suspecting a much more far-reaching compulsion from
large-scale patterning of grammatical categories, such as plurality,
gender and similar classifications (animate, inanimate, etc.), tenses,
voices, and other verb forms, classifications of the type of 'parts of
speech,' and the matter of whether a given experience is denoted by
a unit morpheme, an inflected word, or a syntactical combination.
(Whorf 1956: 137)

This compulsion is most associated with grammar. Yet it is not
grammar as such, but 'large-scale patterning' of 'grammatical categories'. Whorf gives a useful checklist of them here. But no item on the
list on its own carries this meaning in a strong or evident form. The
effects come from combining meanings, none fully conscious.

This is the object I see as Whorf's discovery: the idea of *language-
and-thought as a vast, infinitely complex, largely invisible network of
meanings*. This is an object on the scale of Durkheim's 'social fact'
(1952), similar to Geertz's idea of culture as a web of meanings
(1973) and Bonfil's 'cultural matrix' (1987). They are not precisely
the same, but it is useful to bring them together in fuzzy forms in a
framework for social semiotic analysis on this scale.

Whorf's linguistic intuitions were guided by his distinction between
'overt' and 'covert' categories (1956: 88). Overt categories have some
overt marker, such as masculine and feminine gender in Latin, Greek
and Romance languages. Covert categories are marked only by what
Whorf calls 'reactances'. These are displaced signs, other words or
signs enshrined in rules, forbidding or requiring certain elements in
that place.

I can still remember my exhilaration as I first explored Whorf's
ideas of covert categories applied to gender. Outcomes of this
research were published in Kress and Hodge (1979) and later applied
to Chinese (Hodge and Louie 1998). At that time I was keenly interested in issues of gender but had supposed that English no longer
had grammatical gender, unlike Latin, Greek, French, etc. Then I
read Whorf's confident statement that yes, indeed, English does have
gender, but it is covert, marked only by the use of pronouns – 'he',
'she', etc. I used the pronoun test to reveal my personal gendered map
of reality, physical and social, whose existence I had barely known,
whose function I had not seen, acquired during my socialization.

Whorf generated some crucial questions. How far does reality
motivate this fact of language, and how far is the 'fact' generated
or constituted by other forces in society? With the gendered reality
revealed by the pronoun test it became possible to ask: Why is this

or that constructed as female rather than male? For example, for me and advertisers in England in the 1970s, 'flowers', 'nature' and 'cars' were feminine (Kress and Hodge 1979: 81). 'Idea' in Greek and Latin is feminine. I wondered: Does covert gender along with animism survive in Chomsky's 'colorless green ideas'?

In Chinese I found the same principle (Hodge and Louie 1998). Chinese, like English, does not mark gender. It has gender, but it has gone underground. For instance, the binary pair *yin* and *yang*, female and male principles in Chinese philosophy, are usually claimed to represent complementarity and balance between these two principles in an ideal of gender harmony. However, in Whorf's terms they have different 'reactances' (patterns of use). There are thirty-four compound nouns with *yin* in Chinese, twenty-three of which (68 per cent) express negative sentiments, and only three (9 per cent) positive sentiments (Hodge and Louie 1998: 52). Of twenty-one compounds with *yang*, only two (9 per cent) are negative. A useful term from grammar is 'marked forms'. There are many asymmetrical pairs of forms in language, where the less common is marked in some way: possible but marked as exceptional. Unmarked forms in contrast are presented as 'normal', to be taken for granted: grooved, sustained by the grammar. *Reactances are often fuzzy asymmetries.* The ideological message coded into these gender terms is a contradiction. It is not so different from English and European forms of a gendered ideological complex.

Networks of signs, each so small as to be nearly invisible, maintain gender systems in all societies. Feminists have successfully attacked the use of gendered pronouns in English (Pauwels and Winter 2006), but this has not changed the whole system. That does not show that no change has happened, only how complex and resilient the system is.

In a story published in 1975, the US science fiction writer Ursula Le Guin challenged the unconscious dominance of gendered pronouns by creating a world of androgynes in which the default pronoun was 'she'. This produced sentences such as:

4.10 When this picture was taken the young king had her back against the wall. (Le Guin 1975: 94)

This story illustrates the nature and power of the 'compulsion' exercised through grammatical items such as pronouns. In this case the writer deliberately breaks the rule for pronouns in a sentence that Chomsky might star as ungrammatical because 'king' has male gender. Of Le Guin's experiment we might ask: Why not use the available term 'queen', which has the correct gender and can mean a ruler? Why defy language, when language seems sufficiently inclusive? Yet on closer inspection the gender issue is more complex. 'Queen' does not simply mean a female king. It more usually means the female wife of a male king. As with Chinese, *gender systems work through hidden asymmetries*. They give with one hand then take back double with the other.

The compulsion to see the world in an ideological way is hidden from individuals under the seemingly neutral compulsion to use words correctly ('king' versus 'queen', 'he' for individuals who are males, etc.). As Whorf points out, those decisions are linked together in a network of 'reactances', no less powerful for seeming largely 'natural' and obvious.

Gender and popular culture

'Culture' is used in a slightly different sense when it refers to 'popular culture', but both forms need to be integrated in social semiotic analysis. I illustrate with the closing line from a song, 'Rose Marie', as sung by the American singer Slim Whitman.

The song was composed in 1924 for a highly successful Broadway musical. Whitman's version was recorded in 1955, when it remained at no. 1 in the UK hit parade for eleven weeks, a record not broken for forty years, even by famous names such as Elvis Presley, the Beatles or the Rolling Stones. As I listened to the song on a flight from Australia to New Zealand in 2011, I wondered what meanings it might have had for so many Britons in 1955. In the final line, repeated three times, the singer addresses Rose Marie directly, as a queen.

I begin the analysis with the humble pronouns, 'I' and 'you', major items in the grammar of deixis. 'I' is interpreted initially with reference to the singer, Whitman, but also to his persona as the lover of 'Rose Marie', then adopted by listeners who identify with the singer. 'Rose Marie' is a proper name, deictically pointing to this imaginary lover. Two clauses contain this relation between 'I' and 'you', but the two persons swap roles: in one clause, 'I'd choose you'; in the other, you (understood) 'rule me'. In the first, the male lover is the agent, the one 'choosing', as in the dominant gender ideology. In the second, the woman 'rules' over a willingly passive male lover, contradicting the dominant gender ideology.

I turn to the semiotics of the song as song. Whitman's distinctive yodel ranges between a man's range and the higher pitch of a woman. It is androgynous: the masculine is dominant but the feminine keeps breaking through. Whitman's interpretation of the song created gender ambiguity around the pronouns, similar to Le Guin's conscious experiments with gendered pronouns. Whitman switches between low and high pitch, masculine and feminine, to give a complex gender meaning to the 'I' who loves the supposedly female 'you'. In the dominant model, men rule. The other is a subversive world in which men desire to be ruled.

On its own, Whitman's song has too many ambiguities to be usable for cultural analysis. For instance, we cannot be sure what date it reflects – the 1924 of its original performance, or 1955, when Whitman gave it an overlay of musical meanings. The 1920s were a brief moment of sexual liberation; 1955 was two years before *Syntactic Structures*, in the heart of the anti-gay paranoia associated with McCarthy. It was also the year dominated by the ambiguous sexuality of James Dean, star of *Rebel without a Cause*.

Popular culture allows counter-realities to be expressed more richly, at the price of remaining largely unconscious, unacknowledged, without clear effects. But in a study drawing on much more data, Whorfian concepts of grammar could identify unobtrusive threads that lead deep into the ideological morass of the changing cultural matrix, while recognizing how difficult it is to identify its component meanings, much less change them.

The meaning of grammar

This chapter has used the word 'grammar' in many senses as its focus. To complement that approach and draw the various threads together I list meanings associated with grammar which are often expressed by other words, in English as in other languages. A central meaning I identify for these purposes, the candidate relative universal, is the idea of *a small set of rules generating great diversity*, as in Chinese *yŭfá*, 'language + law'. Some analogous words in English are as follows.

1　*Code* (from Latin *coda*, 'a tail') This word comes from a convention in early books, where basic principles were gathered together at the end. This kind of tail truly wagged the dog. It was the word used by war-time code-crackers such as Alan Turing, later used extensively in computer programming. It was also the term used by Crick and Watson for the generative principles of DNA. The meanings of code and grammar could usefully be brought together in a powerful new fuzzy meaning.

2 *Alphabet* (from the first two letters of the Greek alphabet, *alpha, beta*) Representing the phonemes of speech was an early breakthrough in a digital understanding of language, capturing the principle that a small number of elements could produce the sound of every word in the language and more. Crick and Watson used this analogy from language, too. Although it is more limited in scope than 'grammar' or 'code', it can co-exist with the others.

3 *Axiom*, from mathematics, has a similar sense applied to mathematical systems. However, both *code* and *grammar* have greater flexibility and scope. The same is true of *algorithm*.

4 *Meta-language/communication Meta-* comes from Greek, one of whose meanings is 'after'. Aristotle used it influentially for his philosophy, *metaphysics*, coming after physics, like a coda explaining all general principles. So meta-communication has come to mean communication about communication (Jakobson 1962; Bateson 1973). Grammar could be reframed around this as its primary function. If so, grammars might look very different – more like Chomsky's *Syntactic Structures* (1957), Whorf's *Language, Thought and Reality* (1956) or Halliday's *Language as Social Semiotic* (1978).

5

Reading and Meaning

In this chapter I revisit themes and ideas I have already touched on. I develop a broader basis and a deeper, more complex understanding of these in a social semiotic framework and show them doing social semiotic work. I connect especially with psychology, philosophy and literary studies to complement and extend semiotics and linguistics. But my focus remains on meaning as the main node linking language, meaning and society.

The concept of 'reading' links theory and practice across all modes. Reading verbal texts is of obvious practical importance. Reading is the point of entry into the written code for everyone in literate societies, equally indispensable in the digital age. Yet controversies rage over what reading is, how it can be best acquired and developed. What role might social semiotics play in understanding the various things that reading is and might be, with what practical importance? Conversely, what can existing research on reading contribute to social semiotics?

For social semiotics, reading goes beyond deciphering letters and words. 'Read' comes from Old English *raedan*, 'to counsel, interpret, read'. Some of this semiotic scope survives in English today, as in the use of 'read' for decoding body language. I use this etymology to support a semiotic argument that *different semiotic modes are interpreted in similar ways that can be equally illuminated by social semiotics*, building on a common term like 'reading'.

Reading as theory and practice

Meaning is a theme for many disciplines. In this section I connect social semiotic ideas to two disciplines in particular, philosophy and psychology. At the same time I use key texts as a focus for examining the semiotics of reading itself, as deployed on these often difficult texts.

Wittgenstein on meaning

Philosophy has a long tradition of illuminating reflections on meaning, from Plato and Aristotle to modern philosophers such as Peirce, Heidegger, Husserl, Habermas, Austin and Grice. My focus in this section is Ludwig Wittgenstein, arguably the most influential figure in the philosophy of language. His texts present highly complex meanings, demanding powerful reading strategies. I show how social semiotics can frame and enhance these high-order strategies of reading as a practical contribution to analysis. At the same time I hope to enrich social semiotic ideas of meaning by reading his influential ideas on meaning better.

I begin with a passage from the early *Tractatus* of 1921:

5.1 A proposition is a picture of reality. A proposition is a model of reality as we imagine it.
At first sight a proposition – one set out on the printed page, for example – does not seem to be a picture of the reality with which it is concerned. But neither do written notes seem at first sight to be a picture of a piece of music, nor our phonetic notation (the alphabet) to be a picture of our speech. And yet these sign-languages prove to be pictures, even in the ordinary sense, of what they represent. (Wittgenstein 1971: 4.01, 4.011)

Paraphrases are fuzzy and approximate, usually good places to start analyses of complex meanings. I begin with my paraphrase of Wittgenstein's meaning: he proposes a relationship between propositions and pictures such that a picture is equivalent to a proposition. I see this as similar but not the same as the picture underlying my own definition of meaning, that it is a socially inflected version of reality.

My next semiosic act is to compare the two pictures, his and mine, as complex analogue forms. In doing so I could emphasize differences or similarities. Either way I co-construct a meaning for myself as for Wittgenstein that is subtly different from either. *The two pictures come together as a paratactic syntagm*. This produces a new compound picture with unpredictable new meanings: mine after I have read Wittgenstein, Wittgenstein's in the light of my reading of him.

I do not impose my meaning on Wittgenstein. I use it to bring out unexpected implications of his picture. His was a brilliant semiotic account of language before semiotics had been invented. It is a multimodal theory of meaning in which analysis of verbal propositions depends on their non-verbal form as analogue signs, as 'pictures'. He uses an analysis of other 'sign-languages' as a decisive part of his analysis, reflecting on the comparable digital codes of letters and musical notation.

I now drill down deeper into this text and its meanings. Wittgenstein follows the first statement by changing 'picture' to 'model', adding 'as we imagine it'. This is a paratactic structure, juxtaposing two statements without specifying how they are to be related. Is a 'picture' the same as a 'model'? Does a 'model' include elements lacking from 'picture', such as generalizability? More generally, does the second sentence completely subsume and cancel the first? If so, why include it?

This text is built up of units of different lengths which are paratactic structures, pivoting around a partial negation, usually an adversative ('but', 'yet'). These small words play a potent role, in Wittgenstein as throughout English. Adversatives like Spanish *pero* and Chinese *dànshì* have a similar range of meanings and functions. Crain (2012) argues that logical operators seem to be expressed in comparable ways across all languages. Here, as often, they have a complex effect on meaning. What goes before 'but' is partly negated, not as true as what follows. But it still remains as a meaning, its 'picture' partly but not completely erased. Usually 'but' has a social meaning and function. It marks what the speaker thinks or says. Before it is what the opponent says. It is what Derrida (1976) calls 'under erasure', a *meaning which is seen but not seen*.

In the same section Wittgenstein proposed another metaphor:

> 5.2 A proposition constructs a world with the help of a logical scaffolding, so that one can actually see from the proposition how everything stands logically *if* it is true. (Wittgenstein 1971: 4.023)

This is a different metaphor. If we follow Wittgenstein's argument we have two pictures, two worlds projected by the propositions. I have problems with the term 'scaffold' here. The logical relations Wittgenstein talks about seem more integral than a scaffold. I use the metaphor as something to think with. Logic here seems like paradigmatic structures organizing syntagmatic structures. I am aware that I am not identifying what Wittgenstein meant so much as seeing problems connecting what he said to possible meanings.

I add a third text, this time from late Wittgenstein:

5.3 The *questions* that we raise and our *doubts* depend upon the fact that some propositions are exempt from doubt, as it were like hinges on which those turn. . . . If I want the door to turn, the hinges must stay put. (Wittgenstein 1969)

'Hinge' is a third metaphor, suggestive, profound, and not entirely consistent. For me it connects more with the scaffold metaphor as I redefined it, an extension of the idea that meanings ramify out into a world that exists or is constructed from a single proposition. But the hinge metaphor complicates the whole structure of meaning.

A final stimulus I take from Wittgenstein is his discussion of the duck–rabbit illusion (2001). Wittgenstein reflected on an ambiguous image of the kind Gestalt psychologists analysed. Some saw a duck, others saw a rabbit. Wittgenstein argued that the image was not ambiguous, since observers could see only one or the other at one time, not both. I connect this with Saussure's discovery of the principle of incommensurability, in his opposition between synchronic and diachronic.

I have not fixed what Wittgenstein really meant. On the contrary, for me these *meanings are more interesting, generate more meanings, even if, even because, after strenuous efforts I remain uncertain what his intended meanings were.*

I have also complicated the question of what 'Wittgenstein' is to whom these meanings can be attributed. In one view of the relationships of wholes to parts, a concept of 'Wittgenstein' or 'early/late Wittgenstein' should override the interpretation of individual sentences or arguments. In this case I showed a fissure across every level, a dialectic between two meanings or more, multiple Wittgensteins. It is this generative core of Wittgenstein's thought I looked for, but in his meanings, not instead of them.

Reading reading

I continue my experiments in reading by deploying social semiotics at the conjunction of two fields, psycholinguistics of reading and semantics, as a branch of linguistics. Both fields have a complex play of digital and analogic codes and different perspectives on the issues that arise from them.

I begin with the psychology of reading and the work of Frank Smith. Smith (2004) drew on an exciting explosion of work in psycholinguistics in the 1960s, stimulated by the Chomskyan revolution, to become a seminal theorist on reading. His ideas on how this process works bear on the fundamental social semiotic issue of how parts can be different from wholes of which they are part in interpreting meaning.

As a psycholinguist, Smith integrated the psychology of perception and thought with linguistic analysis. He saw the process of reading as a complex whole, a dynamic interaction between readers, texts and language, in which readers play decisive roles. With reading he distinguished between initial stages in the process, the identification of elements, to later stages of interpretation. Readers go from mediated understanding (dependent on analysing elements before the whole) to immediate understanding (where the whole is directly grasped in itself). This end point is exemplified in 'fluent reading'. Smith's theory emphasized the role of holistic perception of what I call analogue forms, but digital analysis plays a key role too. He drew on digital concepts from information theory, which calculates 'information' as the mathematically calculated reduction of uncertainty, to explain how readers scan texts and context for clues and cues. Readers compare wholes to wholes through the presence or absence of distinctive features. Their guesses are digitally structured.

No one doubts that 'fluent reading' exists as an empirical fact, and it is an ultimate goal for every reading programme. Fluent readers have a remarkable ability to perceive larger, significant wholes directly, mobilizing their knowledge of relevant models or wholes. But Smith's 'whole language' approach to teaching reading has proved controversial in detail. Proponents of 'phonics' insist that young learners specifically need to learn the system of correspondences between sounds and letters.

In a multiscalar theory of parts and wholes, this opposition dissolves. Wholes at lower stages can be equally complex at that level. The system of correspondences between sounds and letters is actually highly complex at its own level, as Marilyn Adams (1994) recognized in her judicious review of the controversy. In multiscalar semiotics, readers need to be able to go up and down relevant scales. When good readers strike a problem in their grasp of a whole at any level, they need to backtrack to lower levels, decomposing the whole at a higher level. The passage from level to level cannot be taken for granted.

In what follows I apply social semiotic strategies of reading to read texts about reading, to develop the theory in tandem with the practice. My first example comes from a text by Alan Cruse, from his excellent introduction to semantics. He explains a key principle on which formal semantic analysis rests, the 'principle of compositionality':

5.4 The meaning of a grammatically complex form is a compositional function of the meanings of its grammatical constituents. (Cruse 2004: 65)

I use this sentence to explore both its content and my strategies for understanding it. I begin by noting that Cruse's sentence strikes me as difficult. I imagine it would seem so to others too. So I begin with a paraphrase, my provisional sense of the whole:

5.5 The meaning of sentences comes entirely from adding their parts.

I'm aware this summary leaves things out. On reflection, I find the full sentence was too complex to communicate directly. There was no 'immediate meaning'. Faced with this difficulty, I go back to the parts. I know all the letters, so I do not revisit the alphabet. I know all the words, so I do not stop to look them up in a dictionary. The process would be too slow, and I would still not understand the sentence.

The problem is not the component words but how they come together. As a reading strategy, the principle of compositionality, breaking everything down into component parts, does not work well for me in this case. Some parts make me pause – for instance, the phrase 'a compositional function of the meanings'. I interpret the phrase first by reconstructing a new whole, a full sentence:

5.6 Compositional meanings are functions of the grammatical meanings of their components.

I still have problems with this expanded form. 'Compositional' is one word, but it plays a crucial role. It helps if I decompose it into its parts. It is an adjective, as signalled by '-al'. That adjective comes from a noun, as signalled by '-ion'. That noun comes from a verb, signalled by '-it-'. As I track back though these processes I come to a verb, 'compose'. I use etymology to aid comprehension. Tracking further back to its Latin roots, I find con- ('with', 'together') and pon- ('put' or 'place'). This is intriguingly close to the Greek syn-tagm, 'arranged together'. This comparison brings out a curious quality in the sequence. Across its journey, a word that was about putting things together has come to refer to a condition of remaining separate and separable.

In this process I have used a *strategic multiscalar approach*, in which I move between wholes at different levels, decomposing them into lower constituents, recombining them in new wholes. In this conception, holistic approaches and phonics can co-exist. Phonics deals with challenges of relations between letters, sounds and meanings that are highly complex at that stage but which need to be routinized and become part of the grammar.

That stage is essential in learning to read, just as semiotic analysis of component signs is never redundant. But every stage must be taught as an open system, *moving from lower levels, also open, to higher levels without any prior level being superseded.* Readers of Wittgenstein and Cruse should never forget the ladder they climbed to get there, while children reciting sounds and letters should know these are rungs, not destinations.

Wholes and parts

In this section I continue my dual strategy, developing methods of reading to bring out the meaning of key texts about meaning. Here I use this apparatus to look at a sentence of Aristotle's *Metaphysics* containing his principle of totality:

> 5.7 In the case of all things that have several parts and in which *the totality is not, as it were, a mere heap, but the whole is something besides the parts*, there is a cause. (Aristotle 1935: 1045a8-10)

Aristotle's sentence contains more than the totality principle (italicized). I begin with the grammatical structure, usually a useful guide to reading. The totality sentence consists of two propositions, a paratactic structure, related by 'but', which, as with Wittgenstein, leaves the relation between the two unclear. Each proposition is also a paratactic structure, again related by partial negation. Aristotle's first negation distinguishes between two forms, a totality and a heap. The meaning at this point is carried at the level of words, not higher-level structures.

The Greek word translated 'heap' is *soros*, opposed to *holon*, a similar opposition as English 'heap' versus 'whole'. In this case differences between the languages are not decisive. What carries and constrains the meanings across languages and epochs is the structure, Wittgenstein's 'scaffolding'. Yet in both languages there is the same problem of meaning, the same ambiguity.

This interpretation colours the second statement, often paraphrased as 'the whole is more than the sum of its parts'. Aristotle's claim is more ambiguous. The whole is something – i.e., it exists. It is 'beside' the parts, but they exist also. With both versions of the phrase there is a crucial doubt. Does Aristotle mean that the whole is *not* the sum of its parts but something completely different? Or does he mean that the whole is both the sum of its parts and also something else?

The difference is huge. In the first interpretation, Aristotle would oppose componential analysis. In the second, he includes it alongside holistic analysis. He invented both logical analysis, which is digital, and holism, so he may be supposed to have entertained both meanings, both pictures, both world views. As we saw, there are fundamental divisions in Wittgenstein also. In both cases, *meaning is dialogic, in which different positions or voices co-exist in unresolved, undeclared tension.*

In both cases, interpretation (reading) reaches a problem, not a clear meaning. This outcome is not usually desired by beginning readers, yet these questions raise basic issues for the theory and practice of reading as interpretation. Neither outcome – a single interpretation or awareness of complexity – is always right or wrong. But important continuities of skills and knowledge cross these approaches which should find a place in a single reading curriculum.

My analysis is an example of 'reading as analysis' (Carbó 2001), where linguistic analysis, including grammar, is integral to interpreting meanings. Critical reading of this kind is an advanced mode of reading, a legitimate target for a reading programme. It rests on habitual practices of interpretation which include grammar and multimodality, including all the modes by which meaning can be encoded and circulate. All this can exist alongside the journey to fluency that Smith emphasizes, with its own dialectic between wholes and parts on different scales. Its focus may be at any level where parts and wholes are in complex relationships, between and within texts. In this process, something like a 'principle of compositionality' has a role to play, in a dialectic which attempts to apprehend new wholes.

Holistic syntagms

The miraculous way humans enter language has rightly fascinated many fine linguists and psychologists, including Jakobson, Carol and Noam Chomsky, Halliday and Hasan, Brown, Kress, Piaget, Vygotsky and Freud. How do children go from having no language to mastering it? How do they learn to mean? What is happening on their way to this achievement?

Many researchers tend to look at this as a fascinating but inherently simple stage which we adults go beyond. I believe this linear model of progress is misleading. In this section I look at child language in a complexity model, in which languages at any one *stage include a heterogeneous set of forms from earlier stages, operating as a loose system.*

I will not comment on the 'pre-linguistic' stage, except to note how dynamic it is. Jakobson (1962) found this a highly creative stage in developing the sound system. Halliday (1975) found children develop a rich set of language functions before progressing to adult functions and syntax. Piaget (1956) observed the emergence of important cognitive capacities before verbal language. After the pre-linguistic stage, children enter into a stage characterized by one-word utterances commonly called 'holophrastic' (Greek *holon*, 'whole' + *phrasis*, 'speech'). This stage lasts from roughly twelve to eighteen months and is followed by syntax involving two elements, *paratactic* structures. The final stage sees the emergence of *hypotactic* (hierarchical) structures, involving three or more elements subordinated.

This sequence is often seen as a simple progression, from lack of syntax to simple syntax to complex syntax, with each stage seen as superior to previous ones. However, from a semiotic perspective, *all three stages have syntagmatic forms, creating meaning out of significant links between elements in paradigmatic sets.* Holophrastic utterances are commonly connected to the immediate environment. They also have an expressive element, carried by intonation and gesture. *Holophrastic language is already multimodal.*

The two-word stage lasts for around a year. Its vocabulary seems mostly continuous with the third stage, but its syntactic rules seem to be those of a different language. But all three forms or grammars survive into adult language. From a semiotic perspective I ask: How do they function as a system? To answer this question, I look at a song John Lennon and the Beatles sang on TV, broadcast live by satellite on 25 June 1967 to 400 million viewers from twenty-six countries:

5.8 All you need is love, love, love is all you need.
Love (nine repetitions)

At the exact centre of the first line is 'love', repeated three times, followed by nine repetitions in the next line. The first and third 'loves' could be seen as parts of sentences, but the central 'love' functions more holophrastically, as a self-sufficient syntagmatic form whose meaning comes from different contexts and intonations. As I interpret it, all three 'loves' are captured by the holophrastic principle, partly detached from the sentences in which they occur, more free to have a holophrastic richness of meaning. In nine repetitions of the chorus, 'love' becomes more detached from the syntagm.

As a holophrastic sentence, 'love' is primitive but complex and profound. 'Love' as a meaning is arguably a relative universal, an organizing principle in every known human society. In every society it is exploited, manipulated and opposed by many people, and that is equally a relative universal. Lennon's strategy, reimmersing the word in an early form of language, reclaims the potency the word can still have.

The song has regressive syntax in other ways. 'All you need is love' is derived from a hypotactic, 'You only need love', transformed into the paratactic form of a definition: 'all-you-need' + 'is' + 'love'. Lennon's voice fuses these elements, 'all-you-need', so that they function more as holophrastic utterances, an equivalent to 'love'.

In my interpretation, Lennon is overlaying the three kinds of grammar, holophrastic, paratactic and hypotactic, not replacing the later with earlier forms. As a fully adult verbal artist he drew on all forms, which still co-exist in adult language. Earlier more 'primitive' forms still have powerful meanings and effects. This illustrates a more general social semiotic principle: *successive forms co-exist functionally in new, complex configurations in complex but unstable wholes.* We saw this in the continuing relevance of sound (and other systems) in the interpretive repertoire of readers at every level.

The point of view which minimizes or ignores this fact is influenced by a limited, linear idea of evolution, which sees a simple narrative of continuous progress, with species evolving to become better and more complex over time as earlier inferior species disappear. So it is useful to draw on biology to correct this assumption. As Lynn Margulis (1998) emphasizes, the world of microbes did not disappear with the advent of multi-celled organisms. They flourished, indispensable to the existence of humans and their planet. Without our assemblage of bacteria in our guts we could not function. Without the input of micro-organisms into the mechanisms of Gaia (Lovelock 2000), our planet could not host human life.

This principle can be seen in the continuing relevance of all prior modes of human expression, bodily, spatial, in regimes of orality: in the continuing relevance of oral modes in literacy regimes and all of these in the electronic age.

Paradigmatic structures and reading meaning

Meaning is a socially inflected version of reality in which a crucial role is played by paradigmatic structures and processes. These

structures and processes perform a complex and extensive part in
the creation and interpretation of meaning. In the following sections
I bring out some aspects of paradigmatic structures and paradigmatic work.

Reading culture

There are many ways of using social semiotics to read 'cultures', of
different kinds for different purposes. 'Reading cultures' is a major
focus and function of social semiotics. In this section I continue my
interdisciplinary heuristic use of Wittgenstein's ideas, connecting his
notion of 'logical scaffolding' with semiotic ideas of paradigmatic
forms. This is a social semiotic strategy for cultural analysis which I
apply to Homer's *Odyssey*, focusing on two lines in eighth-century BC
Greek. The text consists of a modern translation, (a), plus two aids
to follow the argument in (b) – literal translations, word by word,
immediately above the relevant part of the Greek text. Readers can
follow the argument by referring only to (a):

5.9a Bright-eyed Athena sent them a driving breeze,
A driving West wind, roaring on the wine-faced sea. (Homer 1974:
2.421-2)

5.9b To them then following tail-wind sent bright-eyed Athena
Tois d'ikmenon ouron hiei glaukopis Athene
fresh Zephyr, roaring on wine-faced sea.
akrae Zephyron, keldont' epi oivopa ponton.

Following Wittgenstein's idea of pictures of pictures, its serial multimodality, I build up the 'picture' projected by this text. Homer's
sung text was transcribed into Greek writing, and this was translated
into modern English. Across this series of analogue signs, a remarkably stable basic picture emerges, describing a journey by Telemachos,
son of Odysseus, one of the Greeks who sacked Troy.

Homer's Greek had a similar syntagmatic architecture as modern
English. The basic sentence form analysed events in causal terms,
with agent, action and object, with here a third participant who ben-
efits from the action. Greek had a case system, in which each of these
roles was explicitly marked. As Fillmore (2003) showed, English has
a similar case system, but covert.

The picture communicated by the Greek and English versions is
comparable. Common to the English and Greek is a physical reality:
a favourable wind drives a ship. But there is also 'something besides'.

The overall 'shape' of the sentence directs how these components come together in a single meaningful picture, with differences in the 'scaffolding'. The physical agent of this action, Zephyrus, the west wind, is the object of the main action, 'sent', whose subject, the main agent, is the goddess Athena. Zephyrus is grammatically both object of the main verb and subject of the participle *keldont'*, 'roaring'. He is both god and part of the natural world, at the meeting point of two major paradigmatic categories.

Athena has no special marker to indicate she is a goddess, but Homer's readers, then and now, know that she is. It is part of the cultural meaning of the name. But that meaning, the fuller picture it constructs, makes sense only if we build into the model a major place for divine causality, attached to a different paradigmatic structure. Most of the time Homer describes natural causality with human or non-human agents following the laws of physics as then understood. But sometimes, as here, he describes the actions of gods, usually behaving like powerful humans. In these cases, this second level of causality operates in complex ways. Athena has the power to 'send' lesser gods such as Zephyrus, but sometimes lesser gods dissent.

This is an example of Wittgenstein's 'scaffolding', the network of assumptions that make sense of this world. But in this short passage we have two cases of a superimposition of two systems of causality, two systems of scaffolding. I need to modify Wittgenstein's stated model. Instead of just one picture, utterances may project two pictures, two worlds, each incompatible with the other. But, as we saw, this duality applied to Wittgenstein's practice, too.

Wittgenstein's 'hinge' metaphor pushes me to look outside the text for an aspect of the logic that underpins different positions, equally taken for granted by both. In this case one such proposition may be that reality or causality is both fully divine *and* fully material. Existence precedes that division which seems so inescapable to modern thought. Yet modern readers have a 'hinge' too, equally invisible, in which that division has always existed.

This kind of analysis contributes directly to both literary and anthropological analysis, since it brings out basic meanings that make this a major text for both fields. For social semiotics it would remain incomplete without questions that bind this text to its social world. Why would the militaristic thugs Homer describes in his poem, similar to the aristocrats he sang for, be bonded by this double view, a view whose duality remained invisible for everyone in the society?

Conceptual structures

In this book, 'meaning' is seen as produced by interactions between paradigmatic and syntagmatic planes, structures and transformations. In this section I look at how work on concepts in psychology, philosophy and linguistics can illuminate accounts of paradigmatic structures.

Aristotle was a giant in European philosophy. His theory of wholes and parts has been taken up in complexity theory today. His linear ideas of logic, on taxonomies or classification schemes, were even more influential. Far from this contradiction making him an inadequate thinker, it shows a breadth and capacity for contradiction which lesser thinkers lack or conceal.

Aristotle developed a strategy to produce hierarchical (hypotactic) classification systems based on two digital principles: sameness (in relation to higher categories) and difference (in relation to categories at the same level). This scheme produced crisp definitions. For instance, red is a colour, like blue, green, etc., but is different from other colours, preferably by just one criterion. In modern physics, one criterion would be wavelength.

Aristotle's scheme is simple and powerful. The taxonomies it produces still underlie much of science. Jakobson's structural analysis of phonology is an adaptation of this kind of process. The idea of categories it produces seems like common sense. Yet the scheme has inconvenient consequences. It not only emphasizes boundaries, it creates them where they do not exist in reality. It overemphasizes digital systems of meaning and misses or distorts analogic meanings. It excludes the multiple criteria which are usually present.

The Russian psychologist Lev Vygotsky in the 1930s proposed two kinds of concept developed by children (1978). One type, which he called 'scientific', was essentially the Aristotelian form. But he noted that children enter school with different kinds of concept using what he called 'complexive thinking'. Children given a sorting task, for instance, might group objects using more than one criterion, so that a natural group, equivalent to a 'concept', might contain objects each of which is connected to something in a group, but not by the same principle. A colour – e.g., red or blue – may be a factor but not a criterion. The 'concept' formed in this way lacks both the sharp boundary of Aristotelian concepts and Aristotelian unity. It is more like a network.

The later Wittgenstein (1968) challenged Aristotelian categories along similar lines in his concept of 'family resemblances'. He observed that we can recognize that different people are related as members of the same family, even though they do not all look exactly alike, and some members at the extremes may not look like each other at all. They have a family resemblance rather than a single feature in common.

The psychologist Eleanor Rosch (1978) used experiments to support what she calls a 'prototype' theory of concepts, in terms of which concepts have an internal structure, such that some examples of the concept are closer to the understanding of the concept than others. They have a better 'Goodness of Fit' value.

In chapter 1, I introduced the work of the engineer Lotfi Zadeh (1973), with his idea of fuzzy sets, fuzzy categories, fuzzy boundaries and fuzzy rules. He claimed that fuzziness is not just an alternative to scientific, crisp thinking. It is a powerful corrective to scientific thinking, even in the domains of science and engineering, especially in conditions of high complexity.

All these proposals see a continuum of membership of items and concepts. That is an analogic model, which produces a different picture of concepts. In the digital perspective, boundaries are high with no internal differentiation that matters. *In an analogue perspective concepts have low, permeable, fuzzy boundaries, tolerating heterogeneous and shifting structures.*

An influential attempt to develop cross-cultural taxonomies was proposed by a team from anthropology and linguistics, Brent Berlin and Paul Kay (1969), who focused on colours, examining what they defined as primary colour terms (dedicated colour terms) in a large number of languages. Their bigger target was universals. What they found was surprising and interesting – a basic repertoire of eleven terms organized by comparable paradigmatic structures. These colours were not found in all languages, but where they were found they followed a consistent pattern. All languages had the first three: dark, light and red. If they had later ones in the sequence, such as pink, then they would always have earlier ones, such as red, blue and green.

This pattern is broadly similar to the paradigmatic structures of phonology in Jakobson (1962), a universal process producing actual diversity. In paradigmatic structures like this, individual elements change their value in different systems. So red or blue, for instance, in a five-term system is likely to have a different scope and meaning to the same colour in an eleven-term system. It will be more heterogeneous, fuzzy and inclusive. As with all paradigmatic structures, they have meaning as they intersect with syntagmatic forms and social contexts. I illustrate with Homer's text (5.9). In terms of Berlin and

Kay's scheme, colour was coded differently in Homeric Greek compared to English.

For instance, Athena is called *glaukopis*, translated as 'bright-eyed'. But *glauk-* could refer to blue or grey as well as bright. It is one of Berlin and Kay's two most primary terms. The colour of the sea is *oinopa*, 'wine-faced'. This diverges from the colour English speakers would call the sea. But Homer often calls the sea *phoinix*, which covers red and purple. It spans a range of what would be distinguished in the English colour system. But if there are no sharp boundaries between red and blue the sea can be the same colour (*phoinix*) as wine. In this case there is a binary scheme overlaid by complexive thinking, in which sea and wine are grouped together in the same concept, also linked by other features they share. This has a similar effect as metaphor, in which strong (deep-red) wine and the dangerous sea are brought together because they have a similar colour, from a fuzzy perspective, plus other properties the poet sees as relevant (e.g., fascination and danger).

It is not that Homer has a defective colour vocabulary (and, as some would infer, defective visual capacity) compared to English speakers. Colour terms for Homer, as in modern English, are *organized by both digital and analogic/complexive paradigmatic structures, in different proportions, with different effects of language and meaning*. The meanings and forms of meaning encoded in colour terms are different from the meanings of the colours themselves, but *terms signify deeper paradigmatic meanings, points of entry into cultural analyses*. They can be used equally well to analyse verbal texts and representations in other modes, in art and reality, literature or advertising alike.

Boundaries

Every complex dynamic system in language, society or biology is constituted by flows and barriers, internal and external, in relationships of reciprocity. Without barriers there is no structure and no identity. But barriers that are too high or too strong block the flows on which social and biological life depend. *Most boundaries have a dual function, to act as barriers yet also to allow some flows.*

In language and society alike, semiotics plays a major role, because material barriers can be constituted or reinforced by signs, and vice versa. As I observed in Mexico City airport, signs in tandem with material barriers are ideal ways to manage the ambiguities of barriers, to allow both flows and exclusions, to combine the reality and illusion of freedom with acceptance of control. The same principle applies to syntagmatic and paradigmatic structures. Syntagms of control organize bodies in space and time, spatial and social, drawing on paradigmatic structures that identify who can and who cannot do given actions or receive categories of object. In tight systems of control there is a one-to-one correspondence between social categories and the distribution of power. But normally both systems need fuzziness, blurred and ambiguous categories for negotiable relationships of power. That throws special weight on these boundary categories and events.

Anthropologists have made important contributions to a social semiotics of barriers. Arnold van Gennep (1960) proposed a universal scheme of what he called 'rites of passage' which has proved impressively durable. He saw a common pattern in the various rites that mark the passage of individuals through stages of life. Ritual time and space allow the contradictions between stages to be negotiated for individuals for their relationships to be separated from the old dispensation and incorporated into the new.

A complementary idea can be found in Victor Turner's work on the role of liminal spaces and times (1974). Turner is one of many cultural anthropologists whose work can be seen as major contributions to social semiotics.

Lévi-Strauss's structuralism (1963) included an intense interest in structural boundaries. The British anthropologist Mary Douglas (1970) pursued some of these ideas in contemporary life as well as in 'primitive' communities. She focused on the paradoxical role of major boundaries, 'thresholds', especially as they manifested in 'taboos', powerful prohibitions on particular words, things or behaviours. Taboos arise around mixtures of major categories. Yet those mixed categories can also generate the most potent meanings for that society. For instance, the boundary between what is inside the body and what is outside it is strongly marked and protected from violation. So excreta – faeces, urine, blood, milk and semen – form common sites of taboo.

The psychoanalytic semiotician Julia Kristeva (1982) explored a similar complex particularly affecting women's experience of their bodies through the term 'abjection'. Blood, especially menstrual blood, is often represented as a site of power as well as pollution. In some societies, in some circumstances, all excreta can be symbols of high but dangerous potency, not just objects to be rejected.

For social semiotics, this makes *the study of taboos, sites of intense ambivalence, especially valuable for studying contradictions in basic paradigmatic categories as they intersect with syntagmatic rules organizing social life.*

I illustrate this point with an analysis which combines taboo things with verbal language in order to show how a semiotic perspective helps to understand meanings and effects which drive what is going on in words. On 13 January 2012, Reuters press agency circulated a story about a video which showed US marines urinating on some bodies, identified as Taliban. In terms of media effects, this was similar to the photos of abuse of prisoners in the US Abu Ghraib prison in Iraq. In both cases, simple digital technologies produced analogue images which went viral.

5.10 Outrage over video of Marines urinating on Taliban corpses

The double effect of taboo comes across in this act. It is an outrage, by values shared by Americans and the Taliban, yet the fact that it is an outrage expresses even more power. By this means, these soldiers express meanings which are normally suppressed from discourse – hatred and contempt for their enemy which high-status people such as presidents and generals normally do not express.

This crossing of forbidden boundaries has complex, contradictory effects. Between the soldiers it created high cohesion. They laughed. Clearly it would have the opposite effect on the enemy. On all but the closest allies of the soldiers it would have an alienating effect. Officers might viscerally reject this raw assertion of power from below. Other US citizens may be divided.

In far-from-equilibrium conditions, the same structure of meanings can have opposite effects. When primary paradigm categories, such as inside and outside the body, interact with social categories of them and us in semiotic objects and in semiosis itself, *paradigm collapse produces explosive, uncontrolled reactions.*

Social complexity, complex meanings

In this section I use Halliday's words as a heuristic guide: 'Language is as it is because of the functions it has evolved to serve in people's lives' (1976: 4). If this is so, we can reverse the gaze to ask: If language clearly has certain properties, what does that tell us about its social forms and functions?

In this section I look at two properties of human languages, metaphor and ambiguity. What do these properties imply about the social contexts of language? What role can they play in social semiotic analysis of language in use?

Metaphor

More than any other contemporary linguist, the American George Lakoff has given metaphor a central place in linguistics. 'Our ordinary conceptual system, in terms of which we both think and act, is fundamentally metaphorical in nature' (Lakoff and Johnson 1980). This Whorfian kind of statement sets the ground for social semiotic disciplines to think about thinking.

Metaphor is strategically useful for the social semiotics quest to bring cognate disciplines of meaning together. Poets are expected to use metaphors, but linguists and literary scholars alike usually see them as a distinctive property of only literary language. This division shadows a more fundamental one, between analogue and digital codes, and their different ways of producing meaning.

The word 'metaphor' is itself a metaphor, probably invented or given its definitive form by Aristotle. It comes from *phero-*, 'carry', + *meta*, 'over', 'after' or 'across', between words and things and between different domains of discourse. *Metapherein*, the verb, meant either 'carry over' or 'transform', so Aristotle's term may have meant both. What is carried over is always analogue: *metaphors are analogue forms*. In many ways metaphors are part of a general theory of transformations.

Aristotle plays a suitably ambiguous role in the Western tradition on metaphor. As he defined it, 'A metaphor is the application of an alien name by the transference either from genus to species, or from species to genus, or from species to species, or by analogy' (Aristotle 1951: 1457b). Aristotle constructs metaphor as an elemental relationship between A and B, such that A is B. Yet it is always the case that in some respects A is *not* B. B is 'alien' (*allotrios*, 'other', 'different', 'alien', 'strange'). So, in metaphor, A is both A and not-A to some degree.

This is the normal effect of fuzzy logic on Aristotelian logical categories. Fuzzy logic deals with combinations of A and not-A as normal. Metaphoric thinking works with fuzzy categories and relationships. As the US psychologist George Miller (1979) noted, in order to come together in a metaphor, both aspects, A and B, should be indistinct, or, in Zadeh's terms, fuzzy.

Ambiguity

Like metaphor, ambiguity has been marginalized in linguistics, yet the two are closely related, equally fundamental qualities. Metaphor can be seen as a broad class of forms of ambiguity. *Both represent conditions of meaning that are indexical signs of social difference and conflict.* That makes them good sites for social semiotic analysis.

Halliday's concept of multidimensionality (1956) produces a model for mapping ambiguity. Chomsky discussed syntactic ambiguity in the example sentence:

5.11 Flying planes can be dangerous. (Chomsky 1957)

Chomsky saw this as the structurally ambiguous product of two sentences, one transitive (X flies planes), the other intransitive (planes which fly). He did not emphasize the fact that different structures corresponded to different meanings, and he did not ask how and why meaning functions in such instances. Even so, he includes ambiguity as a defining property of language, demanding that adequate theories should explain it.

Inserting 5.11 into a Freudian framework I see it as an example of a fundamental category of transformation I call fusion transformations (chapter 1). In fusion transformations, surface texts combine two or more sets of meaning associated with different authors, interests or aspects of the self. *Ambiguity is the normal product of co-construction of texts and meanings, in explicit or implicit dialogic processes.*

Reading ambiguity is a powerful tool for social semiotics. People from different disciplines have contributed to it. The literary critic William Empson (1930) drew discreetly on Freud in influential work that showed many grades and kinds of ambiguity in literary works.

The linguist and psychoanalyst Julia Kristeva (1980) carried Freud's ideas deeper into the study of language and social meaning to analyse terms of the kind in which Mary Douglas was interested, where powerful, ambivalent ideas and feelings clashed in women's experience of such taboo topics as menstrual blood. Seana Coulson (2001), from cognitive linguistics, showed many occasions in everyday discourse characterized by what she called 'concept blending'. She traces how people mix and match different qualities in a phantasmagorical process sometimes surprisingly like a Freudian dream state.

Ambiguity in action

Mainstream media discourses are full of examples to analyse to show how metaphor and ambiguity serve purposes in given contexts. One *Time* magazine cover featured an image of former President Reagan photoshopped to look as if he was embracing President Obama. The accompanying text said:

5.12 Why Obama ♥ Reagan
And what he's learned from him
BY Michael Scherer and Michael Duffy
Reagan at 100 –
Why he still matters
BY Richard Norton Smith (*Time*, October 2011)

This text is ambiguous in many ways. For instance, this is a multi-modal text in Kress and van Leeuwen's terms (2001). The single page communicates through words, pictures and composition, including the insertion of a red heart in the key sentence. *Multimodality allows many opportunities for ambiguity.*

Neither man here is called 'president'. Obama was the current president, Reagan a former president, now dead. So, strictly speaking, Obama was president and Reagan was not. Yet the meanings from the semiosic subtexts seem to say the opposite. Reagan looked fully alive, at the centre, still the real president.

Staying with meanings from the visual mode, I pick up the colour red, used for the heart and for Reagan's tie. The red of the heart is a saturated colour, a prototype red, in Rosch's terms, where Reagan's tie is a more complex colour and has stripes. One effect of that is to draw attention to it. It also has a cultural meaning. The heart is red because it signifies emotions. In the same simple, binary code, blue is the opposite, signifying the coolness of reason. Obama's tie on this occasion is grey, not blue, but, as with Athena's eyes in Homer's lexicon, they mean the same.

These colours also have political meanings. Colours conventionally signify political positions, a binary code, red for the left, blue for the right, though in America red for Republicans, blue for Democrats. But here right-wing Reagan has the red tie and Obama, accused by his enemies of being too socialist, has a non-red tie. These are metaphor-like processes which create ambiguity. Reagan is radical yet conservative and Obama is conservative yet radical.

The ambiguity can be resolved in each case, but the resolution is asymmetrical. Reagan is presented as really radical at the same time as he is a true conservative, but Obama is a pale imitation of both positions. In this reading, *ambiguity itself is ambiguous*. As in Douglas's analysis of taboo, Obama's contradiction signifies weakness, whereas Reagan's signifies power.

Applying Lakoff's frame analysis, I see further apparent

contradictions. The emotionality of the heart metaphor seems to evoke the progressive frame or complex, a nurturant president loving and loved by his people. But both are viewed through this frame. Reagan seems as warm as Obama while still being firm. We can see from this how easily Lakoff's frames can be manipulated in practice.

I guess these various meanings were skilfully arranged by the *Time* team to cleverly convey a hidden negative judgement on Obama and the Democrats while praising the Republicans. But newspapers have to appeal to a range of political views. One way to do this is through ambiguity, constructing texts which can be read in different ways by different kinds of reader. In such cases, *ambiguity both reflects and manages difference.*

Meaning in crisis

One basic proposition of this book is that language, meaning and society take different forms under different equilibrium conditions. They can be understood in their everyday forms only by seeing how they function in extreme, far-from-equilibrium conditions.

Bateson's model

Gregory Bateson's work on schizophrenia (1973) in the 1950s has proved controversial in psychology, but it remains seminal for social semiotics, so important that it warrants a whole section here. Its value comes from the fact that it deals with a case at the limit where the forms and functions of meaning are massively and systematically distorted, so much so that most people dealing with schizophrenics supposed that their discourse was meaningless. Bateson's model brought out the nature and functions of that meaninglessness. His general model is still important for social semiotics.

Bateson started from one feature of normal discourse, play, which is usually ignored as too trivial to bother to analyse. Bateson noted that play in all its modes has a rule-governed relation to reality, such that players know that the signs of play are not intended seriously or literally. He proposed that this is done by a cybernetic process through what he called a meta-communication loop, which calibrates signs and practices against reality.

In Bateson's analysis, the problems needing meta-communication loops came from the omnipresence of contradictory messages in everyday discourse. He called these 'double messages'. Others had noted that the nonsense effect of schizophrenic discourse is substantially due to the presence of what are called 'word salads' – strings of ideas apparently collapsed into each other – and excessive use of metaphors. Bateson saw metaphors as part of normal language. The distinctive quality of schizophrenic discourse, he argued, was that their metaphors were not recognized by schizophrenics and their audiences. Their problem, in his view, was not metaphors as such but the weakness of meta-communication loops.

Bateson used a kind of inverse analysis to connect these practices with social contexts and forces, asking what kind of universe makes sense of apparently aberrant communication habits and behaviour of schizophrenics (1973: 177). He classified these aberrant responses in three typical forms (1973: 183): paranoiac (seeing too much meaning), hebephrenic (seeing too little meaning) and catatonic (withdrawal from meaning and action). This simple model for social semiotics *showed the social conditions for different pathologies of meaning in language and action.*

In Bateson's view, schizophrenics are relentlessly bombarded with particularly intense, irreconcilable double messages and lack meta-communication loops to cope with them. The double messages are damaging and painful because they carry opposite affectual meanings from someone important to the schizophrenic, usually a parent. Bateson formalized this as a socio-logic that would produce these behaviours, steps in his theory of the 'Double Bind' (1973: 178–9).

1 There are two or more persons, including the schizophrenic. This is a crucial premise: causality for schizophrenic patterns of meaning comes from a *social system, not only from an individual.*
2 There is repeated experience. Schizophrenic behaviour is grooved, as in a grammar. In this sense we can say that *Bateson's rules form part of a grammar.*
3 There is a primary negative injunction. This is a prohibition, backed up by threats of punishment.
4 There is a secondary injunction, conflicting with the first. This is a particular kind of double message, where the contradiction is intractable. It is often non-verbal, so *Bateson's model is functionally multimodal.*
5 A tertiary negative injunction then prohibits the schizophrenic from escaping from the field. This prohibition often has a positive form, an expression of love, seeming positive but negative in its effect. In practice, as well as the contradiction between these

injunctions, there is normally a contradiction within each. *They are all. double messages.*

6 The double-bind system is normalized, so that small events can trigger massive and seemingly excessive responses. *The system becomes a generator of butterfly effects.* These are then interpreted as a mark of schizophrenics' dangerous irrationality and serve to further entrap them.

Lakoff's two frames underpinning his analysis of US political discourse represent competing models of the family (2004; see chapter 3), so I look at them through Bateson's lenses. The two frames, strict father and nurturant parent, correspond to the two halves of Bateson's schizogenic parent. Lakoff presents them as distinct ideologies held by two political tribes. He claims that one tribe, the Republicans, consciously and manipulatively uses its own frame and translates from the other frame. Insofar as this is conscious, we can suppose that the tribe has access to a meta-communication loop.

Lakoff's analysis could be seen as providing the meta-communication link that the Democrats lack. He helps them to be more effective and contributes to their mental health. However, Bateson's model complicates this judgement. Bateson emphasizes not just the frames as such, as meanings which can be present or absent, but the semiosic conditions at play. Lakoff's tactical advice to Democrats is consciously to reframe issues in terms of their own model, but this may have semiotic effects on Democrats themselves. Do the Democrats really mean these reframed utterances? Are they just tactical meanings? Or do they always know?

In practice, the problem Lakoff reports is the effect of the Republicans on political discourse, on the conditions of political thought. According to Lakoff, the Republicans used think-tanks and other mechanisms to understand Democrat frames and cynically used them against them.

This cynicism seems to have direct effects in winning debates. It also perhaps has schizogenic effects on Democrats. These effects may not be obvious, because *they are not meanings in themselves but conditions and constraints on meanings.* These conditions and constraints may have greater effects and consequences than any set of meanings in themselves. For this reason, social semiotics can be as interested in *semiosic conditions as in specific sets of meanings; interested in the specific meanings as indexical signs of these processes; and also interested in semiosic processes because they are a key to what those meanings will mean in social practice.*

Language and therapy

I argue that linguistics and social semiotics need to take on board a broad range of forms of language and meaning that are classified as 'abnormal' or 'aberrant'. Given the current politics of disciplines, this means purposeful collaborations with like-minded professionals engaged with different kinds of interaction commonly labelled as 'therapy'. Bateson's work pioneered this connection. In spite of the practical and ideological difficulties, I believe there ought to be many more collaborations between therapists, linguists and semioticians.

In systemic-functional linguistics, Rochester and Martin (1979) showed how illuminating was the concept of cohesion (Halliday and Hasan 1976) for understanding the aberrant discourse of schizophrenics. More recently David Butt and some of his systemic-functional colleagues collaborated with a team of psychotherapists, including Joan Haliburn and Russell Meares, in a fine example of linguistically orientated social semiotic analysis of pathological discourses (Butt et al. 2007). I reanalyse one fragment from their extended analysis of a patient, 'Jennifer', diagnosed with a borderline personality disorder and dissociative identity disorder. This is a slightly different condition from schizophrenia, but they have many similarities. Jennifer was treated by Haliburn, whose long, detailed account of the case I draw on for the analysis.

Jennifer had suffered sexual abuse from her father, who also punished her physically until he was removed from the home when she was seven. Her mother was 'unavailable, critical, and punitive' (Butt et al. 2007: 266). This is a family structure similar to the one Bateson modelled, with both parents classic sources of double messages. But unlike Bateson's account, where family dynamics alone seem to account for the symptoms, Jennifer was actually sexually abused when young. She later suffered a 'vicious sexual assault', which also really happened. Material events also need to be factored in to the model. The session pivots around her report of a visit to her sister's place (ibid.: 280):

5.13 *Therapist*: Mmm hmm.
Jennifer: (decreased volume) They have a few acres/ and they've got horses. /mm/ A few of us went out to see the horses. Everything was fine, it's like, it's really disgusting. But everything was fine and we go to start going back and they had a pony there, fairly tall for a pony, and as he was relaxed his penis was out.
Therapist: Mmm hmmm.

Jennifer: And I just had, that's when I think, is it me or is there
                     a connection?

Butt and his colleagues comment on two significant moments in this
text where forms of language carry diagnostic meanings. The switch
of tenses is dramatic and ungrammatical, projecting a fractured world
and time that Jennifer feels – symptoms of a dissociated personality.
The use of 'it' is also symptomatic. In chapter 3 we saw how important
and slippery deixis is. Here 'it' is ambiguous in the extreme: there are
too many possible referents with no organizing meta-communication
loop to keep Jennifer's message or self coherent.

This multimodal transcript records non-verbal aspects, which
even in this minimal form are revealing. The lowering of Jennifer's
voice is clearly significant. So are the therapist's two vocalizations. As
reported here there seems a difference between the two vocalizations.
The first seems reassuring and encouraging, phatic communication,
and Jennifer launches into her story. The second comes just after
the shocking revelation about the horse's penis. It seems reported as
louder and perhaps more anxious, involuntarily expressing a slight
shock. Perhaps to Jennifer it sounded judgemental. Whatever the
case, she alters direction sharply, stopping the story of the horse. She
resumes it only many moves later, when the therapist reintroduces it.

This therapy team is highly aware of the effect of the therapeu-
tic situation and the role of the therapist in it. Haliburn is highly
competent in the tradition to which Bateson contributed, which
social semiotics can learn from and contribute to. The points this
analysis raises are as valuable to social semiotics as to therapy.
Together they are reminders of basic principles of semiotic analysis
of meaning.

1 *In far-from-equilibrium as in 'normal' conditions, meanings are decoded
  and interpreted by reference to the interaction of the three dimensions:
  the reality referred to and constructed by participants, the logic of the
  semiotic code and, finally, the complexity of the social relations which
  are topic and context of the exchange and the situation.*
2 *As each of these three dimensions is clarified, the others can come into
  sharper focus, so that everyone involved can come to understand better
  the nature of the complex, the meanings and experiences that constitute
  the problem.*
3 *These processes of social meaning are continually affected by semiosic
  conditions, sometimes as a continuous background, sometimes changing
  to small or large degrees even across a single exchange.*

Schizogenic society

Schizophrenic and schizogenic conditions are not always diagnosed as such. In many cases they are features of what is classified as everyday practices. I illustrate with an example that came to me from the British independent media *Schnews*. To the shock of the *Schnews* team, they learned in 2010 that 'Mark Stone', a familiar member of Britain's tight-knit radical community, was really Mark Kennedy, a police officer who had penetrated radical circles and maintained deep cover for six years (Lewis and Evans 2013). After this revelation many more details leaked out about this highly secret operation, which involved cover so deep that it included long-term sexual relations and apparently complete adoption of an alternative lifestyle. The whole episode is strange, bizarre and full of implications.

One merit of systems analysis is that it draws attention to effects on all participants on a number of scales, not just intended consequences for intended targets. I limit myself to one impact of it which is highlighted by Bateson's model.

In January 2011, two months after the first revelations about 'Mark Stone', *Schnews* staff ran a long article on the affair. They claimed not to be 'quite as shocked as elements of the mainstream media have been'. They commented that 'to be an activist you've got to get used to the idea of surveillance'. Yet in spite of that pose of indifference it would be strange if they were not affected. They discovered a government website ('Gateway') was a prolific source of postings on the alternative media outlet *Indymedia*, and they reprinted and categorized these postings. Some they classified as incitements, some as demoralization, some as sowing division. I analyse one to show the multiple effects these postings have before and after they have been exposed.

5.14 No – stuff that – SHUT the place: Let's not all stand around like lemmings – lets shut THE place! Bring ladders and wire cutters. If there are enough of us we can shut it! Posted by Militant Band on 26.06.2009, 08.48.

Schnews classified this as incitement but noted that genuine activists could have been just as extreme. In the media as in meetings, these undercover police pushed activists towards the violence that, as police, they were meant to prevent. In the process, their convincing parody of radical discourse delegitimized it once they were exposed.

Schnews's analysis of the Gateway postings was an attempt to re-establish a badly damaged meta-communication loop. Before the unmasking, the meta-communication rule was simple and clear. Communications from enemies were not to be trusted. Communication by allies may be right or wrong but could be trusted to be sincere. The undercover operation corrupted all the signs that previously established membership. Instead of strong bonds of solidarity among activists, one of their greatest social assets, it left everyone wondering whether their friends, colleagues or sexual partners were perhaps undercover police.

The activities of these deep cover police, according to Lewis and Evans, were hugely costly and ineffective in their own terms. However, the conspiracy and its unmasking produced massive unintended collateral damage. It created paranoia in the activist community and a form of madness among the undercover police. This may have spread widely in the police force which authorized the operation. *Conditions of semiosis can be invisible causes and effects of political policies, responding to and creating far-from-equilibrium conditions.*

PART III

Meaning and Society

6

The Semiotics of Reality

'Reality' plays a crucial but contradictory role in the operations of meaning in society. Human action is based on beliefs about how the world is. Most of our crucial beliefs about reality come from others, from meanings they send and we receive. But Umberto Eco (1976) defined semiotics as the study of whatever can be used to lie. Goffman (1959) portrayed social semiotic animals as producers of signs intended to mislead, scanning the signs of others to discern meanings they can trust. 'Reality' is carried by meanings, distorted by semiosis. Social semiotic analysis in large part consists of searching for reality through and in spite of flows of signs and meanings.

Yet unreality is also fundamental to social and mental life. Creativity and criticism, thinking and imagination produce new realities, without which individuals and societies could not change the world. Unreality is a social semiotic resource. This chapter explores the play of these two opposing factors, which produce the problems and triumphs of reality, the ambiguities of imagination, and the possibility of criticism.

Reality as problem and solution

'Reality' became divisive in the social sciences in the so-called culture wars, battles between structuralism and poststructuralism, modernism and postmodernism, 'positivism' and interpretative sociology. These battles produced heat not light. In this section I use social semiotic analysis to clarify the debate and restore 'reality' as a basic term for social research.

Battles for 'reality'

Orwell's novel *1984* ([1949] 2011) provides a useful framework for analysing language and the politics of reality. Orwell's reference point was the perversions of language and meaning in Soviet Russia, but he saw similarities with contemporary Britain. He identified three common political deformations of language and meaning.

One was *the systematic reconstruction of history*: 'who controls the past controls the present'. In Orwell's satire, this went beyond changing versions of the past to forging the evidence on which those versions were based. A second was *the omnipresence of contradiction*, as in such slogans as 'war is peace'. A third was what Orwell called 'double-think', a *pathological state of mind produced in pathological semiosic conditions*.

'Reality' plays a key role in all three pathologies. Propaganda overtly twists reality. In times of war, war is used to legitimate distortions, lies and half-truths. In peace, Orwellian effects flow from undeclared wars between contending parties, including academics. Orwell's insight was to recognize that *distortions of reality need to surround individual lies with what Wittgenstein ([1921] 1971) called 'scaffolds'*, networks of propositions about reality which sustain individual claims.

Orwell noted the omnipresence of contradictions, an idea captured in the social semiotic concept 'ideological complex'. But appeals to 'reality' are part of analytic solutions as well as problems. 'War is peace' is less symmetrical than its form suggests. In *1984*'s reality, the slogan justifies war, not peace. 'Double-think' is a dysfunctional response to contradictions, an inability to connect two-dimensional contradictions in slogans to three-dimensional reality.

A form of the reality–ideological complex was deployed with great success in the 'culture wars', using many Orwellian features. I illustrate with the response of Luke Slattery, a journalist for *The Australian* newspaper, to the attacks of 11 September 2001:

> 6.1 Wake up and smell the cordite. . . . Did September 11 mean the end of postmodern relativism? Here's the reality check. Let's just say I'm a postmodernist intellectual (neither term is likely to apply but this is just for the sake of argument). (*The Australian*, 24 October 2001, p. 30)

As a critical discourse analyst/social semiotician, I am not indifferent to reality, but the contrary. *The search for reality in all its forms is intrinsic to social semiotic analysis*. That search always takes me to reference points outside any text, in social and physical realities, using whatever empirical research methods I can.

A famous phrase in early Derrida, *Il n'ya pas de hors-texte* ('there is no outside-text') (1976: 158), has been taken as a premise of Derrida and poststructuralism, that there is no reality outside the text, that his kind of analysis in principle made no appeal to reality. He later claimed (1988: 130) that he was mistranslated, and that he really meant to say in a provocative form that context was everywhere. I admire Derrida generally but, like his later self, I disagree with this slogan. So it becomes interesting that it has been used to define 'poststructuralism' and its twin, postmodernism.

Social semiotics includes many tools to detect traces of reality in every text and situation. Slattery's text leaks with intended and unintended versions of reality. Goffman's distinction (1959) between signs 'given' (consciously produced) and 'given off' (revealed less deliberately) is an invaluable guide for social semiotic analysis. *Presuppositional analysis (Karttunen 1974) can pick up many phantoms created or constructed in texts, royal roads that lead out of texts.*

Slattery claims to be interested in 'reality', condemning 'postmodernists' who ignore it. I am interested in many realities, including the materiality of his text, around 6000 words, published in a newspaper, still stored in an online archive. In it he refers to 'reality' only five times and 'terrorists/terrorism' only three. In contrast, there are eight references to 'intellectual', sixteen to 'postmodern/postmodernist'. This reality of his text implies that he is not really interested in reality or terrorism, in spite of what he claims. His real target is 'postmodernist intellectuals' or 'relativism'. This target does not have the same kind of reality as 'more than 5000 people' dead in his article. On the contrary, this label is his main means to construct the enemy whose defeat he proclaims. Slattery ignores the terrorists, who probably did exist, and concentrates on 'postmodernist intellectuals', whose existence is less certain. 'Postmodernist' linked tightly to 'intellectuals' functions like 'Bernstein' in Orwell. The Party created Bernstein to caricature valid criticisms so ridiculously that they provoked instant derision.

Slattery's first argument seems surprising for an apostle of reality. Instead of attacking the real words or actions of these postmodernist intellectuals, he offers a fantasy of himself as a postmodern intellectual, instantly disowned before he then continues with it. In this role he literally constructs his object of attack. He invents his own nonsense to show what nonsense these people spout. It seems a strange argument to use by this guardian of reality. His figure of 'more than

'5000' is big. Later estimates by the US government report (National Commission on Terrorist Attacks 2004) brought this 'reality' down to 2606 killed in the buildings, plus 266 passengers – a total of 2972, 41 per cent fewer than Slattery's '5000'. Slattery did not know these numbers when he wrote, but the confidence and inaccuracy are indexical signs of his indifference to the real figures. People seriously interested in real figures are more cautious.

Slattery does not count any other deaths which may be associated with this act, such as non-American deaths caused by American military action. His exaggerated 5000 are presented as absolute numbers, and all other deaths disappear. Herman and Chomsky (2002) gave figures showing that the American media tend to exaggerate deaths caused by America's enemies and minimize deaths caused by the USA and its allies. They called this 'propaganda'. Slattery disseminates this 'propaganda', then constructs a scapegoat, 'postmodernism', whose function is to imply by contrast how much he respects reality. This is the reality–ideological complex at work. It rests on contradictions as extreme as Orwell's 'war is peace'. Slattery claims to respect 'reality' in order to trash it. He cherry-picks facts as he condemns relativism.

The propaganda assault on 'postmodern intellectuals' has been remarkably successful, repeated so often it has become hegemonic, in the USA and Britain as well as Australia. As Orwell recognized, the greatest damage propaganda does to a society is not in the effects of individual distortions but in *the cumulative creation of semiosic conditions which discredit reality itself.*

The social construction of reality

A doctrine often named 'constructivism' has been used effectively in academia to achieve similar effects to Slattery's 'postmodernism'. Social semiotics includes a form of constructivism, so here I bring out distinctions that are lost in the attacks on it. 'Constructivism' was influentially described in Peter Berger and Thomas Luckmann's 1966 book and title:

6.2 The social construction of reality.

In this title, 'reality' can be analysed as a transformational process, starting with 'X says/judges Y is real', finishing with '-ity' to signify this is a noun. Over this process, the agents, acts and objects of judgement, have been deleted. 'Reality' is made to seem like a singular thing. It has been 'reified' (from Latin *res*, 'a thing', also root of 'reality').

This transformation happened before any current users like Slattery, Berger or Luckmann existed, seemingly in 'language' itself. This antiquity gives authority to the existence of the word, which seems to guarantee the existence of the thing, 'reality'. But 'reality' here and in Slattery is literally a linguistic construct.

Berger and Luckmann wrote:

> 6.3 The most important vehicle of reality-maintenance is conversation. One may view the individual's everyday life in terms of the working away of conversational apparatus that ongoingly maintains, modifies and reconstructs his subjective reality. (1966: 172)

At the heart of this proposal is a cybernetic idea. Berger and Luckmann's 'apparatus' is homeostatic, acting through negative feedback loops to maintain existing versions of reality. They do not envisage positive feedback loops, which might produce dramatic changes in versions of reality. They see the process as conservative and hegemonic.

This text is full of signs brought out by presuppositional analysis (Karttunen 1974). Some of these signs reveal Berger and Luckmann's assumptions about reality – in Goffman's terms, signs that they 'give off' as against signs they seem to intend. For instance, 'conversation' projects a taxonomy of language genres, everyday versus formal and public. All project the kind of society in which they have a place. In Stalinist Russia conversations as envisaged by Berger and Luckmann would not happen so easily.

Especially noticeable to twenty-first-century readers is 'his'. The gendered pronoun was normal and obligatory in 1966, but now stands out. This sign is 'given off'. 'His' implies a reality in which male actors are privileged and represent all humans. This gendered world view was maintained by Berger and Luckmann every time they used this pronoun, as by their readers then who did not notice its implications. Their language continually constructs meanings and realities. The first sentence is surprisingly definite. It uses the simple present, 'is', which implies there is no doubt about the truth of what is claimed. Far from putting reality in doubt, Berger and Luckmann cannot communicate without taking it for granted, in general and in particular, as soon as they try to say something, even to state their doubts about reality. In Wittgenstein's terms, 'reality' is a hinge proposition for those who doubt it as much as for those who affirm it.

Berger and Luckmann are clearly right: *the language they use is socially constructed and, in turn, constructs versions of reality of which they themselves are not always aware*. However, that fact does not paralyse analysis; rather, the contrary. Social semiotic analysis analyses both reality and the meanings that are opened up by the dialectic between reality and meaning.

A social semiotic model

Herman and Chomsky's *The Manufacture of Consent* (2002) reflects Chomsky as an activist, not as a linguist. This is an opposition my book seeks to dismantle. In this section I compare the propaganda model to the model I reconstruct from his linguistic theories. I include a Hallidayan perspective in order to bring out pathways between structuralist and functional linguistics and between linguistics and activism.

Herman and Chomsky called their model a 'propaganda' model, which aimed to explain systematic bias in the American media. The model incorporated the linear sender–receiver model then common in mass communication studies (Silverstone 1994). In their version, Herman and Chomsky focused on sender as a primary site for manufacturing not just news but 'consent' on behalf of powerful interests in government and big business.

In figure 6.1, I represent the effect claimed by Herman and Chomsky, that unequal, hostile relations between the media as sender and the mass market as passive receiver generate systematically distorted versions of reality in the interests of the powerful.

Chomsky's linguistic model in *Syntactic Structures* (1957) was not

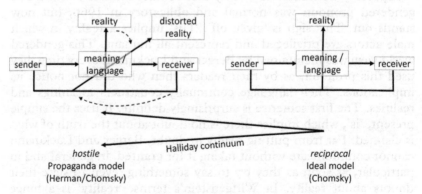

Figure 6.1   Social models of language and reality

designed to model social uses of language, but I put it alongside the Herman–Chomsky model to see how the two might relate to each other in a social semiotic framework. The linguistic model assumes that senders and receivers are interchangeable. In the propaganda model they are opposed. In both models, language transmits meaning transparently, which I represent as a single object, language/meaning. In the ideal/linguistics model, a direct arrow goes from language/meaning to reality, but in the activist/ propaganda model that ideal relation is rotated around an axis to produce systematically distorted versions. I use a dotted curve to show the receiver repositioned to see reality rotated to seem like actual reality. Herman and Chomsky's propaganda model incorporates a fundamental assumption of social semiotics: *social relationships in semiotic processes can override meanings as versions of reality*.

I add Halliday's analysis of 'antilanguages' (1978) to the bottom of figure 6.1 to situate Chomsky's two models. Antilanguages arise in excluded groups who construct a different language to exclude outsiders, to create group solidarity, and express their distinctive defining reality. Halliday saw the antilanguage phenomenon as one extreme of a continuum, and he remodelled the social relations at issue in a V-shape. At its apex is total solidarity and common language meaning and reality, as in Chomsky's linguistic model. The further apart are the sides of the V, the greater the social opposition, and the greater the differences in language, meaning and reality.

In this picture, Chomsky's two models do not contradict each other; they merely represent different positions along a fuzzy continuum. The Herman–Chomsky model lies towards the antilanguage end. Orwell's model is even more extreme. In *1984*, senders conceal the extent to which they feel licensed to trick receivers. The same is true of the masters of propaganda. *They create a second more dangerous unreality, the illusion of consensus.*

The Herman–Chomsky model (2002) applies well to the Murdoch-owned newspaper *The Australian*. Herman and Chomsky demonstrated with massive empirical detail how highly concentrated are the American media, including Murdoch's stable, and how often they support the views of their wealthy owners. In analysing this process, *Chomsky's linguistic and activist models are complementary, as framed by Halliday's functional model.*

Linguistic models and semiotic research

In this section I revisit and reinforce a major methodological point of the book: *a social semiotic framework can transform purely linguistic theories, which can then contribute better to general semiotics.*

Grammar and reality

I regard the work that Gunther Kress and I did on linguistic modality (mechanisms in language for signifying and managing relationships between utterances and reality) as one of our most important contributions to linguistics. We devoted three chapters to a detailed account of linguistic modality in English in *Language as Ideology* (1979). *Social Semiotics* (Hodge and Kress 1988) had a chapter on semiotics of modality, and *Children and Television* (Hodge and Tripp 1986) had a chapter on visual modality.

I begin with a possible source of confusion of terms. Kress and I used 'modality' from linguistics, following Halliday's usage (1985). Halliday followed traditional linguistics, where words such as 'may' and 'can' attached to verbs are called 'modal auxiliaries'. However, non-linguists find the term difficult. To complicate matters further, in Kress and van Leeuwen's seminal work on 'multimodality' (2001), 'modality' referred to semiotic modes. In this book I use 'multimodality' in that sense.

We drew inspiration from three linguists. Whorf (1956) supplied a powerful explanatory framework in which 'reality' had a key place, plus many particular insights so original that most of his readers did not notice them. Halliday (1970) studied linguistic modality as a system connected to a function. He embraced more features in modality, including intonation, and he made a broad-brush distinction between high, median and low modality in a fuzzy continuum. Chomsky's account (1957) of the structures and processes of verbal auxiliaries as a device complemented those of the other two linguists. From these sources Kress and I built a comprehensive theory of reality-markers and evaluations across all semiotic modes.

I illustrate forms and functions of reality-markers in language with a scam email I received:

6.4 I will like to discuss about a deceased client's Fixed Deposit Account with Wing Ling Bank. (Received 23 December 2011)

I initially reacted sceptically, using the social dimension of my reality-evaluations systems. My email brings me floods of 'spam', communications from a predatory social world. I have defensive strategies to filter out 'real' communicators and messages I can trust.

This kind of scam is so common that I quickly recognized signs of the genre. Usually I read no more. Genres carry presumed levels of reality-value, which give a general reality-value to texts in that genre. I have internalized a structure of genres in all semiotic modes, visual and verbal, as a first line of defence against tricks. This kind of email has low reality-value for me. However, I continued to read. I noticed the string of words 'will + like + to'. This seems a heterogeneous list of elements. 'Will' is an auxiliary of tense, signifying future time. 'Like' is a main verb. 'To' is a preposition, signalling that the verb is in what traditional grammars call 'infinitive'.

These heterogeneous elements work as a single set, all with the same function, in Halliday's terms: to establish complex reality-values. I identify two properties of linguistic reality-value systems from this. Firstly, *reality functions and meanings are carried by many different structural elements*. Second, conversely, *reality-value is often only one of the meanings of carriers of reality-value*.

One of Whorf's most brilliant insights was to recognize *that systems of tenses carry meanings about reality as well as time*. Tenses in English such as 'will' fix the time of the action of the verb, past, present and future. But they often have a modal reality function as well. The future tense 'will' here is not about the future. Its meaning is social, not temporal, to project polite deference. The order of the three words (will + like + to) signifies the order of steps in an underlying process – three successive modifications of the main verb 'discuss'. I understand this phenomenon in terms of a Chomskyan 'device'. In *Syntactic Structures* (1957: 65) Chomsky proposed that a set of similar transformations act on base strings to produce negations, modal auxiliaries, questions and emphasis.

Each is a separate operation, but these transformations can be applied successively. There are other reconstructions, but in mine of 'John cán't come', the sequence goes: John comes ➜ John can come ➜ John can't come ➜ can't John come? ➜ cán't John come? ➜ John cán't come. Each transformation leaves a trace, an indexical sign of the operations, a history that signifies a complex reality-value. Chomsky explicitly avoided referring to function or meaning to ground his rules, so it is significant that operations he groups together purely on formal grounds turn out to express similar functions as in Whorf and Halliday.

Those meanings all concern aspects of reality-value carried by different parts of the grammar. The present tense ('John comes') has high reality-value because it is presented as unquestioned. 'John can come' uses a classic linguistic modal auxiliary: perhaps he will come, perhaps not. With 'can John come?' there is further uncertainty about John's coming. 'Can't John come?' adds a negative, but paradoxically this makes it more positive and forceful than the simple question. Finally, the stress on 'cán't' implies there has been a previous negative answer, meaning that the request has been refused (a low likelihood of John coming). But the pressure is intensified, so maybe John will come after all.

This brings out another quality of reality-value systems in all semiotic modes. The grammar gives sets of signs with reality-value. But since language exists in social exchanges, these signs and claims can be overridden by their value as indexical signs. I reacted negatively to the excessive string of auxiliaries in the scam letter. Emphatic stress usually suggests conflict and, paradoxically, arouses doubt.

Reality-value systems have a double face. Signifiers of reality-value are only claims, interpreted against background assumptions about producers of messages and the reality to which they refer.

Cybernetics of reality

Cybernetics offers a valuable approach to modern media effects. Cyberculture is populated with new digital forms and processes, which cumulatively have transformed the possibilities for political and social action. Cybernetic models of feedback loops and counter-loops help analyse the continuing role of the fuller range of semiotic modes. Here I analyse a micro-instance of intersections of cyberculture and political action in order to show the complex role of reality and reality-values at small scales.

In September 2011 the hacktivist group Anonymous supported the Occupy Wall Street movement, an activist campaign that demonstrated in New York's iconic centre of capitalism.

Digital media and cyberspace are potential game-changers in the contemporary environment for social activism. In the 1980s Herman and Chomsky critiqued a seemingly monolithic media hegemony, built around TV and the press. Now activists such as Edward Snowden and WikiLeaks act as counter-feedback loops, channelling alternative more plausible versions of reality. They reveal what governments and big business really thought about their citizens and their allies. They use new media to sustain older notions of 'truth'.

As hackers, Anonymous specialized in another role. The group disrupted normal business by hacking websites, using their web connections to spread the word in cyberspace and beyond. I first encountered them in a newspaper article plus photograph I read in Mexico – evidence of their global reach. The article reported on the still flourishing protest in New York in December, three months on. The photograph showed a man wearing the iconic smiling Guy Fawkes mask, holding a placard:

6.5 Arrest One of Us; Two More Appear. You Can't Arrest an Idea!
(*La Jornada*, 28 December 2011, p. 23)

Reality-values work in parallel in visual and verbal media and follow similar principles: *linguistic and other semiotic modes can only be understood as components in a multimodal system, at the level of individual texts as well as at higher levels.*

Like words, visual signifiers often carry both content and reality-value. For instance, the photograph shows the event. It also carries the conventional reality-values of photographs. In my internalized taxonomy of semiotic modes, photographs have high reality-value. This is a conventional meaning, not a guarantee of reality. Press photographs can be altered digitally. This fact has altered their reality-status, but still only slightly.

The man holding the placard is in the centre, looking at the camera, with no one else in frame. This is a compositional sign (Kress and van Leeuwen 2001). It includes indexical signs that this photographer takes him and his message seriously, and that the two are complicit in posing for the message. The text is crudely handwritten, in large letters. These indexical signs communicate reality-related messages. Handwriting signifies rejection of print, with its mechanically produced symmetries, and hence conveys authenticity. Hacktivists jump over print media to exploit digital technologies. Here handwriting signifies an alliance with old technologies. The size is probably designed to be seen by TV and press cameras, signifying awareness of the power of mainstream media and a desire to appropriate it. Anonymous's strategy is *multimodal, uniting many modes in a distributed network.*

Modal auxiliaries repay analysis here. Halliday (1970) noted one curious feature of the English linguistic system. It has two sets of modal auxiliaries. One is a small, closed set, such as 'can', 'may' and 'could'. The other is larger and more open, for example, 'possibly' and 'probably'. The smaller set has systematic ambiguity between social and reality-based judgements. So 'can' means either 'have the capacity' or 'is allowed'. Ambiguity is often removed by context or by terms from the second set (e.g., are able/allowed to).

As a functional theorist I ask: Why would a language allow systematic ambiguity? The Anonymous example suggests one reason why ambiguity is functional. The first clause is technically an imperative but does not function as a command. Protesters lack the power and status to order the police to do anything. Even if they did, surely they would not want to be arrested. In Austin's speech act theory (1962) this is an aberrant command. But its function here is reality-related. It corresponds to a conditional 'if' clause: if you arrest one of us, then two more will appear. 'If' clauses have lower reality-value. The second clause states what will happen if the first clause becomes reality.

On this occasion Anonymous uses no modal auxiliaries but, rather, the simple present, 'appear' – a tense with high reality-value in English. The effect of the second clause with its high reality-value is to negate more strongly the first: 'don't arrest' anyone (because the consequences are certain).

This analysis of these simple forms shows that *this system can produce bewildering complexity, in which reality-values are built up from continual partial negations of negations.*

The second sentence uses a different kind of reality-signifier, carried not by ambiguous signs but by reference to competing versions of reality. 'You can't arrest an idea' has intriguing similarities to Chomsky's famous phrase about 'colorless green ideas' that 'sleep'. For Chomsky, combining 'ideas' and 'sleep' caused reality problems for a world view in which 'ideas' cannot be agents in human activities like 'sleep'. Anonymous claims the same problem with 'ideas' as object of the verb 'arrest'. Police can only arrest humans, not 'ideas'. Yet Anonymous also attributes human-like agency to ideas. The protesters have a contradictory position on the agency of ideas. Ideas cannot be arrested, yet they have a magical Hydra-effect, doubling their numbers with every arrest.

Anonymous's verbal reality-structures allow for ambiguity. 'Can't' compresses two Chomskyan transformations into one syllable. 'Can' has its normal ambiguity here: power (police have no right to arrest ideas) and possibility (if they try to do so they will fail). Both blur together in the negative, as both kinds of impossibility support each other. In this case the protesters deny the logic they attribute to the police, that ideas can be arrested, but they keep open their core belief that ideas are so powerful that, from the point of view of the police, they probably should be arrested. *The ambiguous modality of the negative, working together with the modal auxiliary 'can', creates an indeterminate space in which contradictions flourish.*

A cybernetic framework includes all the older modes and their reality-values alongside new multimodal systems within which political processes play out. The resulting multimodal system functions as a single system yet is full of ambiguity and incoherence. *Relationships between meaning and reality are as complex as ever, and reality still plays an ambiguous and decisive role.*

Reality flip-overs

In this book I use chaos theory as a heuristic resource for models and concepts in order to help explain phenomena in language, society and meaning that seem especially non-linear and unpredictable. In this section I deal with what I call the 'reality flip-over'. Reality-value systems are typically continuous, but there are sometimes sharp breaks – 'phase transitions' as they are called in chaos theory (Prigogine and Stengers 1984). Far-from-equilibrium conditions see more frequent examples of non-linear causality, such as inversions, contradictions and butterfly effects (small causes triggering large and different effects).

My first example comes from psychology. In the 1960s and 1970s, when linear effects models dominated media research, Seymour Feshbach (1976) conducted experiments to demonstrate what he called 'the catharsis principle'. His focus was TV violence, claimed to cause real-world violence. Today video games provoke similar concerns. Feshbach took 'catharsis' from Aristotle (1951), who described the effect of seeing tragedies as *catharsis* (purification, purging) of emotions. Aristotle distinguished emotions generated by aesthetic texts from emotions arising from everyday life. In some experiments Feshbach showed direct cause and effect between TV violence and aggressive behaviour, as other studies had done. But this occurred only when viewers believed it was real. If they believed it was fantasy, aggression was sometimes greatly reduced.

I explore some of the conditions under which reality flip-overs happen in order to illustrate the proposition that, *in some conditions, reality-values can rapidly invert, and, when they do, behaviours also change dramatically.*

Herman and Chomsky modelled a society in which governments ally with mainstream media to 'manufacture consent'. But this consensus has to be ongoingly constructed and maintained by mechanisms that include Berger–Luckmann apparatuses. It is always vulnerable to the chaos lying in wait to dismantle it in reality flip-overs.

I am writing this section in Mexico in 2015, observing a scandal unfolding that currently threatens to destabilize the government of President Enrique Peña Nieto. The scandal was precipitated by a probable massacre of forty-three students at Ayotzinapa, Guerrero, in September 2014. A Mexican commentator wrote:

> 6.6 The practice of using language to cover the truth, and leave a door open to impunity . . . is as old as humanity. . . . The same thing happens today in Mexico when the word 'massacre' is annulled, to be replaced by 'disappearance', to refer to the 43 students killed in Guerrero with impunity. (Carlos Vigueras, *La Jornada*, 7 March 2015, p, 36; my translation)

The 'facts' in this case are still not certain or verified, as is common in far-from-equilibrium conditions. But fuzzy facts are valid starting points for social semiotics in such circumstances. In this case, all sides agreed that forty-three students were missing. Five months later the government was still trying to control the rest of the message.

On 26 February 2015, the federal chief prosecutor, Jesus Murillo, gave a press conference to announce that the case was closed, though there had still been no trial and the main accused had not been captured. Murillo showed a 26-minute video and claimed, in a widely reported phrase:

> 6.7 Esta es la verdad histórica de los hechos. (*La Jornada*, 26 February 2015; 'This is the historic truth of the facts'; my translation)

The phrase 'verdad histórica' went viral, usually in quotation marks, usually mocking Murillo's claims. Within two months he had resigned, his and the government's credibility in tatters. The government's credibility was already damaged by a concerted campaign over many months, not just by a single official's single sentence. The whole process deserves a full analysis. Yet analysing this one sentence reveals many important things.

Verdad functions like English 'truth'. For politicians to call their lies 'the truth' is so common it hardly deserves comment. But in this case Murillo adds further signs of reality-value. '*La*'/'the' are deictic (pointing) words which have a similar reality-value in both languages. *The singular in both languages also has reality-value, part of the linguistic modality-value system.* 'The truth' is more weightily true than 'a truth' or 'truths'.

Murillo adds other words to build reality-value. *Estas* ('this') is a deictic with high reality-value, pointing to something so close and evident that supposedly no one could deny it. Like many deictics, it is ambiguous, referring here to the video that has just been seen or to the official version Murillo is repeating. *Los hechos* ('the facts') in both languages imply that what they refer to is true beyond doubt, though in both languages the word comes from roots meaning 'made' (Spanish *hacer*, Latin *facere*).

But Murillo's biggest mistake was the word *histórica* ('historical'). He probably intended this word to reinforce 'truth', to turn a contested statement in the present into something enshrined in a history textbook. He is doing what Orwell observed dictatorships do, constructing history to control the present. But, as he piled on signifiers of reality and truth, the excess reached a tipping point. Instead of convincing his audience of the reality of what he was saying, he had the opposite effect. Most found his phrase and his government absurd. The reality flip-over destroyed his career.

Most functional theories, including Halliday's, assume that normal functions always prevail. This case shows how 'normal' (homeostatic) functions of a form can be inverted. *Functional analysis clarifies possible intentions, not inevitable effects*. It also shows how far-from-equilibrium conditions can affect and be produced by regular Chomskyan reality-value devices. At certain points *the accumulation of signs of reality, perfectly produced by a device, can topple over into a cascade of unreality effects*.

Power/truth

This episode throws new light on Foucault's influential statements about the nexus between power and truth:

> 6.8 'Truth' is linked in a circular relation with systems of power which produce and sustain it, and to effects of power which it induces and which extend it. A regime of truth. (Foucault 1980: 133)

In this formulation, power is related to truth in a cybernetic loop so tight that each is the effect of the other. Truth is an effect of power and induces effects of power. Foucault seems to be saying that, in normal conditions, whatever the powerful say within systems of power becomes the only available or effective version of truth.

But this proposition does not apply to every condition under which power is exercised. On the contrary, it best describes the world as it seems to the deranged, pathological rulers of Orwell's *1984*. 'Truth' in 'a regime of truth' has an Orwellian inverse meaning – propaganda, lies. This idea of power is a delusion, leading to isolation, distorted information, and loss of power. I invert Foucault's proposition to say that *capacity to know the truth may also be inversely related to power*. His theory of power is like an anti-model against normative models such as Habermas's 'ideal speech situation'.

In relation to the Mexican example, Foucault could be describing *rules by which the powerful commonly self-destruct*. Foucauldian 'regimes of truth' produce far-from-equilibrium conditions which magnify the contradictions of power and lead to reality flip-overs. The Murillo moment as reality flip-over briefly reveals general contradictions and limitations of power.

Uses of unreality

Bateson's study of reality-values in crisis (1973) was complemented by his work on play. He saw reality-values surrounding play as relatively universal, also found in many non-human species. Play for him was fundamental to human learning. So were the feedback loops that mostly managed these reality-altering processes.

In a similar vein, Alison Gopnik (2009) used the term 'paracosmos' to refer to the coherent alternative worlds some children create, a practice that she claimed supported creativity and imagination in children's development. A paracosmos is not just unreal, it is coherent, built on the negation of few basic premises of what I called a Wittgenstein scaffold.

Unreality is invaluable yet vulnerable to attack or abuse, since it draws on the same set of mechanisms that underpin normal healthy communication. That makes unreality one of the most difficult yet important objects of semiotic analysis.

Negation

Negation is at the centre of the set of processes that produce both creative and dangerous unrealities. Freud provides a rich link between semiotic and psychological processes pivoting around negation:

6.9 With the help of the symbol of negation, thinking frees itself from the restrictions of repression and enriches itself with material that is indispensable for its proper functioning. (Freud [1925] 1961: 236)

The 'symbol' of negation here refers to the linguistic apparatus of negation. For me, it includes all reality devices in all semiotic modes.

Negation has a paradoxical relationship to repression. Negation seems parallel to repression. Negation acts on signs, repression directly on thoughts. But Freud claims that symbolic negation frees thinking from repression. In cybernetic terms, it partly cancels repression while or by mimicking it. It makes rich material available for thinking, under cover of a surface denial of the reality of that material.

Rationalistic political discourse analysis has a strained relationship with psychoanalysis. But Lakoff (2004) used the double message inherent in negation in a book title. If you say *Don't think of an Elephant*, he said, everyone thinks obsessively about elephants.

As I argued, all the linguistic reality devices I analysed in the Anonymous placard are different ways of saying partial no's, but the ambiguities they produce go beyond simple political analysis. The positive command 'arrest one of us' has the effect of a negative command: 'don't arrest us'. Yet the protesters have still used the positive form. The phrase is positive at one level, negative at another. But perhaps it is positive again at yet another level. Perhaps while rejecting arrest they invited it, for publicity or street cred. These multiple negations allow them to project a counter-world which is different from their political programme, containing more contradictions than any programme could sustain. Yet, as in Freud's account, it is this rich set of meanings which drives them, revealed and concealed, indispensable to their proper functioning as humans who are also activists.

To illustrate the complexity of negation and its world-building capacity, I look at a famous painting by the Belgian surrealist René Magritte, which so impressed Foucault (1983) that he wrote his most extended semiotic analysis on it. Under the title *La traison de las imagenes* ('The treachery of images'), Magritte painted a realistic image of a pipe, from side on, against a light beige background. As part of the painting he wrote:

6.10 *Ceci n'est pas une pipe* (This is not a pipe).

As an acute semiotician, Foucault analysed the handwriting itself as a set of signs. He noted how stiff and conventional it was, like unsophisticated writing on a blackboard. This gives a social meaning which is also a reality effect. These are the words of a conventional mind, not of a complex surrealist (so Magritte could not have believed them).

Yet the paratactic form combining the simple phrase and the equally simple image is an endlessly generative contradiction.

The French sentence uses similar enough forms of deixis and modality to English to be translated unproblematically. The caption seems to contradict the painting. The contradiction can be resolved by seeing ambiguity in the deixis. *'Ceci'*, like English 'this', points in two directions: to a world outside the painting, which contains pipes like this one, and to the painted pipe, which is not real. But this interpretation rescues the rationality of the painting at the cost of its surrealist effect. Both statements remain true, the positive and the negative, co-existing in the same place like a visual illusion, like Wittgenstein's duck–rabbit. This both is and is not a pipe. It is both sign and reality, or two kinds of sign relating to the same impossible reality.

Iterated negation can create infinite complexity. In art and everyday life it can create rich alternative worlds or problems of interpretation. In pathological forms it is Orwell's 'double-think'. Such a contradictory range of outcomes creates difficulties for theory, for lamppost theorists who prefer to study only what is illuminated by their theory. But *it is better to understand and manage complexity than to deny it.*

I saw another more popular use of complex negatives on a plane from Sydney to Los Angeles in 2011. The front cover of the inflight magazine depicted Kermit the frog in sharp detail. Underneath was the caption:

6.11 At last, a frog you can believe in.

Yet Kermit is not a frog you can believe in, because he is not a frog. He is a puppet. This sentence was juxtaposed with a large, crisp image of Kermit in which the sewing is clearly visible, as are the ping-pong balls crudely attached as his eyes. This is not illusionism, but the opposite. Yet, paradoxically, it creates a positive reality effect. Kermit is a real puppet even if he is not a frog. The words use linguistic reality systems skilfully. 'You can believe' is ambiguous in the ways typical of that form. You can believe, if you want to. It is your choice. Or this frog enables you to believe.

I interpret the image as contrasting with politicians, whose discourses can no longer be believed. But this frog, the caption playfully suggests, can save the whole collapsing political discursive system. This is contradiction at work. The cure for the unreality of political discourse is the deliberate unreality of the Muppets.

The image itself, however, was also promoting a new Muppet

movie starring Kermit. Behind the scenes is another carefully hidden reality, the economic clout of the US movie industry, which ultimately made more than $US100 million profit from this movie.

I treat the counter-realities of Magritte, the Muppets and Slattery differently. I trust Magritte more than the Muppets, the Muppets more than *Inflight* magazine, and both more than Slattery, and Slattery more than Murillo, and probably Murillo more than my email scammer. Trust as a fuzzy, multilayered sign is the key to my fine-tuned reality-evaluation device. Those judgements could change. But *reality effects always incorporate judgements about social relations between producers and receivers of messages.*

Reality and three-body analysis

I finish this chapter using a three-body model to reflect on the role of reality, using Bateson's work as my point of departure. Bateson's theories were controversial. He was positioned on one side in the long-standing battle in psychology between 'nature' and 'nurture', physiological versus social determinants. Bateson, as a biologist and the son of the eminent evolutionist Sir William Bateson, recognized the role of biological forces, but he did not include them in his model. Three-body analysis does more justice to the scope and complexity of his thought.

Figure 6.2 shows unreality at the centre, as the product of three interacting, mutually conditioning forces. For Bateson, social relations (schizogenic families) produce schizogenic semiotic systems. 'Physiology' as the third body breaks this closed binary system. It can include genetics, hormones and drugs, which increase or damp down inputs of social and semiotic forces, to produce further unreality effects. Three-body systems are dynamic and iterative. Each body is continually modified by interactions with the others, so that each becomes fuzzy. I show three iterations schematically, starting from social relations (thick line). The second iteration has a dotted arrow producing second versions of the body, and a corresponding version of unreality. The third iteration is shown with an arrow of dots and dashes. It again affects all three bodies and produces a new version of unreality.

This complex, dynamic picture allows observers to zoom in at specific stages to understand something of the complexity of the full process from that point. Three-body analysis like this produces simpler, more manageable versions of systems which have too many bodies in too many relationships to be easily grasped by human minds.

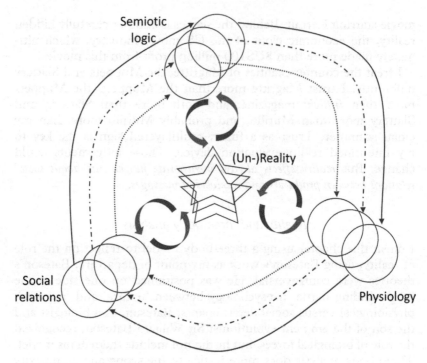

Figure 6.2   Reality in a three-body system

Bateson understood schizophrenia as a systemic aberration of normal semiotic systems, creating and affected by dysfunctional social relations. The model as I redrew it, including physiological factors, can be applied to many major social phenomena, all involved in producing unreality in some form. But, in my model, unreality is not always a pathology.

1 *Love* In spite of its problematic and central role in many ideological complexes, love is probably a relative universal, essential to the survival of humanity and found in many other species. I see it as a *genetically implanted, naturally occurring mind-altering substance*, with relatively few negative physiological effects and many life-changing social effects. Love is a highly fuzzy term, which has meant that it is hard to generalize about or study it. In terms of the model, love is the inverse of schizophrenia. Its unrealities are generated by intense union, not conflict.
2 *Addiction* Not all addictions involve mind-altering substances, but many do. This model includes social relations and semiotic

systems along with physiological forces in a holistic approach. With every addictive substance, *three-body analysis takes account of different physiological effects as they impinge on and are affected by society and meaning.*

3 *Entertainment* The entertainment industry, including high and popular culture, is *built around unreality as its principal commodity.* Unreality for these purposes is especially *valued as a condition that heightens the sense of meaning.* In ancient Rome, the triad 'wine, women and song' represented the main forms of what Romans saw as anti-social irrationality. The 1960s slogan for youth rebellion, 'Sex, drugs and rock-and-roll', has a homologous structure. Combined in a three-body system, these are seen as especially dangerous, needing to be suppressed and controlled.

4 *Religion* The demise of religion was widely prophesied in nineteenth-century Europe, but no one doubts its continuing potency in the twenty-first. Secular critics who attacked its doctrines as contradictory or untrue missed the point. As Tertullian is said to have stated 1800 years ago, 'I believe because it is impossible.' *Purveying unreality is not a problem for religion. That is what it does.*

Marx famously wrote of religion (1971: 116): 'Religious suffering is at the same time an expression of real suffering and a protest against real suffering. Religion is the sigh of the oppressed creature, the feeling of a heartless world and the soul of soulless circumstances. Religion is the opium of the people.' For Marx, religion has an ambiguous relation to 'reality'. It expresses suffering and also negates it. It produces feelings out of the negation of feelings and meaning ('soul') by negating soul or meaning. In his final sentence he connected two reality-altering strategies, drugs and religion, so closely that I invert them. *Drugs can be seen as the religion of the people.*

The nineteenth-century philosopher Friedrich Nietzsche also proposed links between intoxication, religion, and social action in religious rituals:

6.12 Not only does the bond between man and man come to be forged once more by the magic of the Dionysiac rite, but nature itself, long alienated or subjugated, rises again to celebrate the reconciliation with her prodigal son, man. . . . Now the slave emerges as a freeman; all the rigid, hostile walls which either necessity or despotism has erected between men are shattered. (Nietzsche 1946: 23)

This English translation, like Nietzsche's German, has traces of Dionysian syntax. It has mainly paratactic structures (alongside each other). The first is both–and ('not only . . . but also'). The rest consists mostly of strings of short sentences alongside each other. However, two binary either–or structures are inserted into these larger structures: 'alienated or subjugated' and 'either necessity or despotism'. But these are compressed, subordinated and negated. They act like traces of linear rationality still preserved in a Dionysiac syntactic flow.

Nietzsche described pre-Classical religion in a present tense, which normally has high reality-value. This combines the remote past with a glowing future, both more real than the present in which he wrote. In this sense he was rewriting history, as Big Brother did in *1984*. But the two cases are different, in terms of the following two important complementary propositions.

1 *Unreality becomes more problematic and dysfunctional when driven by conflictual social relations, expressing the will to manipulate and deceive others.*

While, at the same time,

2 *Unreality is the site where conflictual social relations can be renegotiated, by those who retreat from battles as much as by those who seek to change their outcomes.*

7

Ideology and Social Meaning

This chapter asks basic questions for social semiotics. What is its relationship to social theory in general and Marxism in particular? Social semiotics is not a branch of Marxism, but its debt to Marxism is huge, complex and open-ended.

Marxism has been ferociously attacked and misrepresented for nearly 200 years and equally distorted by its friends. In dogmas, social meanings override referential meanings, disconnecting them from the realities they purport to explain. Marxism is not immune from this basic proposition of social semiotics. Yet this fact is not just a problem for social semiotic analysis, but a challenge and opportunity. Social semiotics thrives on negotiating multiple, shifting, contested meanings.

At the same time I want to strengthen links between social semiotics and sociolinguistics, and both with Marxist and other social theories in a three-body system. Blommaert (2005) criticized CDA for ignoring some relevant branches of sociolinguistics, and the same can be said of social semiotics. In this and the next chapter I respond to that criticism.

Sociolinguistics as an applied science deals with problems and tries to solve them. Marx and Engels stated: 'The philosophers have only *interpreted* the world, in various ways; the point, however, is to change it' (1970: 30). The world has changed greatly since they wrote. In this chapter I am especially concerned with changes in society and meaning associated with globalization and how to respond. Marx and Engels foreshadowed globalization, but its new realities are so vast and complex they need the best that social semiotics can do.

Ideology

'Ideology' has been an important yet problematic term for analysing language and social meaning for 150 years. Many have used it in different senses, so it is hard to get an agreed definition (Williams 1976). But it is too late to put the genie back in the bottle. Besides, this 150-year old genie still does magic. It played a defining role in the manifesto for critical linguistics, *Language as Ideology* (Kress and Hodge 1979), and in British cultural studies (Hall 1996).

Marx and Engels used the term extensively in their early work, *The German ideology* ([1845] 1976), a massive critique of the dominant German Hegelian philosophy of the time. This contained a striking image of ideology:

> 7.1 Consciousness can never be anything else than conscious being, and the being of men is their actual life-process. If in all ideology men and their relations appear upside down as in a *camera obscura*, this phenomenon arises just as much from their historical life-process as the inversion of objects on the retina does from their physical life-process. (1976: 42)

This is a metaphor and model rather than a definition, but more useful for that. It emphasizes ideology as representation, as analogue sign. It also focuses on the relations of signs to reality, which it sees as so functionally distorted that it invites attention both to the semiosic dimension and to the political and social reasons and forces which create it. *Ideology as analysed by Marx is an exemplary instance of social meaning.*

In similar terms, the French Marxist Louis Althusser incorporated a complex combination of representation and systemic distortion in his claim that ideology represents 'imaginary relations of individuals to their real conditions of existence' (1971: 169). Althusser added an implicit cybernetic dimension by invoking the idea of a device, an 'apparatus', which sorted the population along class lines in their relation to ideology to reproduce a society consisting of dominant and subordinate groups.

Gramsci used the term 'ideology' innovatively in what he called the 'ideological complex'. He employed this strategically to explore the co-existence of different ideological forms, old and new, representing different positions and stages, in dialectic with each other. This perspective identified *contradiction as an important quality in ideological forms*.

The British cultural theorist Stuart Hall gave 'ideology' currency in cultural studies, adding a concern with race and ethnicity to class analysis. He drew on Gramsci's 'ideological complex' to distinguish between 'British racism in its "high" imperial period and the racism which characterises the British social formation now' (1996: 435).

With Gunther Kress, I developed 'ideological complex' in a different, overlapping sense as a key concept for social semiotics: 'a functionally related set of contradictory versions of the world, coercively imposed by one social group on another on behalf of its distinctive interests, or subversively offered by another social group in attempts at resistance in its own interests' (Hodge and Kress 1988: 3). Where most other analysts look for an oppressive unity in ideology, and impose it where they do not find it, this version of the term allows analysts to see contradictions that are always present as systemic and functional.

As for Gramsci, contradictions come from and signify struggles, in the present and the past. They are diagnostic. Yet they can be functional, sources of effective power, not only sites of weakness. In cybernetic systems, contradictions can match contradictions and incorporate the complexity of those to be ruled. From this follows a paradox: *successful ideological forms contain and manage deep contradictions.*

As illustration I take Lakoff's two frames (2004), discussed in chapter 5. These pivot around two central figures, stern father versus nurturant parent. Although there is a polemical opposition between these two figures and the ideologies that accompany them, there is also functional contradiction within each. The sternness of the father is countered by his role, in patriarchal ideologies, to support and sustain the family. He is more punitive than the mother but still nurturant. Contradiction in the other frame comes through the overt stress on nurturance, opposed by the implicit role of parents as responsible adults who exercise power over their children.

The two frames are both ideological complexes which work for their respective constituencies. Together they form the two halves of a complex for an America that is still mainly patriarchal and still plays lip-service to the role of women. Yet the differences exist and are strategically important for activists and lobbyists. Contradictions are not fatal weaknesses in ideology, but they provide guides to points of vulnerability in each.

Ideological complexes in a postcolonial globe

Marx and Engels developed their theory for a world in which the primary struggle seemed to be the war to the death between capitalists and workers. They recognized the role of colonialism in capitalism, but today we can see that the effects of imperialism have been deeper and more complex than they thought. The concept of class is still relevant, but it is not enough on its own for social semiotics. Ideological complexes are still potent forces in confusing opposition and maintaining the dominance, but they take symptomatic new forms for social semiotics to analyse. I illustrate with three major examples of ideological complexes in a globalizing world.

Orientalism   I begin with what the Palestinian theorist Edward Said (1978) influentially called 'Orientalism' (see chapter 2 for discussion). Orientalism referred to strategies used by European colonial powers to govern dominated territories in what was constructed as 'the Orient'. Said explicitly used Foucault's theories. His *Orientalism* is a classic in social semiotics and critical discourse analysis.

As a strategy of governance, Orientalism as described by Said had different tasks, which led to contradictions which I see as instances of the *Orientalist ideological complex*. Ideologues of colonial rule were required to provide sound information about these subject peoples and also to justify the right of the rulers to rule. For this second purpose, colonial subjects had to be represented as inherently inferior to their rulers, incapable of independent rule – in Kipling's famous phrase, 'white man's burdens' carried dutifully by white men driven only by the desire to serve.

There was a contradiction here. Civilization was invented in Africa, the Middle East and Asia when ancient Britons were running naked into battle coated in blue paint. European culture was not obviously superior to Asian and Middle Eastern culture in the 1500s, when European colonization began in earnest. How could the European colonizers claim to be inherently superior when they gazed at Egyptian pyramids, Teotihuacan, the Taj Mahal or the Great Wall of China?

The great trick of Orientalism exposed by Said was to claim that the descendants of these great civilizations did not truly know themselves until European experts arrived to explain their own mysteries to them. The colonized were constructed as the Other who did not know its own self until Europeans came as the new Self, the sole source of that knowledge. The Orientalist paradigm allowed colonizers simultaneously to celebrate and to despise the colonized.

But there were contradictions in ideology and practice, as can be seen in the case of Sir William Jones, discussed in chapter 1 as a founding figure in linguistics. Jones was also a founding father of Orientalism who read a famous paper on the origins of Indo-European languages to the Burmese Orientalist Society he founded. Said wrote only a few pages on Jones, emphasizing the fact that, as a British judge, he used his extraordinary linguistic abilities to translate legal texts, clearly to benefit British rule. But Jones genuinely went beyond what any Indian or European scholar of the time knew about the origins of Sanskrit. He used this insight to praise Sanskrit, ancestral language for modern Hindu, as superior to Latin and Greek, themselves regarded at the time as superior to modern European languages such as English and French.

This argument went against British prejudices of superiority over their Indian subjects, as Jones well knew. It shows that the Orientalist complex is inherently unstable around this point. If Jones could use it against the dominant British attitudes, so could Indians. This is a general point about ideological complexes: *their strategic maps of contradictions can be used by anyone against the interests of the ideologue.*

The neo-liberal ideological complex   Orientalism arose in the specific context of European imperialism in its high phase, between 1800 and 1940, when European powers exercised more or less direct rule over their colonies. After the Second World War this system broke down, ushering in an era which has been called 'postcolonial', where former colonies won independence, often through armed struggle. Yet the former colonies did not simply win their freedom, and the colonizers did not simply concede defeat. A movement emerged that Hardt and Negri (2000) call 'Empire'. In their controversial thesis, the old order of dominance morphed into the new. It inherited some of the old mechanisms and ideological forms, including Orientalism, and forged them into new forms, as powerful as the old.

Following writers such as Bourdieu (2003), Chomsky (1999) and Harvey (2005), I call the current ideological face of global capitalism *neo-liberalism*. One value of this term is that it brings together both ideologies and practices at the global level and practices in individual nations and in institutions within those nations, including universities.

In an alternative way of seeing this picture, I invoke the term 'globality', a term theorized by Roland Robertson (1992) to capture a new sense that has recently emerged and which, he claims, has a sense of the planet as a single, interconnected whole of concern to everyone. Alongside the economic and political processes of international capital, he sees, there are institutions of globality. These may be weak and poorly resourced, easily captured by major nations and economic interests, yet still surprisingly important and effective. Are they just the soft face of global capitalism's new ideological complex? Or are they fragile but real signs of possible change?

I illustrate this issue by analysing a text by one neo-liberal institution of globality, the World Trade Organization (WTO), defining what the organization means by 'developing' nations:

> 7.2 Definition of a 'developing country' in the WTO.
> How is the selection made?
> There are no WTO definitions of 'developed' or 'developing' countries. Members announce for themselves whether they are 'developed' or 'developing' countries. However, other members can challenge the decision of a member to make use of provisions available to developing countries. (WTO website)

There are traces in this text of contradictions inherited from earlier ideological stages, as in Hall's understanding of ideological complexes as consequences of history. Behind the contrast between 'developed' and 'developing' nations is an earlier, harsher binary between 'developed' (industrialized nations of the West) and 'underdeveloped' or 'undeveloped' nations. After de-colonization, this binary was deemed too harsh and offensive. The new term, 'developing', allowed these nations, many of them former colonies, to see themselves in a better light. That better light, in Althusser's terms, was a more flattering relationship to the same reality.

The key contradiction in this text is the ambiguous renunciation of power by the WTO and the powerful nations it represents. On the one hand, it seems to leave 'developing nations' free to define themselves. In Said's definition of Orientalism, colonial powers took to themselves the right to define the colonized others. This text seems a refutation of Orientalism, into a new equality. But, on closer inspection, the freedom is illusory. Other members (powerful nations) can challenge this naming process. That challenge, as the text goes on to explain, affects all the special provisions that go with the status of 'developing'. As in Marx's camera obscura, disadvantage is inverted into seeming privilege, and the text does not mention all the special conditions that turn neo-liberal help into indebtedness.

Specific forms of language support this ideological strategy. Transformations are frequent. For instance, 'How is the selection made?' turns a statement into a question attributed to the reader. It is as if the WTO is not imposing information, merely responding to requests. 'Selection' is a nominalization, turning a sentence with a verb, 'select', into a noun. In the process it loses the agent of the verb, the one who selects. *The ideological complex frames and guides many individual linguistic forms and moves.*

In the neo-liberal ideological complex at every level, in the institutions of globality, in multinational corporations, in neo-liberal universities, the basic message is the same: the power of the powerful and inferiority-with-benefits of the governed. Yet this message often comes second, given less space, and clothed in complex, ambiguous language.

The new rulers of the planet want to rule more comprehensively than anyone has ever ruled before, but not to claim to do so. The neo-liberal ideological complex is designed to allow them to pull off this contradiction. Social semiotic analysis of ideological complexes can show the trick and suggest lines of resistance.

Flexible governance   One of the mantras of neo-liberal discourse is 'flexibilization', which Nancy Frazer (2003) critiqued as a new strategy in post-Fordist capitalism. 'Participation' is another in a family of terms that claim new freedoms for workers to be paid less to do more, to have illusions of power and self-determination without the reality. Yet these positive terms should not be thrown out just because of the role they play in an ideological complex. Ideological complexes appropriate precisely what the dominated most want. *The ideological complex wins a double victory if it damages the meaning as well as appropriating it.*

Alongside the seemingly unstoppable processes of political and economic globalization I see another current, which I regard as far more positive. Many friends, colleagues and movements I admire espouse an alternative political model which emphasizes participation, interaction, solidarity, whose practitioners are more inclined to accept chaos, complexity and uncertainty. This model has been around since at least the birth of 'democracy' in ancient Greece, but doubts have always arisen about an apparent inherent contradiction: How can power be power if it is dispersed? Is it always based substantially on a fiction, as it was in ancient Greek democracy? What can social semiotics contribute to clarifying these issues, in principle or in practice?

This kind of case cannot be made by analysing texts alone. What is crucial in ideological complexes is not only contradictions in texts but also their relationship to reality, as well as analysts' relations to the semiosic context. *Social semiotic analysis of ideology needs careful empirical analysis of social and material reality in order to understand specific functions and effects of ideology.*

'English' as ideology

Language policies and practices are extensively studied in socio-linguistics and applied linguistics. This is an area of study where sociolinguistic interests and methods converge with social semiotics. Policies always involve attitudes to language as major factors, and those in turn are always mediated by ideologies. In this section I bring out the contribution the concept of ideological complexes can make to this area. Without it, the dominant ideologies of language are likely to confuse and paralyse those who want better practices. That is precisely what ideological complexes are designed to do.

These ideological complexes make sense only in relation to a complex multiscalar political map. In this section I focus on English as a candidate 'global language', in the context of shifts in the global landscape generated by new flows of people, ideas and languages.

This topic has special importance for my book. I write in academic English as an L1 English speaker, using examples mostly from English, for readers assumed in the first instance to be university-level L1 English speakers. The default interpretation of what I am doing is that I replicate a sense of the 'natural' dominance of English. However, I use this privileged position to critique the dominance of English, and I try to write in a way that can reach many L2 readers with my meanings. The global reach of English helps me spread this message. This is a contradiction, but that alone does not trouble me. In ideological complexes contradictions are omnipresent. They can be part of strategies of critique or of resistance. The test comes from outcomes.

It is often claimed (especially by L1 English speakers) that English is the leading global language today. There are some grounds for this claim. According to Wikipedia, there are an estimated 949 million English users in the world, of whom 335 million are L1 speakers, and another 614 million who use it as an additional language. But there are probably more L1 and L2 Chinese speakers, and Spanish also has a large base.

Assuming these figures are broadly true, they still contain a contradiction. English is important in some way for nearly twice as many non-L1 as for L1 speakers. It is only this aggregated English which is a global language, not its L1 form. L1 speakers of standard English are a minority of this part. *The English which is a candidate to be a global language is fuzzy English.* But the industry which feeds and profits from this global fact acts as a gatekeeper to ensure that the English they promote is standard English, not global English.

The British Council is a government-funded body that has to make sense of these contradictions on behalf of the interests of the nation. It sponsored a report on English as a global language in 2006. Lord Kinnock, then head of the British Council, wrote in the preface:

> 7.3 Monoglot English graduates face a bleak economic future as qualified multilingual youngsters from other countries are proving to have a competitive advantage over their British counterparts in global companies and organisations. (Graddol 2006)

This is no celebration of the prestige of English but a wake-up call to Britons today. Relying too much on the privileged status of English paradoxically threatens the power of English people and their language. But this referential syntagm is complicated by social syntagms which act on its interpretation and likely effects. For instance, Kinnock the speaker has high status in English life. He is a British peer, head of the British Council, reporting on the work of David Graddol, a well-reputed British linguist. This is a tight chain of authority. Each link enhances the others to make them representatives of official British opinion. The statement is in good standard written English produced by a fluent L1 speaker. *Yet the referential content critiques the dominant ideology of English as a privileged language.*

In the book, Graddol directly criticized 'English as a Foreign Language (EFL)', the dominant approach to teaching English to non-English speakers. As he comments, 'English' here is taken for granted as the standard language, the language of elites in Britain and its colonies, past and present. This devalues the English of many L1 speakers, even in Britain, who use non-standard forms. The word 'foreign' then constructs these learners in a binary opposition, seen from the point of view of English speakers. Graddol sees this approach as 'designed to produce failure' (2006: 83) for most 'foreign' learners. Any time learners deviate slightly from standards established by elite speakers they fail to be fully like them, however interesting or important may be what they have to say. This is a triumph for the ideological complex. Like Althusser's 'ideological apparatus', it is an instrument of control, classifying, sorting and assigning positions and values that reproduce the dominance of the dominant.

Graddol considers a range of models, all more inclusive than EFL. He favours a more radical model, English as lingua franca (ELF), in which English plays a key role in a 'multilingual ecology' (2006: 87). The two terms 'multilingual' and 'ecology' signify a complex meaning about complex forms of social and linguistic organization. They also identify and legitimate a community of researchers, learners and teachers of English who see the language in this way and want it taught like that.

The point of this analysis is not to be seduced by the positive aspects of this ideological complex but to reflect on what it signifies and what opportunities it offers for those who can take them. The EFL juggernaut rolls on, sustaining and sustained by a massive global industry. The dominant ideological complex may subsume ELF to legitimate the status quo in language teaching. The EFL model has deep pockets and big battalions.

But Kinnock's analysis is not mere ideology. He has good reasons to claim that the new competence within which English must operate is minimally multilingual and will have to operate with fuzzy English and other languages just as fuzzy. ELF is not constructed by the ideological complex but appropriated by it. It exists in the minds and practices of many very good teachers and intelligent learners. *Ideological complexes are weapons, not truths, double-edged swords in battles whose outcomes are not fixed in advance.*

Models and processes

Conflict and cooperation

Marx is commonly seen as the founding theorist of conflict models of society, opposed by sociologists who emphasize collaboration in effective, functional societies. To represent sociology I quote Alberto Martinelli, president of the International Sociology Association from 1998 to 2002:

> 7.4 At the core of sociological inquiry lies the basic question asked by Georg Simmel: how is society possible, that is, how can cooperation be fostered so that basic needs are met, social reproduction guaranteed and conflict regulated. (Martinelli 2014)

Martinelli here overtly emphasizes collaboration as the main goal of social theory. Conflict appears, but only in a final two-word clause. Yet it still exists, as an object to be regulated. Cooperation is a goal, not an omnipresent reality. Martinelli's statement presupposes and inflects a model in which conflict is basic to society.

In practice, all models of society in Western and Eastern traditions recognize *dimensions of both power and solidarity, both cohesion and conflict,* though in different forms and balances. Marx and Engels described society in the *Communist manifesto*:

7.5 The history of all hitherto existing society is the history of class struggle. (1970: 35)

This explicitly states that struggle and conflict are omnipresent, open and hidden, between 'oppressors and oppressed', as they called them. Yet in English, as in German, the singular is used for 'society' (*Gesellschaft*). This struggle could not take place unless processes of solidarity constituted 'society' as an entity, divided strongly or weakly into classes. The term 'class' here (German *Klassenkämpfen*) is ambiguous in scope, with a fuzzy meaning. It could refer to the socio-economic classes of nineteenth-century capitalist Europe but, in keeping with the historical sweep of Marx's claim, it could also refer to any social group on any scale.

Marx and Engels use 'is', a present tense of complete certainty in English and German, to bind their radical audience to support their statement. But they knew, as they said in this manifesto, that most leaders and countries in Europe were afraid of this certainty and opposed it, in the name of an idea of nations harmoniously ruled by their rightful kings and leaders. They were also contesting Hegel's dialectical view of history (1977), in which the motor for history was the 'spirit of history', the *Geist*, whose self-divisions drove material history. Their meaning was also dialogic.

Conversely, Martinelli does not mention Marx but can be understood dialogically. He silently countered Marxism, as sociologists have done for over a century. Simmel, a nineteenth-century sociologist and younger contemporary of Marx, was not of Marx's stature. By placing him at the head of the sociological tradition in place of Marx, Martinelli strikes a silent symbolic blow against Marx. But both Martinelli and Marx acknowledge conflict and community. *The co-existence of conflict and collaboration is a 'hinge' concept for modern social thought.*

As part of the sociological tradition, social semiotics takes *power and solidarity, hostility and cohesion as primary social meanings, as relative universals.* It looks for potential conflicts, to make sense of meanings, social and referential, of semiosic acts which initially do not seem to express conflict. It seeks links between opponents which hold them together in a common system. *It identifies important conflicts which were not recognized before and major sources of cohesion that were undervalued.*

Difference engines

Critics of Marxism often use the history of the Russian Revolution as
proof that Marxism must be fundamentally wrong. Social semiotics
distinguishes between ideologies and practices and tries to identify
meanings and models at work in their often complex contexts.

Here is Lenin, the architect of the first successful Marxist-inspired
revolution, writing in exile in 1902, fifteen years before his triumph:

> 7.6 We are marching in a compact group along a precipitous and diffi-
> cult path, firmly holding each other by the hand. We are surrounded on
> all sides by enemies, and we have to advance almost constantly under
> their fire. (Lenin 1947: 11)

This image captures the duality of conflict and cooperation in his revolutionary practice. The 'we' group is compact, with high solidarity,
even intimacy, metaphorically holding hands. Lenin implies that this
high solidarity is needed because of the intensely conflictual context.
He also implies that the core group is a small minority, facing a
hugely superior enemy. This image is an analogue basis for his discursive practices. Lenin, like many on the left, was highly combative,
fighting others on the left as well as capitalist enemies. Here he is
writing against 'revisionists' who reinterpreted Marxist doctrines,
including Bogdanov and others from his own Bolshevik faction, itself
product of a split with the Menshiviks:

> 7.7 It was only the revisionists who gained a sad notoriety for them-
> selves by their departure from the fundamental views of Marxism and
> by their fear, or inability, to 'settle accounts' openly, explicitly, reso-
> lutely and clearly with the views they had abandoned. (Lenin [1903]
> 1938: 90)

Lenin's opponents here are from the same social class as he was, committed opponents of the czarist regime, so it does not express a class
struggle. He has a double criticism: they departed from Marxism and
refused to recognize it. The split is too fuzzy for him. They pretend to
be the same. He wants their difference to be unambiguous.

The content Lenin produces implies a paradigmatic system,
which I represent in figure 7.1. This is the familiar tree shape I have
suggested (chapter 4) is a kind of universal across biology as well
as language and society. Across all these domains it can be understood as a digital device which multiplies divisions. It is fractal-like,
producing self-similar forms at every level. This model implies that

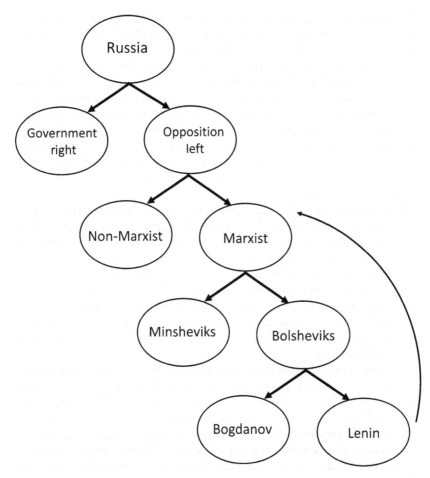

Figure 7.1   Tree diagram: the evolution of Leninism

Lenin's specific debates, and the context for his writing and practice, were shaped by a system which pre-existed his struggles. As Marx wrote: 'Men make their own history, but they do not make it just as they please; they do not make it under circumstances chosen by themselves, but under circumstances directly encountered, given and transmitted from the past' (1970: 96).

Lenin was both product and creator of this process of continuous division. Like Chomsky's analogous device, the ideological form of his device had recursive loops which jumped over the divisions he made. He identified with Marxism, two levels higher, with the left in general, and finally, after he came to power, with Russia itself. As in his image for his group, Lenin imagined high solidarity through his identity with a larger group. In effect this denied in fantasy the isolating consequences of the logic of his actions.

The tree structures and the kind of device are familiar. In this case it produced endless divisions on the left, Lenin's own side. All these involved conflict. They made successive groups ever narrower as they tended towards an impossible purity. It also fragmented the Czarists, preparing their fall. In terms of chaos theory, this sounds like cascades of catastrophes as in the theories of Per Bak (1996), who called it 'deep chaos'. This sequence of Russian history exhibits the classic exponential form of a power law. In chaos theory, not all chaos is the benign creator of new order.

This device, to call it that, has some specific characteristics. It is programmed with a crisp logic which maximizes and enforces divisions within categories and classes that are adjacent and almost the same. The outcome is paradoxical, a rejection of these almost allies as ferocious as the common enemy. This pattern probably responds to the context, opposition parties in exile. The context functions like the environment in evolutionary theory, acting on emerging forms to select between them. In this case, Lenin's group emerged triumphantly and, by a series of lucky breaks, became rulers of a new state, the USSR, in 1917.

In some respects this produced a disconnect between this device and the new context. In this situation it produced massive suspicion across the leadership. No one could trust the hand they supposedly held, in Lenin's metaphor, which like their own hand probably held a knife. Lenin initiated the 'Red Terror' to remove suspected subversives whose possibility was created by the difference engine. Lenin's successor, Stalin, intensified state terror on a systemic scale over three decades.

This device does what it does, formed by and creating the context for the unfolding of the core social meaning, just as epigenetic environments shape the realization of genes. It produces outcomes that are not inherent in the original meanings and may be dysfunctional. Some common devices are pathogenic. The point of analysis may be not just to understand but to change.

I use this compressed account of a complex history to suggest some tentative generalizations:

1 *Conflicts exist within as well as between groups, of all kinds and on all scales.*
2 *Bonds of solidarity as well as power can produce distortions of meaning.*

3 *Differences of all kinds (social, semiotic, biological) can be produced by difference engines. They operate, partly independent of context, to produce outcomes that may be dysfunctional for that context.*

4 *Contexts can change, sometimes turning a functional fit between device and context into a dysfunctional system.*

5 *Where devices produce dysfunctional outcomes, social semiotics can usefully identify the logic at issue and seek ways to dismantle it.*

What I have called a 'difference engine' can be seen in terms of Durkheim's 'social facts' (see chapter 2). Social facts for Durkheim are social forces acting to shape individual behaviours in ways that individuals themselves do not perceive. Something like a 'difference engine' in Lenin's case came from outside him. The logic was driven in the first place by the czarist regime. This produced divisions which led to its collapse. It also created the paranoiac state which Bakhtin theorized against and Orwell satirized in his novel *1984*.

Understanding multiculturalism

Multiculturalism as a term has few friends today (Hodge and O'Carroll 2006). Nationalists on the right proclaim that it has 'failed', though their preferred policies produce suffering and dysfunction which they blame on multiculturalism. Critics on the left often see it as compromised, a neo-liberal strategy of governance not a vision of social justice.

In this section I draw on two strands of social semiotics. I treat multiculturalism as an ideological complex whose contradictions leave it open to these critiques. I also use social semiotics to uncover the logics which drive these processes.

The problems of multiculturalism are exacerbated by movements of peoples and cultures across and within national spaces and with typical responses to those movements. Some responses are positive, the emergence of what Ingrid Piller (2011) calls 'intercultural communication' as a new major context for language use. Others are punitive, setting up and policing borders.

The Holocaust is a potent fact and a symbol of genocide as the extreme expression of racism. I see these destructive responses as one of the most dangerous threats facing humanity today. It is also intractably complex – a 'wicked problem', in Hulme's terms (2009). In this section I use social semiotics to understand some key dimensions of these problems as they manifest in events, texts and debates.

Racism

Racism is a key term in organizing violence and discrimination between different groups, yet in some ways it seems deceptively easy to combat. Racism is defined and banned in most developed nations, including Britain, the USA and Australia. The idea of multicultural-ism seems triumphant enough. Yet, as all citizens of these nations know, 'racism' is alive and well. Its signifiers shift bewilderingly. Its fundamental meanings morph like the heads of Hydra.

The following example of everyday racist discourse caught my attention while I was in a small shop near Brighton, UK, in 2010 (see figure 7.2). The *Daily Star* is a popular newspaper. I begin with an auto-ethnographic account of my reactions. I thought: 'Oh no! This isn't a paper I would buy.' My reactions reflected a quality of the article. It is meant to be divisive.

This aspect of its social meaning is picked up early in my encounter with the text. It rapidly establishes the cast of players and the rela-tions expected towards them: Muslims versus non-Muslims, men versus women, with sex a catalyst for conflict. In this way it creates social syntagms which reach out of the page. This is a difference engine, like Althusser's ideological device, which grasps some readers and rejects others.

There is another difference engine at work here, not signalled in the text itself. A popular newspaper such as this understands its readers as a demographic – in this case, lower class, with presumed reading levels and interests. *Class analysis is not obsolete. It is still embedded in common sense practices of business and the media.* To bring out the diversity of readers included and excluded by this text, I 'make it strange', imagining how it might be read by L2 speakers of English in Britain and outside Britain by L2 readers of my book.

The language seems simple but would present some challenges for L2 speakers, especially outside Britain. For instance, 'rev up' con-sists of two monosyllables, but it is colloquial, not standard English. It is a phrasal verb (verb plus adverb), a difficult form for L2 English speakers. It has the effect of excluding them. So does the familiar reference to Clarkson, as host of a British TV show. The show's title is given, but its connection with driving has to be inferred. The simplicity is deceptive. British lower-class L1 English speakers are enclosed in a club from which L2 English/'foreigners' are partly excluded.

Multimodal analysts will be struck by the balance between words and images. In the image which dominates the gaze, five words

Figure 7.2 Front page of the *Daily Star*

occupy 80 per cent of the space. This typographic convention, for British readers, has a well-known social meaning: lower-class. In Voloshinov's terms (1973), *typography is a multi-accentual sign*. It signifies social and class differences within a common stock of conventions.

Kress and van Leeuwen (2001) show how aspects of composition are important signs. The format of white letters on black, with the face of a Muslim woman looming out of the darkness, makes the words seem like white reason against formless female/Muslim darkness. The size of the letters also signifies. It is the typographic

equivalent of a shout: white rationality responds to Muslim irrationality (madness).

The first two words, 'Burka babes' form a single paratactic
syntagm, one word stacked on the other. It is part of a longer syntagm
which extends below it without ever making full, unambiguous
sense. It never becomes a full sentence in standard English. The
combination of 'burka' and 'babe' in one syntagm signifies conflict.
'Burka' refers to the clothing code for women that signifies gendered
Muslim identity. 'Babe' as a way of referring to women has referential
meaning – young, attractive, sexy. It is also a set of social meanings, a
way of looking at young women associated with US males.

The clash seems so extreme as to be unresolvable. How could the
same woman be a 'babe' and conform to strict Muslim practices by
wearing a burka? Yet paratactic forms are ambiguous, leaving it open
to readers to combine them to make sense. The openness is asymmetrical. There is an obvious meaning which sees the conjunction
as absurd, a racist reading. Yet the other meanings are still possible.

Many other negative meanings are communicated about Muslims
in this piece. But the concept of the ideological complex pushes us
to look for contradictions to this main message. As one instance, in
the top right-hand corner, whose compositional meaning is ideal-
concrete in Kress and van Leeuwen's scheme, there is a large image,
the face of a calm, dignified, beautiful Muslim woman, only her
eyes showing. In the bottom left-hand corner, compositionally signifying non-ideal, non-concrete, we have the smaller face of Jeremy
Clarkson, with a silly look. In this contrast, the Muslim woman radi-
ates power and dignity while the British man looks ridiculous.

This is a similar contradiction to the Orientalist ideological
complex, where the Orient is the object of fascination as well as contempt. In this case the weight of meanings is towards contempt, but
fascination co-exists with it. It does not cancel the contempt or will to
control the Muslim other but gives them more energy.

Identity

Identity is a key concept for understanding major problems of global
society today, a factor in many of the most violent conflicts, yet it
is remarkably ill-understood, full of contradictions, hard to grasp,
analyse and act on.

Identity is embedded in social syntagms on which social judgement
and action are based. Social syntagms consist of statements '[X]
does/does not do [Y]', 'should/should not do [Y]', 'should or should

not communicate [Y]', where [X] and [Y] are the basic paradigms of social action. The paradigmatic structures and processes of identity are keys to social judgement and action. *Change categories, change beliefs, change actions.*

Identity has a disconcerting contradiction at its core. It can refer to sameness or difference. 'Identity' comes from Latin *idem et idem*, 'that one and that one', or 'the same and the same'. This etymology brings out the deictic basis of the word. Identity is not a quality; it is the product of pointing. It groups things or people as being effectively the same (for some purposes) and also different from the rest (for these purposes). As in Vygotsky's complexive thinking (see chapter 5), they may include men and women or older and younger people in the same family, rather than group all old men in the same category. Elements chosen at one moment as 'the same' have differences that on another occasion might lead to different groupings.

In one form identities are constructed by a simple binary device, a difference engine that keeps splitting each element into a new pair of elements. But, as we saw in the case of Lenin, an unmoderated difference engine produces dysfunctional relationships. *Endless difference produces a social pathology.*

Problems with identity arise because so many people believe that identities are fixed, homogeneous, pure and essential. Yet identities in reality are fluid, heterogeneous and intermixed. The beliefs in fixed, homogeneous identities are social facts with social effects. Yet the gap between these beliefs and complex reality is also a social fact with major consequences.

The Indian cultural theorist Homi Bhabha (1994) proposed the concept of 'hybrid' identities as the distinctive product of postcolonial global forces and conditions. I extend the scope of his concept. *Identities have always been complex and fluid, hybrid and more than hybrid. They are always fuzzy.* All thinking about identities needs to use fuzzy algorithms, fuzzy statements and fuzzy identity categories. Wherever crisp identities and crisp identity statements are used, they impose rigidities in the interests of control. By a paradox of the kind that is common in social life, in practice they produce lack of control, problems of governance, counterproductive policies and actions. *Rethinking every identity problem through fuzzy categories is key to more adequate analysis and action.*

In the 'Burka babes' text, Clarkson is given his personal identity through the English name system: first name plus surname. Here this is a unique identity created by multiple applications of identity categories. In contrast, 'Muslims' is an undifferentiated, homogenized collective plural. It is not clear in this case whether it includes women as well as men, British citizens or others. This simplistic logic is used as a weapon against this whole group, a way of gathering all their diversity into a single target, to then dismiss them all. A fuzzy logic analysis is a critical strategy that helps to dismantle that discriminatory strategy.

Yet the presentation of Clarkson's identity is more complex than this suggests. His Britishness is not referred to but is relied on as part of a cultural knowledge that includes his TV show. His gender is not strongly marked, but for those who did not know it already it is evident from his picture and name, confirmed by the pronoun 'his'. While the particular identities of Muslims are covered by the generic category, his generic identities are implied alongside and above his individual identity. *He has a hybrid identity as a product of his class affiliation.* This allows Clarkson to combine the two kinds of identity, unique and personal, generic and collective. He functions as a 'prototypical' Briton, in Rosch's terms: more British than many British men, much more so than all British women. Because of this double level of identity, British readers, especially men, can identify with him more readily even if they disagree with his position or the way he expresses it. Muslim readers have only a single option, to accept or reject the identity ascribed to them.

The asymmetry in the way the identities are constructed communicates negative stereotypes about Muslims. It also constructs the grounds on which the struggle is waged in unequal terms, in which the complex identities and meanings of Muslims are less easily thought of. They make it harder for Muslims to respond in a range of different ways that would be truer to their experience and more effective in practice.

Flows and meanings

In linear, static models of meaning, texts have meanings or not, which have more effects if they reach more people. In a dynamic social semiotic model, meanings exist only in circulation. Texts usually change and do not carry the same meanings even if they look like the same text. The processes are always social, they always carry social meaning, and the social always produces diversity. Faster flows and transformations enabled by digital technologies are characteristic of globalization, with massive effects of meaning for culture and identity.

I illustrate this process by analysing the second half of the 'Burka

DAILY STAR, Wednesday, July 28, 2010   5

Figure 7.3   Continuation of the *Daily Star* article

babes' story, from page 5 of the paper. This concerns a video clip produced by a German advertising agency, Glow Berlin, starring Miriam
Wimmer, whose Muslim identity is not stated, to advertise a luxury
online lingerie shop, Liaisons dangereux. This video effortlessly
negotiates language barriers: made by a German firm and involving a
French trade name and an English punchline. The video quickly went
viral. The *Daily Star* was one of many who picked it up and recycled
it, reproducing six images from the video. Three are reproduced in
figure 7.3. The scale of appropriation and mixing and mashing texts
and images today is seen as a defining phenomenon of the internet
age. It is also found in earlier media regimes. 'Intertextuality' in literary theory has similar features (see Allen 2000).

Bernstein (1981) used the term 'recontextualization' to describe a
class of transformational processes that act on texts as they migrate
from different contexts. The object of these transformations is the
context of utterance, understood as a set of meanings constituted by
links between texts and contexts. These meanings are like an analogue form which is transformed when messages are moved to new
contexts. Social meaning comes from what is transformed in this
process, why and by whom.

The author of the video is Glow Berlin, a German video producer.
Glow Berlin's social meaning is constructed through clues in the

video itself, indexical signs from which viewers may hypothetically reconstruct social meanings. For instance, the video begins with intimate shots of a naked Wimmer, shot tastefully in soft focus from behind. The relationship constructed with the camera, and hence implicitly with the audience, is an analogue sign, here of respect, not voyeurism.

This structure of meanings is not a static object which is transformed by the *Daily Star*. It is constituted by and for transformations. For instance, the video follows Wimmer, self-transformed and fully clothed in her burka, to the window, where she gazes out on the city (presumably Berlin). The camera then switches to the outside, to capture Wimmer gazing out, and the image freezes. Lines of text are added, to make it an advertisement, suitable to be reproduced as stills.

The transformation from video to still image includes many changes, each carrying social meaning. For instance, in the still image Wimmer is part of an advertisement, not the living woman she was in the video. She now looks like a prisoner of her Muslim status, separated from a world outside in which she does not act. Less obviously, she is also the prisoner of her role as an icon in an advertisement. She is only an object to be seen, not a subject to see. The final transformation is the slogan: 'Sexiness for everyone. Everywhere.' Wimmer has been transformed from moving individual to still image in a slogan.

The *Daily Star* version has many significant differences. For instance, there are no signifiers of respect for women or Muslims, as in the video. The images are offered directly for voyeuristic male gazes. That becomes part of their meaning in this new context. The newspaper's story was also a fusion transformation. It recontextualized another story, about Jeremy Clarkson, and some sexist, anti-Muslim comments he made on his TV programme. The story consisted of these two disparate texts-plus-contexts which were stitched together into a fictional syntagmatic string, presented as if Clarkson had actually commented on the video. Both were presented in the new context of the *Daily Star*. This had the effect of reinforcing the Clarkson context, reducing the force of the more complex video context.

Countless texts circulate on the net, each recontextualizing the texts they deal with. As a complementary example I show a different response to the Glow Berlin video:

7.8 Empowering Muslim Women
As an advocate for the amelioration of women's rights, I believe that this ad featuring German model Miriam Wimmer is a wonderful tribute

to Muslim women because it does show that all women have the right
to feel beautiful, love their bodies, dress themselves however they want
to, and yes, wear sexy lingerie if they so desire. ('An American Muslim'
blog: Monday 23 August 2010)

This male blogger's comment, like all comments, can be analysed as
recontextualization. He is conscious that the social meaning of his
text comes from his location (the USA), his gender, and his political
position – 'progressive'. He houses it in the safe space of his personal
blog. It has fewer markers of context but is less exposed to hostile
gazes than the *Daily Star* piece, less commercially driven than the
Glow Berlin video. It is closely related to the original video but carries
an opposite meaning to that of the *Daily Star*. It is only one example
that illustrates *the range of meanings that can be created in response to the
same initial meaning in the far-from-equilibrium conditions of cyberspace.*

Far-from-equilibrium conditions

In this chapter, as throughout the book, I stress the value of focusing
specifically on a far-from-equilibrium framework. Battles over racism
and identity are too full of paradox and contradiction to fit easily into
a linear paradigm.

Schismogenesis

Bateson expanded the scope of the study of identity with work he
did before the Second World War. As an anthropologist, he worked
with traditional societies imploding under pressures from their colonial masters in the twilight of European imperialism. As a citizen
between the wars he became interested in the mechanisms that
produced wars and social collapse in both pre-modern and modern
societies. Bateson (1973) called this schismogenesis, literally 'generating schisms, splits'. It is similar to what I call a difference engine.
Something like this may be a relative universal, found in many social
semiotic and biological processes, in other species as well as humans.
  Bateson distinguished between two patterns of split, affecting two
kinds of social organization. In one kind of split the problem seems
to be difference. This form dominates discussions of racism. For
instance, the Muslim problem comes from the supposed fact that
Muslims are different from Christians, Europeans or whatever. They
are demonized as the 'other'. Bateson called this 'complementary

schismogenesis'. It is a more analogue form. But he pointed out that sameness as well as difference can lead to schismogenesis. It is a more digital process. He called this 'symmetrical schismogenesis'. It is driven by comparisons between near equals, each of whom strives to have more of the same attribute than their rivals.

For Bateson, the pre-war arms race was a prime example. Each side's armoury inspired the other side to outdo it in an exponential progression. Factionalism may be a similar phenomenon, as factions break off in search of a more 'pure' version of their shared ideology.

Bateson's theory has us looking for different patterns of sameness and difference in structures and processes, around diversity, discrimination, racism and sexism. For instance, the 'Burka babes' story is built around two binaries, not one – Muslim/non-Muslim and male/female. In both there is a play of sameness and difference at every level, including images, words, and sentences.

7.9 Burka babe's undies ad fury (*Daily Star*)

'Burka' is the signifier of Muslim difference from 'us' (i.e., *Daily Star* readers), but 'babe' signifies sameness. She is turned into an honorary Western woman who can be addressed as 'babe', regarded as sexy. So she is the same as 'us', yet she is different. Being the same is as controversial and schismogenic as being different.

Because full burkas are all similar (black, covering the whole body, etc.), they signify that all these Muslim women are the same. They create symmetrical solidarity among Muslims, difference from non-Muslims. But burkas even more strongly signify the complementary solidarity of women with their husbands, representing submission to their husbands' patriarchal rights.

This news item creates schismogenic effects in readers through a mixture of symmetrical and complementary identity meanings. Muslim men are ridiculous because they are both too alike (sexist) and too different. Muslim women look different from their British sisters, but they can be appropriated as sex objects because they are so like English women, at least as seen through the gaze of sexist Britons like Clarkson.

Difference engines construct difference out of sameness. That difference may be challenged by underlying sameness, by persisting social and affectual bonds between human beings. It can also be challenged by internal differences which are ignored by the engine. Either way, they respond to and create far-from-equilibrium conditions and effects which are often damaging and sometimes catastrophic.

Effects in times of crisis

Meanings have effects, and they are affected by social factors and forces. That is why it is so important to study the nexus between meanings and effects. But the study of this nexus has been complicated by one dominant paradigm for interpreting it. In a crude form it has been labelled and critiqued as the 'silver bullet' theory, a simplistic linear model which imagines messages as being like bullets, only needing to be aimed accurately at their targets to have irresistible effects.

This model has been discredited many times (see, e.g., Silverstone 1994), yet it retains a remarkable hold on media practices (see Hodge 2011). Part of the problem is that it may be inadequate, but it is easy to grasp. In a simplistic binary logic, if meanings have effects they must be linear. If they are not linear then they are not understandable as effects.

Social semiotics offers a third option. In a fable attributed to Aesop, a Greek slave living in the sixth century BC, at a similar time to the Buddha, the sun and the north wind dispute about their respective powers. They agree to put the matter to the test: which one could make the next traveller take off his coat. The north wind blew ever harder, but the more he blew the tighter the traveller grasped the coat. The sun shone, the man grew too hot, and he took the coat off himself.

This parable has been used to justify the use of persuasion over force. It also illustrates non-linear causality. The efforts of the north wind are not only ineffective, they produce an opposite effect. The traveller holds his coat on even tighter. The sun acts not on the object to be affected but on the conditions in which the object exists. He alters those conditions, and the energy and purpose come from the traveller himself. Translating this into the silver-bullet model, he shoots himself.

The sociologist Stanley Cohen 1972) explored a similar complexity of media effects in theorizing what he called 'moral panics'. These took the form of an irrational explosion of hostility against their designated targets. Cohen included campaigns against refugees among other hot-button issues of his day. He saw this process in earlier societies, but perceived a key role for the media today in 'augmenting' the process.

The phenomenon of 'moral panics' undoubtedly exists today, and Cohen's pioneering work is still a relevant guide. He identifies what I call 'critical incidents' (Hodge and Matthews 2011; see chapter 2). I reframe 'moral panics' as instances of far-from-equilibrium dynamics (Prigogine and Stengers 1984), in which systems can shift far from equilibrium. This leads to non-linear causality (effects disproportionate to causes, sometimes inverted: Lorenz's 'butterfly effects' (1993)) and runaway positive feedback, shifting the system rapidly into chaos and collapse.

Bateson's work on schismogenesis preceded his cybernetic phase, but I translate it into cybernetic terms, as two kinds of runaway (exponential, escalating) feedback, where sameness feeds on near sameness, or where difference does so, to trigger escalation.

I illustrate from the Holocaust, something Bateson did not know about when he wrote. The difference of Jews from 'normal' Germans was exaggerated in Nazi propaganda, because the problem for the Nazi difference engine was that Jews were too alike, not that they were too different. Intelligent, high-achieving Jews such as Freud and Einstein were not welcomed because they were indistinguishable from Germans, but ejected for that reason. The notorious Yellow Star of David to mark Jews was designed to overcome the actual problem of sameness.

I illustrate far-from-equilibrium dynamics with the case of the *Charlie Hebdo* affair, where seven journalists of the satirical magazine were assassinated by two Muslim extremists on 7 January 2015. In the first issue after the massacre, the magazine published a cover cartoon showing a man with strong Arabic features and a simplistic white turban.

7.10 Above him are the words '*Tout est pardonné*' (All is forgiven). A tear rolls down his cheek, and he holds a placard saying '*Je suis Charlie*' (I am Charlie).

I start with the contradictions in this text, connecting them with the conflicts and contradictions in the multi-layered context. *Charlie Hebdo* angered Muslims, especially by printing cartoons depicting the Prophet, which they claimed was offensive, forbidden to their religion.

Laws in various European nations, including France, defend the right to free speech and also ban 'hate speech', utterances likely to provoke racist violence. The two principles are contradictory, but in normal conditions the competing claims can be negotiated and balanced. Far-from-equilibrium conditions destabilize this balance and expose contradictions at the heart of the dominant ideological complex. The assassins' way of resolving the contradiction by shooting the journalists is labelled 'terrorism'. This term's function is to short-circuit all shifting contradictions in the ideological complex and impose a totalitarian unity of judgement and response. In Bateson's terms it is schismogenic.

But *Charlie Hebdo* in this cartoon repeated the offence of which it was accused. The journalists used a racist stereotype. They did not name him as Muhammad, so strictly they committed blasphemy only for those who knew independently who the figure was. But such subtle distinctions do not survive in far-from-equilibrium conditions.

The caption is ambiguous in many ways. It is a passive (*est pardonné*), so it is not stated who is doing the forgiving. *Charlie Hebdo*? Muhammad? The phrase refers to a human act of forgiveness, but it resonates with the characteristic act of the Christian God, who pardons all sins. But 'Allah' is all-merciful, and the word has the same meaning, God, in Islam. So in its deep structure the phrase brings together *Charlie Hebdo*, Allah and the Christian God. To claim they are the same can be seen as an act of reconciliation. By the rules of far-from-equilibrium dynamics, it can also be responded to as an act of aggression, as in this case it was.

The response to this incident exploded worldwide – another sign and effect of far-from-equilibrium conditions. A dominant theme in the pro-*Charlie* demonstrations was the phrase quoted here, *Je suis Charlie*, or its translations. The effect of the phrase is not only to assert solidarity with the magazine but to create a new identity which replaced all other identities. However, the cartoon attributed this to Muhammad, and in effect stripped him of his own identity. The magazine performs the Orientalist trick of speaking for the Other. And meanwhile those who were Charlie for the day were free to resume their everyday identities the next day.

This issue of *Charlie Hebdo* sold 3 million copies worldwide, for a magazine previously close to bankruptcy. The assassins' attempt to close the magazine did the opposite. Yet the assassinations were a response, however inappropriate, to rampant racism and injustice to Muslims in France. There is an ultimately linear chain of cause and effect which follows non-linear lines across the different parts of deeply divided French society. Social semiotics needs to manage the fact that the two kinds of logic co-exist in the same social space.

One lesson from this incident for social semiotics is that *large effects of meaning occur mainly in far-from-equilibrium conditions*. The effects of meaning in close-to-equilibrium conditions are rational but so small that it does not seem worth the effort of analysing them. But because effects may be contradictory in far-from-equilibrium conditions they may seem self-cancelling when averaged out. So linear approaches may not want to study or explain them, since they seem too aberrant.

A second lesson is that *the equilibrium status of conditions is an important object of analysis in its own right.* For instance, the 'Burka babes' story had no demonstrable effects at the time, but it reflected and fuelled a far-from-equilibrium condition.

The final lesson of this chapter is that *contradictions arise from conflict and the attempts to manage those conflicts through meanings.* Social semiotics will do its job of understanding and ameliorating socially dysfunctional situations only if it can *trace pathways between social injustice and deformations of meaning, between the social bases of ideological complexes and their dances of identity.*

8
Multiscalar Analysis

The multiscalar principle plays a key role in this book. Stated simply, it seems common sense. If meaning is expressed through language at all levels, from very large to very small, then linguistics and semiotics should analyse it across this range. Similarly, social forces act across all scales of society. Social semiotics needs multi-scalar analysis.

In practice, both semiotic and social science disciplines have problems working across the full scale of forms of language and society. Scalar systems have some distinctive and surprising problems. If language and society form highly complex multiscalar wholes, then such problems are multiplied by separating linguistic and social analysis.

In this chapter I continue to address Blommaert's challenge to CDA and social semiotics (2005): to incorporate methods and objects from sociolinguistics into a common field. The multiscalar principle is valuable for this purpose, as many sociolinguistic classics involve unmanaged problems of scale.

Analysing scale

I use the term 'multiscalar' non-technically to refer to phenomena which include many scales or levels (*multi*, 'many' + *scal-*, 'ladder') in space and time, the two fundamental dimensions of physical reality and conceptual space–time. I bring out various uses of the term in different disciplines in a common social semiotic framework.

Fractals

I found Mandelbrot's theory of fractals (1977, 1993) a game-changing approach to issues of multiscalar structures and processes, though with important limitations. Mandelbrot brought several different ideas together in his concept of fractals. Central is the concept of fractal itself, referring to non-Euclidean shapes such as pottery fragments (*fractus*, Latin for 'broken'). In semiotic terms, *fractals are self-similar not identical analogue forms*. For Mandelbrot, they are *multiscalar, replicated indefinitely up and down*.

Mandelbrot applied his mathematical theories mainly to scientific fields. I use fractal theory for social semiotic analysis, not to impose ideas from one field onto others but as a heuristic method. *Fractal analysis can generate hypotheses to test empirically in texts and processes.*

Science has some different, complementary multiscalar models. Newton's great synthesis ([1687] 1999) united the very big (celestial mechanics) and the small (terrestrial mechanics), which he bound together by calculating positions as point sources. This is a classical way of producing scale-invariant theory, which applies to phenomena irrespective of scale. Fractals can be understood as non-linear scale-invariant objects. In this form, *Newtonian laws apply to every fractal level.*

An influential multiscalar model from science is Gaia, proposed by James Lovelock (2000) and Lynn Margulis (1998). They suggested cybernetic mechanisms whereby events driven by lowly organisms in the biosphere can profoundly affect apparently larger, more basic levels – the atmosphere and the geosphere. This model is similar to the concept of the Anthropocene (Crutzen 2002), the idea that, in recent times, human activity is changing not only the rest of the biosphere but even the physical planet. In Gaia, fractals are lateral. Very many small organisms repeat the same pattern at the same scale. Consequences rather than similarities cross scales. *Very small things in great numbers can affect very large things*, crossing the scalar spheres of the planet.

Most reflections on scale are concerned with linear causality, in which large-scale entities mainly determine what happens to small-scale entities, such as dinosaurs trampling proto-mammals or societies determining the behaviour of individuals. Fractal theory models a different kind of causality. Where patterns repeat across different scales, the main cause *is the algorithm or device operating at each level*, acting on structures (systems, analogue forms) from the previous level, drawing on resources from that level. *Fractal analysis complements linear causal analysis, and vice versa.*

Mandelbrot developed his idea in mathematics, designing algorithms to implement on computers, producing patterns (analogue forms) out of patterns out of patterns over many iterations. Some define true fractals as mathematical objects and the computer-generated forms they produce. I use the concept more heuristically. Computer modelling is a valuable analytic tool, but I am interested in material processes, not just simulations. *Fractal analysis is a means to a heuristic end.*

Mandelbrot proposed an elemental formula: $C + M \rightarrow C_1$: $C_1 + M \rightarrow C_2$ etc., where the input to the second step is the output of the first. In this formula, C, the fractal, is a complex analogue form, not reducible to a digital equivalent, though it is translated into digital form. The arrow can be understood as signifying a transformation. *Fractal operations are a kind of transformation.* Mandelbrot does not emphasize this, but fractals have a dual structure. C and M combine in a complex structure. For instance, if proto-Indo-European began a fractal series, it must have already been a composite form, like its daughters. *Fractals are heterogeneous, formed by tensions and divisions, which are reproduced in every version, at every level.*

The formula is exponential. Fractals can quickly go off the scale and become chaotic. Because they exist only on computers, Mandelbrot's fractals can go on for ever, upwards or downwards. Fractals in reality soon degrade. This fact has two heuristic consequences. *Mathematical models can project hitherto unsuspected levels of the much smaller or much larger.* Fractal hypotheses can drive research to consider structures and meanings too small or fast or too large or slow to be easily grasped. As quantum physics and nanotechnology show, very small can be powerful. As climate change science shows, the large and slow can also be hard to see and act on. *Multiscalar analysis follows non-bounded extensions of scale beyond the perceptible in both directions.*

However, as the factor M is repeated it is increasingly distorted, so that self-similarity may be recognizable only after a small number of iterations. *If the formula repeats many times, fractal self-similarity may become invisible.* Sometimes clear fractality is lost after only three iterations in either direction, reaching a boundary of incommensurability.

Mainstream linguistics needs fractal theory. It stops at the level of the sentence, with no multiscalar theory, fractal or otherwise, to envisage higher scales. Linguistics strikes a hard boundary above the level of the sentence. But social meaning is made at every level. It does not stop at boundaries between sentences, paragraphs and texts.

Linguistics does have some versions of multiscalar theory.

Halliday's model of language (1978) had a place for large-scale carriers of social meaning. He described his grammar as a rank scale
grammar whose units descend in rank and scale from sentences down
to clauses, phrases, words, then morphemes (Halliday 1985). Fractal
analysis can extend this model in both directions.

Likewise, Chomsky's 'deep structure' metaphor can be used
to project a layered, multiscalar space in which syntactic devices
produce fractal trees. In chapter 4 I argued that these trees resemble
self-similar structures in many aspects and levels of language, syntactic structures, phonological systems and language families. A multiscalar theory of these forms may make new sense of the processes that
unite and divide them. Fractals may be relative universals.

Comparative linguistics diverged from structural linguistics
at the beginning of the twentieth century. But Labov (1972),
often called the founder of modern sociolinguistics, attempted
a Newton-like synthesis of historical and sociolinguistics. Labov
showed similar mechanisms produce language variations over
shorter times. He mapped the social processes that create language
variations, providing a basis for investigating the operation of
sociolinguistic devices driven by fractal-generating algorithms, and
tracked acoustic shapes below the level of phonemes as engines of
linguistic change.

Labov did not use the terms fractal or multiscalar, but I see his
sociolinguistics as *a series of strategies for studying difference engines in
language and society, in a multiscalar proto-fractal theory*. Like many
great linguists, his work is an exemplary basis for social semiotics.

Multiscalar analysis in society

Society is similarly multiscalar. In the past this was managed mainly
through a crisp binary division between 'macro-' and 'micro-' structures, each handled in different ways by different kinds of sociology. This simple division has come to look increasingly untenable,
with growing awareness of global processes crossing all boundaries,
national, political, economic and cultural.

The political geographer John Agnew (2003) developed the term
'multiscalar' to describe the complex determinations of place and
space in a global world. Agnew argued that the old binaries, macro-
and micro-, and the new ones, global and local, are inadequate to
track and analyse relations between different levels in an interconnected world. I adopt this term to describe structures at different
levels throughout systems of language, meaning and society.

Immanuel Wallerstein (1974) influentially proposed the concept of world-system. He gave it a long history, tracking the current world-system back to the sixteenth century. His theory is mainly causal in the Marxist tradition, describing a globe dominated and deformed by the concentrated economic and political power of the hegemonic European powers. This power operates on a large scale, affecting every lower scale, with counter-effects visible as resistance or disruption.

This political-economic structure takes a fractal form, core versus periphery, replicated across every level. Buildings and social organization in the ancient Greek *oikos* (household) had this form, as has been the case with European domestic architecture ever since. Cities evolved with a core–periphery relation to regions, and the same principle produced relations between regions that evolved into the present blocs of nations. At every level this fractal shapes how power is mediated and exercised. Social semiotics asks: Why is this fractal replicated, with what consequences?

Marx was the first great theorist of globalization, and multiscalar principles are relevant to his work. His massive book *Capital* dealt with large, difficult theories. As a revolutionary, he tried to ground it in concrete experience that workers could understand. His exposition was biscalar:

8.1 We have no need to look back into the origin of capital in order to recognize that money is its first phenomenal form. This is repeated daily under our own eyes. (Marx 1971: 131)

Yet the pathway between these two scales is systematically blocked. Here Marx describes the 'mystery' of commodities in capitalism:

8.2 The form of wood is altered when we make a table of it. Nonetheless, the table is still wood, an ordinary palpable thing. But as soon as it presents itself as a commodity, it is transformed into a thing which is transcendental as well as palpable. (Marx 1972: 44)

He begins with actions on everyday scales, where social beings ('we') make material things, in small-scale histories that humans can perceive. But relationships at the second level and over a long history are systematically inverted. Marx's theory of commodification describes a fractal device which produces incommensurability between levels. This structure has only two scales, yet *the fractal device that relates them inverts them and makes them illegible.*

Strategies for multiscalar analysis

Social semiotics includes many strategies for multiscalar analysis. Some start with high-level structures and work downwards; others start from below. Some start with signifiers, words, texts, images and practices and track meanings across different scales. Others start with meanings, signifieds, especially big meanings. I look at both approaches.

Analysis can begin with signifieds, meanings. Teun van Dijk (1972) proposed that 'global meanings' of texts can be self-evident facts of discourse and cognition. Skilled readers, trained to 'read for meaning' in Smith's sense (2004), *can reliably summarize large-scale structures of meaning in low-scale units, words or sentences.* Experts in any field do this with complex meanings. The problem with this method is to find experts you trust and use them well.

Fractal analysis of signifiers can begin with structures at any relevant or convenient level. It looks for self-similar patterns either at extremes, large and small, or at immediately adjacent levels. Either way, this analysis aims *to establish patterns and tendencies that connect higher and lower levels.* On this basis it hypothesizes motives as meanings of the form.

I use a text by Aristotle, in Greek and English, to illustrate. Readers can follow the argument with (a), the translation; (b) gives the Greek text above a word-for-word transcription.

8.3a Every tragedy falls into two parts – complication and unravelling or denouement. (Aristotle 1951: 1455b, 24-6)
8.3b *Esti de pases tragoidias to men desis, to de lysis.*
There is, then, every-of tragedy-of the on-one-hand binding, the on-the-other loosening.

The sentence in both languages contains elements of all Halliday's ranks: morpheme, word, phrase, sentence. However, there are many differences in ranks and meanings between Aristotle's Greek and the English translation. In Halliday's terms, the translator rank-shifts the philosopher's syntax.

Where the English translation has a full sentence with a main verb, 'falls', the Greek has a bound morpheme, the genitive (*es*, *as*), attached to two words, *pas* ('every') and *tragoidia* ('tragedy'). The closest English translation would be the preposition 'of', a free morpheme, but the translator chose a full sentence, a higher rank for the same meaning.

Aristotle communicates important meanings through signifying elements of low rank in another part of his text. The particles *men* and *de* contrast *desis*, 'binding', and *lysis*, 'freeing'. *Men* and *de* point to a moment of balance around which the two words pivot, when *desis* becomes *lysis*. This clause has the same structure, X + pivot + not-X, as he finds in tragedies. Its syntax is self-similar to the structure of his global meaning.

Aristotle describes and theorizes the pivot moment between *desis* and *lysis*, binding and unravelling, at greater length elsewhere. This he calls the *peripateia*, the turning point, when the hero's fortunes turn suddenly from good to bad, and he associates it with a related concept, *anagnorosis*, 'recognition', when this character suddenly realizes a truth that changes everything.

Aristotle here produced global meanings in van Dijk's sense (1972). One sentence summarized a large set of texts labelled 'tragedies'. He also described the meaning they signified, which was a recurring pattern of social action.

In my paraphrase of tragedy's social action, a flawed member of a ruling class suffers total reversal of fortune, from success to disaster, for reasons this hero comes to understand. This generic meaning, repeated in many ways in different versions, signifies a double revolution, one in society, the other in consciousness. Aristotle is a master of 'global meanings', single sentences defining large-scale objects from science, society and thought. If social semioticians find an Aristotle writing on their topic they should gratefully analyse his global meanings in a multiscalar framework. Expert guides can cross many scales.

In ethnography, all members of a culture can be treated as expert but partial guides to the realities they know (Coronado 2009). *Intensive multiscalar analysis of texts containing global meanings is a valuable step towards multiscalar analysis.*

Narrative and myth

Global meanings come in two main forms: multimodal stories and propositions in verbal and visual form. Stories are found in every culture, a relative universal, because what they do is so valuable for all societies. They communicate social meanings and experiences in a multiscalar form about multiscalar reality. Stories are often built around small-scale objects, sometimes a minor event, but they are structured as patterns, analogue signs of meanings and events on larger scales. They have meaning above and below the level of the sentence. Their elements and relationships are mapped onto larger levels by networks of multiscalar paradigmatic structures, linking higher and lower scales.

Literary specialists once colonized the term 'narrative'. However, contemporary ethnographers now use narrative analysis (Denzin and Lincoln 2008). Labov (2013) introduced narrative analysis into sociolinguistic method. Organization studies researchers such as Gabriel (2000) examine how stories and myths construct relationships and identities in organizations and reveal complex social dynamics.

Lévi-Strauss (1963) is a key figure for multiscalar analysis of myths. He took variants of a story – self-similar versions, to use the fractal term. He did not look for the original or best version like most mythographers, but tried to reconstruct the logic, the sets and transformations of paradigmatic categories which generated all the versions and more. He looked for the same pattern within and across versions, in episodes and at the level of words. This gives a four-level structure (words, episodes, story, corpus-of-variants), a multiscalar system of signifiers, able to be systematized and extended as fractals.

Lévi-Strauss's theory was generative like Chomsky's and functional like Halliday's. He proposed that the function of myths in ancient cultures was to represent intractable social and cultural problems of a culture, contradictions at the heart of a society's understanding of itself and its world. Myths, in his view, enacted these contradictions and offered imaginary but culturally convincing resolutions.

The American mythographer Joseph Campbell (1988) popularized what he saw as the timeless relevance of one syntagmatic structure underlying many myths, the 'hero's journey'. In it, heroes, beginning with nothing, set out on quests, passing through dangers and loss, learning lessons they need to know to be constituted, at the end, as heroes. George Lucas famously used this structure as the basis for his *Star Wars* films, showing the long time-scale of this theme – more than 6000 years.

I explore these ideas with a passage from a modern source (see Hodge et al. 2010 for a fuller discussion). The story appeared in *Management Today*, the magazine of the Australian Institute of Management, written by its editor, Jason Day, about David Widdows, CEO of Heinz, Australia. It told how Widdows turned Heinz around through transformative leadership:

8.4 1) 'Internally, it was a very negative "that's not going to work" type culture,' recalls Widdows. 'The rewards for success were probably [outweighed] by the penalties of failure; a punitive culture, is probably the best way of putting it.'

2) Widdows took two measures in the first two months. He sacked 25% of salaried staff, and re-structured the board. He then attacked the culture problem:
3) A saying was agreed upon: 'A great place to work' and everyone was asked for input on what a great place to work meant for them. (My numbering)

This myth has the Campbell structure. This hero's turning point occurred two months after he became CEO. I broke this story into three phases, following its mythic structure, and quoted the text literally. These are the 'global meanings' of Day, an expert in this world, presented in his own words. That allows me to analyse it at two levels, above the sentence and below.

Phase 1 is full of nominalizations, nouns balanced against nouns describing a static culture – a form of *desis*, 'binding', to use Aristotle's term. In phase 2, the pivot, Widdows the hero is active, the agent of four verbs, all destructive acts. In phase 3, he has disappeared as agent. Instead actions are taken by diffused, collective others. As with Aristotle's text, *analogue forms contribute many meanings to the words of the global summary*. This is propaganda, but it also represents the crucial problem of legitimacy this CEO faces. Heinz may be 'a great place to work', but not for those who were sacked. Widdows cannot be a successful leader in phase 3 without renouncing the decisive brutality of phase 2. Conversely, he would not be a successful leader if he had not been brutal then.

The ideological function of this is clear. Legitimation is a common aim of traditional as for modern myths. But, as in Lévi-Strauss's model, this myth also represents the intractable problems of this culture. The two functions and meanings co-exist. As propaganda on behalf of the dominant directed to the non-dominant, Day's message is that this dominance is legitimate and benign. But the myth carries a hidden message for the dominant. There are intractable problems in capitalist management they should never forget. *Myth and ideology coexist, with similar structures but different functions and relations to their audience.*

Paradigmatic categories here, as elsewhere, are multiscalar multipliers, carrying this story up many scales, from one individual in a six-month period to global capitalist management in neo-liberalism. Capitalism seeks to justify itself as a benign system, yet that system is inescapably built on harsh decisions and strong control over its workforce. Fractal analysis of its words and meanings can ultimately link what was said and done, in the article and the incident, to illusions and contradictions of world capitalism.

Big meanings

Big meanings play a major role in sociolinguistics as in social life.
They are inherently multiscalar guides to research which connect
goals and outcomes to broader issues and struggle. 'Ideology' is one
such term, its links to sociolinguistics discussed in chapter 7. Here I
look at sociolinguistic uses of 'capital'.

Meaning as capital

'Capital' is a big meaning in social theory, a key term in economics
for Marxists and non-Marxists alike. It is a fuzzy set of social meanings with immense social, political, social, economic and physical
consequences. As with 'ideology', Marx borrowed this term from his
opponents and never properly defined it. 'Capital' comes by a cir-
cuitous but significant route from Latin *caput*, 'head' – not a human
head but a heading in a table of accounts, listing assets, profits and
losses. As an indexical sign it means that the world economic system
is driven by an accountancy mentality.

Marx began his account of the 'general formula of capital' with
a history: 'The modern history of capital begins in the sixteenth
century with the establishment of a worldwide commercial system
and the opening of a world market' (1972: 131). This is multiscalar
in time, 'modern' versus earlier systems, with the turning point in the
sixteenth century. The defining feature of that turning point is the
emergence of Wallerstein's world-system (1974).

Marx gives a double formula for capital, relating the two key terms,
commodities and money. One formula describes the exchange of
commodities, $C - M - C$, where commodities (C) are transformed
into money (M), which is then transformed back into commodities. The other formula, $M - C - M$, seems the same, but it defines
capitalism. The first formula facilitates trade. The second potentially
produces infinite flows, a chaotic financial system.

These formulae can be understood semiotically. Money signifies
the value of commodities, and commodities signify the value of what
produced them, materials and human labour. Value here is the same
as in Saussure's later use.

However, Marx's semiotics is also social, including agents and
relationships which constitute value. When capitalists extract surplus
value, they also appropriate meanings associated with those values. A
crucial transformation of 'commodity' extended it to include human

labour. Marx called the subjective condition of this appropriation 'alienation'. In this account, *Marx's economic theories are also semiotic.* Capitalism rests on meaning-effects: inversions of processes which misrepresent the whole system, which then come to seem like reality itself. *Capital is a meaning and condition of meaning. Capitalism is sustained by semiosis.*

A number of writers used the concept of capital metaphorically: Bernstein's 'cultural capital' (1971), Bourdieu's social, cultural and symbolic capital (2010), and Putnam's social capital (2000). These theories are all different, from each other and from Marx, but they can co-exist valuably in a multiscalar cybernetic framework. Where Marx noted how commodification turned any quality into a cash value, these others identify loops outside the monetary system. However, these loops, alternative interpretations of 'capital', support the social systems which reproduce capitalism.

I illustrate with Bernstein. His sociolinguistic theories were built on the idea of 'cultural capital' as semiotic capacities appropriated, accumulated and distributed unevenly to reinforce the power of capitalists and the capitalist system (1971: 172). For Bernstein, verbal language was a basic mechanism for managing this redistribution. English has two distinct 'codes', he claimed. By code he meant something close to a grammar or logic, a deep generative principle within an apparently common language and grammar. Bernstein called one code 'elaborated'. It produced complex, articulated forms of language, which he claimed managed complex social relationships with scope for individual agency, and it accompanied complex forms of thought, oriented 'towards universalistic meanings' (1971: 176). The other he called 'restricted'. This was marked by restricted forms of language, thought and action. It was concrete, context-bound and unreflective.

In Bernstein's account, as in Althusser's idea of ideological state apparatus (1971), those socialized into rule have both devices. Those socialized into subordination have only one. They can oppose their bosses in local struggles, but not the ruling class. They cannot negotiate complex alliances and achieve real change.

Paradoxically, Bernstein's thought has been criticized for being too crisp, too binary, unable to envisage change. Labov (1970) argued against what he called misuses of Bernstein in US education programmes. Labov's target was 'Operation Headstart', a federal programme that addressed African-American disadvantage in the US school system, and he acknowledged the scale of the problem. The US education system was and is a device that perpetuates African-American disadvantage. Labov only objected to how this problem was framed and used ideologically by its proponents. His first target was the way disadvantage and difference were constructed as 'deficit'. The educational psychologist Arthur Jensen collected data from poor African-American areas and used it as evidence of linguistic and cognitive deficit, arguing that these children virtually lacked language. Remedial programmes influenced by Jensen devalued and ignored children's actual linguistic competence.

When Operation Headstart produced disappointing results, this was used as evidence for racist assumptions of genetic incapacity. Labov showed it was based on faulty research. Jensen's researchers ignored the impact of their power in interviews, suppressing verbal performance in test situations. Their high levels of cultural capital created the apparent deficit of their hostile young black interviewees. In a brilliant micro-analysis of two texts, Labov brought out the 'logic of Non-Standard Negro English', meanings and capacities encoded in different but equivalent grammars.

Jensen used the term 'deficit', rather than 'cultural capital', and attached it to genes, not culture, but he still used an economic metaphor. Labov showed that racism can contaminate social research. He had no wish to deny the massive effects of discrimination on generations of African-Americans.

Using cultural capital

Australians for forty years have debated the issues raised by Bernstein and Labov around the role of language and education in producing severe disadvantage for many Aborigines. I join this debate with a multiscalar analysis starting with a short piece of text. *The Dreamers* (1982) is a play written by Jack Davis, an Aboriginal writer and activist I knew well and admired.

Davis was born in Yarloop, a small rural town in Western Australia, in 1917 and left school without completing secondary level. He continued to read widely and educate himself. He was also an activist who played a significant role in a successful campaign to change the Australian constitution in 1967 to recognize Aboriginal people. Davis received national honours, an MBE (Member of the British Empire) in 1977, and the Order of Australia in 1985. He helped change the conditions of his people and achieved mainstream recognition in the process. Yet he started life apparently without access to any kind of capital. What does his story say about these theories?

The following exchange from the play involves Worru (performed in early productions by Davis himself), an old man approaching death, and his fourteen-year-old great-niece Meena, doing homework in a messy kitchen:

> 8.5 Meena pours Worru's tea for him.
> *Meena*: Popeye, why do *Nyoongahs* call that one *mahngk?*
> *Worru*: Eh?
> *Meena*: That one Popeye. Why do *Nyoongahs* call it *mahngk?*
> *Worru*: That's his name. You see leaf on a tree, that's a *mahngk*, that one *mahngk* too, tea leaf.
> *Meena*: That's gotta go in my project. (Davis 1982: 103)

Meena's last comment got a good laugh from Aboriginal members of the audience when I saw the play. This was probably delighted recognition of her use of Aboriginal language as cultural capital in non-Aboriginal classrooms.

One social meaning of this exchange is the subtle play between the meanings of the three languages. Meena code-switches between Standard Australian English, including elaborated code, and Non-Standard Aboriginal English. The actress reproduced the distinctive accent as well as vocabulary and syntax when she spoke non-standard Aboriginal English. Worru moved between Nyoongah, the Aboriginal language, and Non-Standard Aboriginal English, mediating between two languages and generations.

This Aboriginal English has qualities Bernstein criticized as too context-dependent. For instance, 'that one' is Aboriginal English. It is more strongly deictic than standard English. Deixis ties speech to context. Traditional Aboriginal forms of instruction tend to be concrete like this. Aboriginal elders draw general lessons from minute observations.

This exchange is triggered by a 'why' question. Meena does not want the word for tea, which she already knows, but the 'cultural logic' behind it (to use an elaborated code term). Worru reflects on processes of word formation like a linguist, using Aboriginal English to show how this alien item, tea, was incorporated into Aboriginal language and culture. Worru also uses 'his' in a distinctive way: 'his name'. Both 'name' and 'his' imply that tea is like a person, who has an Aboriginal name and identity. Worru's Non-Standard Aboriginal English unobtrusively conveys deep meanings of the culture.

Davis does not idealize Aborigines. This family unit as portrayed is dysfunctional in many ways, held together by a strong woman, Worru's niece, Dolly. Most of the men were heavy drinkers, unemployed.

This text carries a didactic message. The new generation (Meena) needs to learn the dominant language in order to acquire the knowledge of the dominant: not just English but elaborated code. Yet traditional knowledge is still being passed down through the language and culture, stronger not weaker because of efforts to operate in both worlds. The two kinds of cultural capital add to each other. The ability to acquire cultural capital is itself cultural capital in conditions where the Aboriginal culture is recognized.

This cultural capital is what Jack Davis possessed. He never translated his forms of capital into monetary form, but he wove them into a basis for power and influence. Davis communicated his understanding of principles of change entirely in restricted code, creating profound analogue meanings. This is meta-communication. This is different from both codes and can be found in either. Davis showed that *different forms of cultural capital can be added, not just subtracted.* He packaged all this in the form of literature, a prestigious genre in Australia, and he drew on it as symbolic capital in Bourdieu's terms, which gave enhanced value and scope to his message. Language framed and labelled in this way is attended to by students, deploying interpretative resources that, for Bourdieu, constitute 'cultural capital'.

If the same students heard the same exchange in everyday life they would probably dismiss it as being without interest. The label 'literature' does a great amount of work. Thirty years after Davis wrote it, *The Dreamers* still appears on English curricula, part of the cultural capital Australian educators deem necessary for Australian citizens.

Davis is a unique individual, but his story and text show one use of multiscalar analysis focused on small scales. *There is equal complexity at small scales as at large, and by analysing them we can see possibilities for agency and change that seem unthinkable at higher levels.*

I complement this analysis with a higher-scale empirical study by Helen and Mark Hughes (2014). These researchers for a right-wing think-tank found similar depressing statistics for Aboriginal education today as in Jack Davis's time. Were all his efforts for his people futile, benefiting only a few gifted individuals like him? Hughes and Hughes broke these statistics down into regions: a multiscalar device that is standard sociological practice. They found that these statistics also applied to non-Aboriginal students in the same schools and areas. Disadvantage owed more to the absence of resources, economic capital, than cultural capital.

But cultural capital of a kind played a role in this situation. The lack of political capital acted to stop equal flows of resources to

Aboriginal people. As with 'Operation Headstart' in America, neo-liberals criticized governments for supposedly 'throwing money at Aboriginal education' when in reality there were fewer resources. *Cultural and economic capital and economic and ideological analysis are related and act together in complex ways across many scales. In this complex, the digital processes of economics drive analogue forms of capital into far-from-equilibrium conditions.*

Models and contexts as meaning

Models and contexts in social processes are often not connected with meaning. Yet models are complex, generative analogue forms. Sociolinguistic studies have produced many insightful analyses of contexts, mainly on small scales. This work can be complemented by multiscalar analysis.

Pragmatics

'Pragmatics' has a long association with semiotics. Peirce and William James co-founded philosophical pragmatism, and the semio-tician Charles Morris (1971) divided semiotics into three parts: semantics, pragmatics and syntax. In linguistics, 'pragmatics' names a vigorous, productive line for analysing meaning. Currently it is seen as a subfield of linguistics, studying meanings that arise from particular contexts and uses (Mey 1985).

One key figure is the philosopher John Austin (1962), who brought a sense of the social into the analysis of language. He analysed speech in contexts as a kind of action: 'speech acts' as he called them. Where Goffman (1959) saw interactions in context as conflictual, Austin looked for rules to stabilize the game. One instance he discussed was 'performatives', where speech acts perform what they say. For instance, when an accredited marriage celebrant says, 'I pronounce you man and wife', the deed is done. Austin looked for the conditions that make this speech act valid. These he called 'felicity conditions', which bind speech and action indissolubly together in a smoothly functioning society.

Austin took for granted the generality of his examples, but from a multiscalar perspective it is clear that most performatives are located at the intersection between public rules and private behaviour.

I use Austin in counterpoint with Goffman in the following analysis. Today my wife and I visited a favourite coffee-shop in Sydney, one of the Gloria Jeans chain, as we often do on Saturdays. The following exchange took place:

8.6 *Woman at counter* (smiles): Hi, Bob. How are you today?
Bob (smiles):   Fine, thanks. Can I have a small flat
                                   white, with skim, very weak, in a mug?

Austin is right that this interaction is rule-governed, in which both the woman at the counter and I perform our roles perfectly. The exchange, perfectly performed by us both, makes her a waitress and me a customer. She does everything right, and I do not ask for anything not listed. I am a 'competent' customer.

Yet there is more going on here which Goffman's perspective can pick up. For instance, she smiles, an easy sign to fake, to 'give' rather than 'give off'. This is part of her job, so it could be seen as inauthentic. However, it looks 'natural' to me. I smile back almost automatically. My smile could be seen as 'given' rather than 'given off' too. Yet it does not feel forced to me. I do feel pleasure. Part of the pleasure comes from the fact that she addresses me by my first name, though I guess that she knows mine because of the Gloria Jeans system. Customers are asked for their name to call them for their order. Like everything in the transaction, *many purposes are managed through multidimensional meanings.*

This whole exchange is closely attached to this context. This attractive young woman can smile and greet me by my first name as if we are old friends without either of us misinterpreting what is going on. This interaction is a performance by the two of us, representing an ideal social relationship, prescribed by a set of rules we both know. These are exploited by Gloria Jeans, not invented by them. Our meaning, the image of the world we co-construct, is an ideological fantasy of a harmonious world created by capitalism, in which the old values of traditional society still live, and cost only $3.50 a cup.

This performance is embedded in a nested set of contexts: this shop, the shopping mall, Australia, Gloria Jeans as a capitalist enterprise, the neo-liberal service industry and, finally, capitalism itself. These rules derived from these contexts act coercively on the young woman, who is paid relatively small amounts for doing her job so well. Her smiles and friendly service are semiotic labour which is expropriated. So is my work as good customer.

The two halves of this meaning constitute an ideological complex which is repeated countless times throughout the global world. It can be seen as a similar cybernetic process as in Lovelock's *Gaia* (2000), where billions of micro-events in a feedback loop sustain a planetary system.

Multidimensional analysis of the micro-events which drive the system is crucial for understanding the system as a whole. So is the semiotic flip-over, where ideological meanings collide with the economic system. In this case, *the capitalist system expropriates semiotic and material labour as surplus value and uses it for both profit and control.*

Context and meaning

In social semiotics, meaning exists only in contexts, in many-body systems in which social relationships and domains of reality – 'contexts' – interact with meanings, each affecting and conditioning the other elements. From this arises the proposition that *context and text and context and meaning are related in loose reciprocal systems in which, under some conditions, contexts overdetermine meaning.*

Here I look at three researchers who have contributed to social semiotic understanding of how context determines meaning. Karttunen and Grice are influential figures in pragmatics. Bateson is usually identified as an anthropologist and a psychologist, but he can be seen as equally important for pragmatics.

Karttunen and presuppositions   In a series of seminal papers in the 1970s, Lauri Karttunen (1974) opened up a rich field of fundamental research in pragmatics built around an old notion, 'presupposition'. In logic, presuppositions are unstated premises presupposed in a statement. For instance, in my Gloria Jeans exchange, my request for a cup of coffee presupposes that coffee exists, along with a whole apparatus to make it and deliver it.

In philosophy and logic, this assumption tends to get bogged down in abstract discussions of universal claims. Karttunen rescued the concept from this fate by relocating it in pragmatics as a field of social research. Instead of having to defend a proposed presupposition in universal terms, he limited his claims to particular contexts, where participants could be more convincingly supposed to have *shared assumptions which could underpin inferences that become part of the meaning.* The process is a relative universal, but its form provides the basis for low-scale local analyses.

In broad terms, this proposal has affinities with Wittgenstein's idea of 'logical scaffolding' (1971), discussed in chapter 5. Putting the two versions of the idea together, I take from Wittgenstein the idea that *presuppositions form networks that construct the basis for reality.* From

Karttunen I take the idea that *there are many such networks, located at different levels in different sites in multiscalar social space.*

The distinction between meaning and pragmatic meaning liberated analysts of meaning to follow pragmatic (context-bound) meanings wherever they lead. I take this distinction one stage further, to propose that *all meanings are 'pragmatic', rooted in contexts which are more or less general in a multiscalar scheme.* From this perspective, presuppositions as analysed in logic are not the primary form, just a special case.

Grice and implicatures   The English philosopher Paul Grice (1991) proposed general principles to promote optimal communication. He then assumed that people engaged in communication probably carried such principles in their heads to guide their practice and interpret what others meant. His 'implicatures' (not just implications, but consequences of implications) are a narrower form of the same principle as Karttunen's presuppositions. *Both override generic meanings to discover or impose meanings derived from a claimed knowledge of context.*

Grice distinguished between 'encoded' and 'non-encoded' meanings. These were similar to Goffman's 'given' and 'given off'. Encoded meanings were transmitted by words. Non-encoded meanings relied on other codes. Grice's theory of implicatures had a place for multimodal interpretation. Like Habermas (1990), he proposed an 'ideal speech situation', but, where Habermas used this as the basis for discourse ethics, Grice used it to interpret meanings in context. He proposed four 'maxims' as rational premises for good communication. The main premise, 'the cooperative principle', assumed that all participants try to speak truth, saying no more or less than they should, being relevant, avoiding obscurity and ambiguity.

Grice claimed they were independent of culture. But these rules are ideological and context-dependent. They construct and assume (construct by assuming) a rational, harmonious world. These rules were more culturally specific than Grice realized. For me they projected an ideal Oxbridge tutorial, which Grice up-scaled to serve as a scale-invariant model for the world.

Bateson and schizogenesis   Bateson's model of schizogenesis, discussed in chapter 6, seems initially very different from Grice's, but the two are *complementary ways of modelling how context can overdetermine meaning.* Grice's cooperative principles are the opposite of those of Bateson's schizophrenics, who do not try to cooperate. Bateson's schizophrenics inverted Gricean logic, using a 'non-cooperative principle'. They talk too much or not enough. Their words are nonsensical or untrue. They express affective meanings through referential ones. They conceal how they interpret messages, their own and those of others. The obsessively repeated but garbled meaning of schizophrenics expresses the incomprehensible irrationality of their situation.

In contrast, the deep meaning of the English philosopher is the complete rationality of his world. Grice uses his model to read what speakers really meant to say, assuming the best. Bateson reads the patterns of meaning as clues for a reverse engineering that uncovers rules and models of this dysfunctional world.

Bateson aimed to intervene in discursive practice. As a therapist, he did not want just to describe the schizophrenics' model. Cybernetics showed what they lack, a functioning meta-communication loop. Grice's model supplied the kind of template they need as content for their missing meta-communication loop. Bateson's rules express and repudiate the excessive power relationship that generates schizophrenic discourse. But solidarity and love can be equally pathogenic. Ambivalent love generates many of the schizophrenic's distorted meanings. Grice's model takes no account of either power or solidarity. But, for elite university students and schizophrenics alike, *meanings are profoundly affected by contexts and relations of power and solidarity that shape them. Interpretation must take account of this fact.*

Power and solidarity

Power and solidarity are present in every social situation. They are given different names by various disciplines and theorists in different languages, but these are the words I use for these core social meanings. They are relative universals. All human and non-human societies seem to have some version of them. Yet they are highly fuzzy and complex, in themselves and in their relationships to each other. They are multimodal, expressed through every semiotic form, and multiscalar, present at all levels of all structures.

In this section I outline a social semiotic understanding of power and solidarity in a multiscalar framework. I look especially at how these complex big meanings work in different branches of sociolinguistics.

Power

Power is acknowledged by all sociologists, but it is not always described or treated in the same way. Marx and Engels put power high on their analytic agenda. Sociologists from Weber (1947) to Foucault (1978, 1980) developed subtle analyses of power in society. Durkheim (1952) emphasized order rather than power, opposed to 'solidarity'.

Pragmatics and sociolinguistics deal with power, but not centrally. Fairclough (1992) defined the primary aim of CDA as showing the unsuspected presence of power and the injustices to which it leads. Social semiotics shares this background and commitment. Foucault's theories of power have been influential in social theory today. I look at two strands of his ideas from a social semiotic perspective.

Regimes of power In a major work on discipline and punishment, Foucault (1977) distinguished between the dominant regime of punishment under the monarchy and new bourgeois forms of rule. Behind this difference he saw changes both to models of power and to semiotic forms.

Changes in models of power are distinct from changes in the semiotic model, but for Foucault they functionally overlapped. Monarchic power radiated from the centre through analogue regimes of spectacle but operated as networks in bourgeois discursive regimes. Yet modern 'democracies' operate with regimes of spectacle as well as discursive regimes. Herman and Chomsky (2002) argue that the interests of capitalism are still supported by concentrated media ownership structures, controlling the mainstream construction of reality as spectacle.

This is the serious point of Jean Baudrillard's provocative claim that the Iraq War did not take place, in his book of this title (1995). He argued that what actually took place in Iraq was so misrepresented by Western media that the fiction replaced the event in shaping Western views. This reinforced the power of Western governments and their allies.

To adapt Baudrillard, Foucault's discursive revolution never happened. Or, to be less provocative, the two models of power and semiosis still co-exist in different configurations across the major changes Foucault reports.

From this discussion I draw two propositions:

1 *Power is exercised through multimodal resources, including verbal discourse, images and other modes.*

2 *Power is exercised through several models, centralized and dispersed, analogue and digital.*

Dispersed power Arising from his analysis of bourgeois discursive power, Foucault proposed a model of power which was not top-down, as under a monarchy. Power in this view is not a mere instrument of the powerful:

> 8.5 Power must be understood in the first instance as the multiplicity of force relations immanent in the sphere in which they operate and which constitute their own organization. (Foucault 1978: 92)

In this complexity model, power is 'immanent' within a society, not imposed from outside ('in the first instance'). From a multiscalar perspective there is a crucial ambiguity with 'sphere'. Where are its boundaries, and how fuzzy are they? If some boundaries are relatively hard, what happens to immanent relations at contested borders?

Resistance has an ambiguous place in this scheme, always guaranteed but pre-empted in advance. 'Power' in this new sense has taken over the functions of solidarity. Since power is constituted by all forces in society, it subsumes them. But the forces immanent in every society include forces of cohesion and solidarity as well as power and domination. Foucault's account of dispersed power needs a new geometry, with power and solidarity as vertical and horizontal axes. In this model, *most power is diagonal, incorporating different proportions of power and solidarity. Likewise, most solidarity is diagonal, including power to different degrees.*

It is these forces combined which distort language, meaning and behaviour. I adapt Lord Acton's famous saying: 'All power corrupts (meaning) and absolute power corrupts (it) absolutely.' Similarly, all solidarity corrupts (distorts) meaning, and absolute solidarity corrupts it completely. *Power and solidarity together shape and distort referential meanings.*

I illustrate the issues by analysing a document from the Australian Research Council, a government body which administers academic research in Australia. It begins:

> 8.6 I, KIM CARR, Minister for Innovation, Industry, Science and Research, having satisfied myself of the matters set out in Section 59 of the *Australian Research Council Act of 2001*, approve these Funding Rules under Section 60 of that Act. (Australian Government 2011)

This is a fine example of Austin's performative speech act. Carr performs the act of approval, writing these words in the correct form as the accredited person to say them, from the right position at the peak of an agreed hierarchical structure.

Carr's speech illustrates Foucault's theory of power/truth. Funding rules are only true if they are announced in this form. Only the minister has the power to make them true. Yet how much power does Carr himself have in the process? He begins with a first-person pronoun, 'I', then refers to himself in the third person, and adds the extensive list of his portfolios. He reports he is 'satisfied', but only that the prescriptions of Section 59 are met. He 'approves' the rules, not the projects funded.

In a small-scale way, Carr's act expresses forms and meanings of a regime of spectacle in a centralized system of power. His power in this apparently power-laden act is confined to his capacity to bestow legitimacy on others, who derive power from that legitimacy. In the Australian system, if ministers try to intervene in the grant process, it destabilizes the system.

In this situation, power has to be immanent, not imposed from outside, always dependent on a network of relations which sometimes negate individual power in order to sustain it. In this case, Carr's performative act, like most of Austin's performative speech acts, works by stitching together Foucault's two models of power, spectacle and discourse. Legitimacy is the basis for power, a diagonal form that links power and solidarity. It is sometimes incompatible with its specific exercise, where solidarity weakens or cancels power. But, as Habermas (1975) argues, legitimacy is crucial for regimes of power, affecting its exercise at every level. *Legitimacy is a fuzzy set of meanings binding power and solidarity across different levels of a social formation. It operates across large stretches of time and social space and has to be both built up slowly and continuously maintained across its range. As a large-scale structure it is often invisible to social actors until it is threatened or lost.*

Systems of power and solidarity

In 1960 Roger Brown and Albert Gilman published a seminal article in the then emerging field of sociolinguistics on 'pronouns of power and solidarity'. I treat this article as exemplary, showing how analysing seemingly minor features of language in a multiscalar social framework can have profound implications for understanding society.

Brown and Gilman's starting point was a feature of many languages whereby different second-person pronouns ('you') are used for intimate versus formal relationships. They called the two options T (from latin *tu*, you singular) and V (French *vous*, polite you, usually plural). They noted that English was once a T/V language but lost this distinction over the seventeenth century.

As an L1 English speaker learning T/V languages Italian and Spanish, I was told that the specific rules for using these forms are so important yet so complex that I should avoid them altogether if possible. Otherwise I would probably cause deep but unintended offence.

Brown and Gilman used three innovations in their consideration of this apparently quaint minor system. They analysed the signifying system multimodally, they connected the meanings generated by the system with primary sociological concepts – power and solidarity – and they used a multiscalar framework over time (back to the fourth century) and space (European languages which still use some form of this model). Their example made use of a multimodal semiotic system that was not recognized by any semiotician at the time. The signs in this system are not just pronouns but also rules for their use. Semiotically, words are well recognized as signs but rules of use are not. Yet, in this elemental system, T has no definite meaning until there is a response. In terms of an epigenetic model, initial meanings of T and V are affected by their epigenetic environment, the context and the contexts of that context.

If A used T forms to B, its meaning was completed initially by A's expectation of B's response. If A saw B as an inferior, A would expect a V response. If A saw B as an intimate equal the expected response would be T. A's meaning is a multimodal syntagm, words plus order. A's meaning co-constructs the relationship. Every usage which goes smoothly reinforces in A's mind, and thence in B's, the reality of this social picture. But, as Brown and Gilman noted, this system was unstable and disappeared from English. Problems arise when A and B do not agree on their positions and do not cooperate to co-construct the unequal social relationship. The most explosive instance is where B refuses the label 'inferior', asserting and demanding equality, either the T–T of intimacy or the V–V of mutual respect. This is an instance of Bateson's 'symmetrical schismogenesis', where competition for equality generates social schisms.

The system relies on contexts in which all identities are crisp, unambiguous, known and accepted, as in small-scale, stable social groups. If not, status needs to be unambiguously signalled by many accepted sign systems, such as clothing codes.

I interviewed Gabriela Coronado, my wife and an L1 speaker of Mexican Spanish, on intricacies of the contemporary T/V system. She reported a trend she saw in workplace discourse in Mexico, where bosses give orders to secretaries in a way that mixes respect and familiarity. Gabriela enacted her analysis:

8.7 *Susanita, me podria usted // traer un cafecito?* which includes the *usted* form but a kind of tone of voice, that uses the diminutive. Susanita is the secretary of this person.
(Translation: Susana darling, could you (*usted*) bring me a nice little coffee?)

Usted is the V form in Mexican Spanish. Gabriela notes contradictory signals in this boss's speech. He (her choice of the gender was no accident) addresses Susana as *usted* but uses the high solidary affectionate diminutive *ita/ito* (literally, 'little') attached both to her and to the coffee he wants her to bring. This boss uses both low solidarity pronouns (V forms) and high solidarity (T forms), both against a background of unstated power.

There are three signifying systems here: pronouns, tone of voice and terms of address. Forms of syntax are also involved. *Podria . . . traer*, 'could you bring?', is a question rather than the command this really is. It implies that Susana is the authority in this exchange, the one who knows whether or not she can perform this act, rather than the secretary that she is. This makes four codes clustering around one message. It illustrates *the massive redundancy around systems which negotiate power and solidarity*. Where messages are as important as these, signalled by such unobtrusive signs, redundancy might make the system more reliable. However, the multiplicity of codes has another purpose. *It allows contradictions between codes and messages supporting an ideological complex.*

Since the response is invisible at the moment of utterance, it is a convenient semiotic mode to convey ideologies and control behaviour. Susana's obedience to the rule system says that, every time she accepts a non-symmetrical position, she accepts her place. By not saying in words that she knows it, she is made complicit in the secret which protects the ideology.

In this example we can see the paradox and problems of power/solidarity behind these rules. For the powerful, *power is compatible with solidarity*, and requires it. For the non-powerful, *power excludes solidarity*. Yet the same system has to manage both premises, distinguishing them clearly enough so that the system of power functions, yet concealing the difference well enough to ensure consent from the non-powerful.

Gabriela set her analysis of this exchange in its multiscalar contexts. Mexican culture and language provide many semiotic modes, including these pronouns, to manage such contradictions. These systems are well adapted to manage relations within the family sphere, where age, gender and status interact. This local system also intersects with a neo-liberal management style that has been called 'soft power' (Courpasson 2000).

This style of 'soft power' is fashionable in Mexican business, regarded as 'new' and 'progressive'. The organization theorist Gert Hofstede (2001) influentially categorized Mexican cultural styles as power-oriented, with power differences clearly marked compared with US styles. The classic T/V system can be seen as a complex that signifies and manages this traditional ideology. But in Mexican offices the two styles have converged, reflecting the ongoing realignment in neo-liberal Mexico towards the American model.

Brown and Gilman's analysis is a fractal jewel. Its design is a model for multiscalar sociolinguistics. Its focus seems trivial, a linguistic form and practice that seemed to have disappeared from modern English. But the study is framed by a pair of big meanings organized by a major ideological complex. The contrast between English now and that of 400 years ago gives diachronic scope to the study. What the authors were able to identify as a result was not a particular form in transition but a kind of fractal device. This algorithm for the power/solidarity contradiction formed *a minimal generative system of meanings, found in practices across all modes, at all scales, in all languages, produced by and producing far-from-equilibrium conditions.*

The role of social semiotics in this case is not to go beyond this wonderful analysis but to recognize how good it was.

9

Conclusions

This chapter offers three different forms of conclusion. I begin by reflecting semiotically on different applications of the term 'revolution'. I then expand the focal length, to speculate how linguistics and semiotics might fit into a larger interdisciplinary project. I finish by using a personal synthesis of social semiotics as a vantage point for looking at how linguistics might function in interdisciplinary approaches to language, meaning and society in action.

Revolutions

In this section I use the term 'revolution' to develop some tentative, personal answers to my initial questions about the past, present and future of linguistics. Is it useful to see Chomsky's theories as marking a linguistic revolution? Is the current explosion of digital forms a genuine semiosic revolution? Is multimodal analysis a revolutionary response to it? Finally, what do social revolutions look like, and how are they revealed and aided by social semiotic analysis?

Linguistic revolutions

I return to where I began, with the relationship between Chomsky's and Halliday's work. Many have claimed that in 1957 Chomsky 'revolutionised the scientific study of language' (Lyons 1970: 9). Is it valid or useful to talk of a Chomskyan revolution?

Chomsky's work is without question original, important and influential. But what is served by calling it revolutionary? 'Revolution' emphasizes discontinuities with earlier linguists. But Whorf's masterpiece (1956) was published just a year before Chomsky's. Jakobson published a major synthesis (Jakobson and Halle 1956) in the same year. These works were not obsolete. Likewise, 'revolution' makes Halliday's work, also original and important, seem counter-revolutionary, a competing revolution, only one of which could survive. Yet both survived. Both are valuable. 'Revolution' acts like a deletion-transformation, to eliminate the existence or worth of Chomsky's predecessors or rivals.

In a multiscalar framework, changes of scale change the answer. At a lower scale the work of Chomsky and Halliday is incommensurably different, not reducible to the other under any rubric of 'revolution'. At the level of the discipline in the USA, we could talk of a Chomskyan revolution which had worldwide impact. Maybe a parallel Hallidayan revolution in Britain split linguistics, which was further split by other revolutions, including Chomsky's successive stages and the work of followers such as Lakoff.

But at another scale I see another trajectory. Saussure in 1917 marked a break to structuralism, the diverse tradition shared by Jakobson, Whorf, Chomsky and Halliday, and Lévi-Strauss and Derrida. *Synergies between these six create something greater than any on their own.* Was that the real revolution? And Saussure did major work in the previous paradigm, stemming from Sir William Jones's revolution of 1786. Jones discovered the deep structure of the Indo-European language family, a tree structure that looked like Chomsky's own tree diagrams. *Was Chomsky important because of the revolutionary break, or in spite of it?*

Multimodality and the digital revolution

Social semiotics has a special relationship to some major changes under way, to do with globalization and the media, which have been called 'revolutions'. How well does that term fit what is going on? How helpful is it?

I begin with the so-called digital revolution. Harvard's prestigious Sloane School of Management published a work with a twenty-word title:

9.1 Race against the machine: how the digital revolution is accelerating innovation, driving productivity, and irreversibly transforming employment and the economy (Brynjolfsson and McAfee 2012: 1)

Critical analysis of this text starts with its origin – management writers from Harvard claiming the revolution for global business. Their presuppositions imply they understand and control it. So after this revolution the same elites will still be in the same place. But this is an ideological complex, with contradictions easy to see. This text uses print media to announce the obsolescence of print media.

The form of this revolution seems to mirror Marx's framework, where revolutions in technology drive revolutions in the rest of the system. But Marx had a more complex, multiscalar idea of revolution. In relation to the previous ruling class, the bourgeoisie were revolutionary, he says. But their revolutions played another role: '[They] cannot exist without constantly revolutionizing the instruments of production' (Marx and Engels 1970: 38). Cybernetically, later bourgeois revolutions were counter-revolutionary.

From a social semiotic perspective I focus on the key term 'digital'. Digital technologies are different from digital signs. *Digital technologies have introduced exponential growth* which has been transformative, producing chaos or new order. Digital technologies have led to a *proliferation of analogue forms via multimedia,* creating *a demand for a new integration of analogue and digital strategies. If social semiotics is widely adopted to provide new ways of managing digital phenomena, in its own small way it will be part of the digital revolution.*

Marshall McLuhan in the 1960s proposed a still relevant account of media revolutions. His theory of communication (1964) was systemic and multimodal. For him, all media were technological extensions of human capacities. All senses and the corresponding media plus other human capacities formed a highly complex system he called a 'ratio of the senses', in which changes in sensory/media regimes impacted on all other systems. A real media revolution in these terms is a 'social fact' in Durkheim's sense, outside consciousness yet affecting social systems and capacities for thought.

McLuhan contributed valuable ideas to a semiotics of media and social revolutions. One is his idea of media as prosthetics: every media extension of humans or societies has costs, extending and numbing senses, offering and closing off areas of reality, enabling or inhibiting social relations. But his hyperbole about revolutions gave the misleading impression that revolutions are total transformations, in which new structures replace the old. A social semiotic review of the data in his history of media comes to a different conclusion. In every media revolution up to the present *the old is modified but survives to co-exist with the new.* Forms and structures change, but common functions remain across all changes.

Body language and art co-existed with speech, speech with writing, writing with print, and visual media with all of them. It is overwhelmingly likely that digital technologies likewise will add new resources and reconfigure their relations, but nothing will completely disappear. Yet, that said, the changes are so great that it may be useful to talk of revolution.

In this new environment social sciences need social semiotics more than ever, to be:

- *multimodal,* including all modes and systems of perception;
- *multidimensional,* aware that many factors and meanings co-exist and interact;
- *multiscalar,* probing the effects of scale on every system and structure, including the very small and the very large;
- *systemic,* including systems and anti-systems;
- *non-linear,* open to omnipresent contradiction, disruption, unpredictability and revolution alongside more linear processes and methods;
- *social,* researching social dimensions and effects of semiotic acts and systems;
- *ethical,* concerned with issues such as justice, love, health and well-being and their absence, in functional and dysfunctional societies.

These changes are all continuous. *Cumulatively they may be so great as to be usefully called a disciplinary revolution, in response to a revolutionary change in human conditions.*

The personal is political

I finish my social semiotic reflections on revolutions with changes that may seem too small and low-key to be termed revolutions. The 1960s in the USA, the UK and Europe witnessed turbulent times and social upheaval, but no political revolutions. Immanuel Wallerstein (1974) created world-systems theory whose scale goes back 500 years. He also argued at a smaller scale that the 1968 movements transformed the form and understanding of political struggle (Schouten 2008) to recognize different social movements which were driven by injustices to minorities of race and gender as well as class.

Wallerstein did not deny the dominance of capitalism, which, like Marx, he saw as relentlessly increasing inequality and shrinking the numbers of elite beneficiaries of the system. But he also saw that system heading towards collapse, as alternative forces and models emerged. The 1968 movements did not remove the dominant system but revealed the existence and strength of emerging alternatives. They altered the terms of struggle in favour of the marginalized and shifted the site of struggle to semiosis.

One slogan was associated in 1969 with the radical 'second-wave feminist' Carol Hanisch:

9.2 The personal is political. (Hanisch 2009: 1)

This phrase shows how global meanings can work. The short title of a short article captured many people's sense of a subsuming meaning for the 1960s. Even without the internet it went viral. Although it projected a two-scale rather than a fully multiscalar structure, it contained two important principles: it *challenged strong barriers between scales*, and it *insisted on reciprocity between supposedly higher and lower levels*. The phrase offered a pathway between multiscalar analysis and radical politics for change.

Hanisch's slogan attacked the form and content of key paradigmatic categories of the hegemonic ideology. It turned a hierarchical structure in which 'political' is understood to be superior to 'personal' into a flat paratactic structure in which they are equivalent. Structures of dominance need difference. Equivalence dismantles them.

These categories carried other potent categories. In the previous hegemonic order the personal was a sphere where gender, ethnicity, age and sexuality were active categories but were excluded from the political, negated by being excluded. The political remained the sphere where older white upper-class heterosexual males rule without their multiple identities being visible or contested. That was the point of difference Hanisch attacked.

Hanisch's struggles and triumphs were primarily semiotic. That may seem to limit their revolutionary scope, especially as none of her causes has won a total victory. Yet total revolutions are not achievable or desirable in a complex world. I believe that *countless acts of meaning-making over long time-scales have changed the settings in which political meanings and actions now are made. Social semiotics can reveal this invisible revolution.*

Racist, sexist interests oppose these meanings, now as then. But I believe that social semiotics is well equipped to recognize and analyse such struggles and, in the process, *contribute semiotic wisdom to participants like Hanisch.*

Grammar, biology and the scope of semiotics

In this book I promote and build towards a radically interdisciplinary form of linguistics and social semiotics, combining leading-edge science with a deep understanding of human systems of language, meaning and society. At current stages of disciplinary knowledge this project may seem abstract and utopian. It is especially valuable, here in my conclusion, to include a concrete example of interdisciplinary practice at a high level.

In his Nobel Prize acceptance speech, the Danish biologist Niels Jerne compared immunology and linguistics:

> 9.3 Immunologists sometimes use words they have borrowed from linguistics, such as 'immune response'. Looking at languages, we find that all of them make do with a vocabulary of roughly a hundred thousand words, or less. . . . [But] we may find a more reasonable analogy between language and the immune system, namely by regarding the variable region of a given antibody molecule not as a *word* but as a *sentence* or a phrase. The immense repertoire of the immune system then becomes not a vocabulary of words, but a lexicon of sentences which is capable of responding to any sentence expressed by the multitude of antigens which the immune system may encounter.
>
> At this point, I shall make a quotation from Noam Chomsky concerning linguistics: 'The central fact to which any significant linguistic theory must address itself is this: a mature speaker can produce a new sentence of his language on the appropriate occasion, and other speakers can understand it immediately, though it is equally new to them. . . . Grammar is a device that specifies the infinite set of well-formed sentences and assigns to each of these one or more structural descriptions. Perhaps we should call such a device a *generative grammar* . . . which should, ideally, contain a central syntactic component . . ., a phonological component and a semantic component.' (Jerne 1984: 220)

This text reports an exemplary interdisciplinary process, in which an eminent scientist reads an eminent linguist, using analogue reasoning. Jerne quotes Chomsky far more extensively than is customary in scientific discourse, creating a rich analogue picture. His reading is based on a metaphor-like juxtaposition of two models.

At the heart of Chomsky's picture/model is his metaphor, the idea of a 'device' which is 'generative'. Jerne identified one problem with Chomsky's model: 'It is harder, however, to find an analogy to semantics: does the immune system distinguish between meaningful and meaningless antigens?' (1984: 220). Jerne's problem with Chomsky's proposal was that the 'syntactic' component is too extensive, leaving the semantic component too little to do. But Halliday's alternative model has a single lexico-grammatical system. The process shows the heuristic value of deep metaphor: it generates insights into the target system, linguistics, which Jerne did not know. Jerne also did not know about Halliday's functional approach, which would have been useful. Jerne takes it for granted that immunological systems are as they are because of the functions they serve: to defend organisms against alien bodies while not destroying hosts. In biological as in linguistic and social systems, this function has similar contradictions.

Jerne does not refer to tree diagrams as common to language and immunology, but he draws some classic tree diagrams. He divides cells into two classes, B-cells and T-cells, the latter divided into Killer and Helper cells. Within each category he has a familiar branching shape, with recursive loops at certain sites which produce multiple clones. Jerne states that B-cells have 'a single-minded desire to express their antibody language' (1984: 213). In this respect they are like genes. T-cells either enhance or modify the action of B-cells, like epigenetic agents, or translate their instructions into action, killing alien cells. I find the idea suggestive that some semiotic forms exist to translate meanings into actions.

Jerne reflects on how genetic systems could produce immunological systems. The same question can be asked of human social and semiotic systems. Is there a deep basis to the analogy between the 'language' of genes, the 'language' of immune systems, and semiotic systems, human and other?

Jerne finishes by envisaging a Kuhnian revolution affecting both biology and linguistics, in which 'linguistics would become a branch of biology' (1984: 223). Even if this outcome is never realized, journeys towards it could be insightful. *Interdisciplinary semiotics could draw on good biology and good semiotics and produce quantum leaps of knowledge in both.*

Social semiotics in a complexity framework

This book has mainly embedded its theory in particular discussions arising from particular analyses in the flow of particular arguments. In this final section I complement that inductive approach by outlining a general social semiotic theory, which I connect loosely with broader theories of chaos and complexity. I arrange general points under five headings, but these are not tightly ordered, with first principles generating later principles. This is a fuzzy, paratactic theory in which areas overlap and interact with each other.

With each point I bring out connections and implications for linguistics in italics. That was one of my main aims. I also bring out some implications (also in italics) for analysing language, meaning and society, to contribute to approaches such as CDA and suggest how they can do their job better in a social semiotic-complexity framework. That was a related aim of the book: to give critical analysis of discourse a more comprehensive theory of language, meaning and society and to build that theory into mainstream linguistics.

1   Semiosic conditions

1.1 Conditions for semiosis (production, circulation, reception and effects of semiotic activity) range between far-from-equilibrium and close-to-equilibrium. Each condition has features which may profoundly affect every aspect of semiosis. Systems of language, meaning and society all exist, separately and together, mainly between close-to-equilibrium and relatively far-from-equilibrium conditions, not at either extreme. Far-from-equilibrium conditions allow chaos and uncertainty, through positive feedback loops, power laws and exponential change, which can rapidly create or dissolve complex forms.

- *Formal linguistics is close-to-equilibrium theory (crisp categories, linear processes) orientated to close-to-equilibrium phenomena (forms, materials, problems). Linguistics needs richer models of complex and chaotic forms, materials and problems, using more fuzzy descriptions, within a single differentiated theory that includes linear forms and processes.*
- *Analysis needs to estimate how far or close to equilibrium its object is. Prevailing semiosic conditions in approximate (fuzzy) descriptions are important objects of analysis.*

1.2 Language, meaning and society are full of complex forms, including systems and networks. Their relationships with other surrounding systems are also complex forms. Complex forms have systematic relations between elements, which produce non-linear causality in which relative wholes have effects that cannot be predicted from the properties of individual parts, and individual elements may have different properties and effects as a result of being part of a complex system.

- *Linguistics already recognizes the principle of complexity (that wholes have meanings other than the sum of their parts). For example, sentence meanings are not just the sum of the meanings of component words. The principle applies to all forms of language, meaning and society studied by linguistics.*

- *Transformations relate complex forms in language, meaning and society. Transformations are recognized in linguistics, but they are more fundamental, complex and extensive than were recognized in Chomsky.*
- *Transformational analysis is a key to all linguistic analysis.*
- *Analogue forms relate complex forms to others, so analysis of analogue meanings should include analysis of relations within and between the forms.*

1.3 Complex forms with different origins, of different scales and sizes, can co-exist in a common space, producing multidimensional forms. They can interact to multiply their forces, to fuse, or produce incompatibility (contradiction, ambiguity, incommensurability).

In far-from-equilibrium conditions, two forms can co-exist but be mutually exclusive, as in Orwellian double-think or Wittgenstein's duck–rabbit illusion.

- *In linguistics, multidimensionality is recognized in Halliday. The concept can be extended far more widely in linguistics and beyond.*
- *In analysis, when one form or structure has been identified, analysts should check whether other structures, comparable or oppositional, may be present in the same space, with what effect.*

1.4 Complex forms may be more tightly or more loosely bonded, with higher or lower boundaries. It depends on contexts and circumstances whether bonds are too strong or too weak, boundaries too high or too low. Bonds that are too strong can be dysfunctional, limiting the scope of one or more elements, whereas if they are too weak the form comes apart. Similarly, different strengths of boundaries can be functional or dysfunctional.

- *Halliday's work on cohesion leads the way for linguistics to use more fuzzy categories and approximate empirical judgements of more and less (strong or weak bonds, high or low boundaries) for all the many situations in the study of language, meaning and society where qualities vary continuously.*

1.5 Given chaos and complexity in the multiscalar world of social semiosis, Chomskyan universals should be seen as fuzzy and multiscalar. Yet searching for relative universals can be a productive heuristic strategy for social semiotics.

- *Every analysis should ask how general a property is, where are its limits, and why.*

2   The nature of semiosis

2.1 Meaning for semiotic agents is constituted in a three-body relationship between at least three interdependent elements or planes: language (means to convey meaning), meaning (concept or version of reality carried by language) and reality (as object of meaning). Each modifies and is modified by the others in a dynamic relationship. Meanings are constructed by language as well as carried by them.

- *Linguistics currently emphasizes the study of carriers of meaning (sound systems, words, syntax) over meaning itself. It needs to integrate the study of language around the primacy of meaning.*
- *All semiotic analysis (including linguistics, CDA) should begin with meanings and their relationship to relevant realities.*

2.3 Meanings construct reality as well as conveying and referring to it. Reality exists outside semiosis, but semiosis constructs versions of reality which guide semiosic agents to act on reality and change it. A normal part of semiosis is to construct and interpret signs of how meaning and reality are related. Distance between meaning and reality constantly changes with and during every semiotic act. In far-from-equilibrium conditions, supposed distances can be so great that they affect interpretation, changing or inverting meanings in reality flip-overs.

- *Starting points for a fuller theory of reality relations in linguistics are Halliday's theories of modality, Chomsky's account of verbal auxiliaries, and Hodge and Kress's critical studies of modality in English. All analysis needs continually to monitor reality relations and effects.*

2.4 Semiosis for human adults normally consists of many languages (systems for conveying meaning) and semiotic modes, organized in functional multimodal complexes. Multiplicity allows redundancy, to overcome the problem of noise, and contradiction, where different or opposite meanings co-exist. So 'English' includes both verbal, visual and mathematical modes and formal and informal forms, usually shaped by multilingual contexts.

- *The minimal framework for linguistic analysis is a complex multimodal, multilingual system.*

2.4 The two fundamental semiotic modes are analogue (where complex forms in language, reality, society and meaning are related to or transform into each other) and digital (where complex forms are analysed and synthesized through repeated binary operations). These two fundamental forms oscillate between each other and co-exist in complex arrangements.

Digital systems underpin generative devices in language, meaning and society which can produce or counteract exponential division ('difference engines').

- *Digital and analogue meanings function and are interpreted differently. Linguistics needs to recognize the differences between them and their consequences for theory and analysis of language, meaning and society.*

2.5 For human semiosis, these processes are deeply embedded in another three-body system, language–meaning–society, in which, over time, society, formed by systematic semiotic relations between individuals and groups, profoundly modifies the nature and scope of language and meaning. The unit of social semiotics is not a sign (isolated elements in a dedicated signifying system) but a small-scale social semiotic act, such as utterances in verbal language, with relationships between language, meaning and reality driven by and affecting social agents and relations.

- *For linguistics, social relations constituting patterns of language and meaning should be included in explanatory frames. Data should come from language in use, preserving traces of social agents, contexts and purposes.*
- *Analysis should always ask questions about social contexts and processes, over many scales, as intrinsic to interpretation.*

3 Psychological foundations

3.1 Human semiosis has a necessary basis in human physiology and neurology, produced over long periods of evolution, affected by particular conditions in individual minds (e.g., effects of drugs or hormones, damage to semiotic organs).

- *Lakoff's principle applies to all linguistic theories, that psychological and neurological plausibility should be used to develop or decide between theories about language, meaning and society.*

• *Analysis of every instance of semiosis should draw on the best available knowledge for fuzzy hypotheses about psychological processes at issue.*

3.2 The role of analogue processes in language, meaning, thought and perception provides important links with some schools of psychology, especially Gestalt psychology, cognitive and developmental psychology, and various psycho-therapy traditions (e.g., Bateson, Rogers). Analogue analysis includes complex relations of language, thought and behaviour in problematic contexts.

• *Studying the interplay between analogue and digital processes can be fruitful for collaborative research in linguistics and psychology.*

3.3 Behaviourist psychology has a linear but powerful form of semiotic analysis.

• *A social semiotic theory with three stages between close-to-equilibrium and far-from-equilibrium could reframe this tradition to allow pathways and connections with other schools and other semiosic conditions.*

3.4 Freud's contribution to social semiotics has been seminal. Yet some of his insights still need a semiotic framework to allow them to be recognized. Conversely, some limitations of the 'talking cure' may be better understood and overcome in a social semiotic framework.

• *Freud's ideas have many potential contributions to make to linguistic theory, not least his analytically powerful functional theories of transformations and negation.*

3.5 Abnormal psychology is well developed in psychology. The concept of far-from-equilibrium provides a good framework for understanding anomalous forms in language, meaning and society as continuous parts of 'normal' systems, mediated by systemic breaks.

• *Linguistic analysis currently emphasizes close-to-equilibrium forms as primary objects of study. Many branches or sub-branches of linguistics deal with aberrant forms, which could be drawn into a larger practice of linguistic theory and analysis. For instance, where mainstream linguistics theorizes situations of ideal speakers and listeners, CDA and forensic linguistics deal with language in conditions where injustice and discrimination are the norm.*

• *Linguistics already studies different kinds of language pathology. Far-from-equilibrium linguistics could provide a coherent, powerful framework for interdisciplinary research.*

4 Social foundations

4.1 Interaction between social and semiotic forces is intrinsic in social semiotics, as are the interrelations of both with forces from and effects on social and physical reality. Social structures are produced by similar processes to semiotic structures, giving rise to many homologies between the two kinds of system. However, in spite of this homology, they operate in different ways to produce the range of social semiotic effects.

• *Linguistics includes many areas where language and society connect, variously described as 'sociolinguistics', 'language in context' and 'pragmatics'. These could be incorporated more strongly into a coherent, diverse discipline which does not oppose social and linguistic analysis.*

4.2 Social life is organized primarily as systems, and social causality is an effect of these systems as embedded in material reality. Cybernetic systems are widespread in society as in biology, always including a semiotic dimension, giving rise to non-linear causality. Social systems are typically partial, contested and incomplete, as are the semiotic systems that correspond to and sustain them. Conflict and negotiation are typically expressed and managed through contradictions, as in ideological complexes. Contradictions can be instruments of control or sites to diagnose weaknesses in a position.

• *A concept of systems is fundamental in linguistics, stemming from Saussure. A critical concept of systems, as in Marx, could be deployed more widely, in soft and amorphous systems of language, meaning and society.*
• *Cybernetics can be a useful framework for analysing complex social forces and effects of language and meaning.*

4.3 Systems are multiscalar, potentially ranging across an indefinite number of scales. Scales normally emerge from below, from smaller to larger scales, where larger, later scales can have new (emergent) properties. As sentences have properties not contained in their component words, nations, classes and other groups have properties not contained in family units. Many multiscalar structures can be analysed in fractal terms, though many multiscalar forms are not fractal. Structures from higher scales can be imposed from above, but with different processes and effects.

- *As this book has shown throughout, multiscalar analysis is important for all aspects of linguistics, for strategic analysis of intersections between language, meaning and society.*

4.4 Paradigmatic systems (sets of categories) encoded in language organize the social and physical world for members of a group, as a taken-for-granted (hegemonic) basis for thought and action. Biological attributes are modified by and contribute to social categories and actions through semiotic processes. Age and race are commonly affected in this way, as are physical and mental strengths, constructed as class systems. Of biological attributes, the most problematic now, as they have been in the past, are those involved in gender, sex and reproduction. Sexuality has proved especially problematic for social theory because it is typically far-from-equilibrium and operates at different levels of the dominant multiscalar structures.

- *Emotions are main drivers of social meaning and action, not well represented in surface forms of verbal language, currently marginalized in linguistics. Social semiotics needs better ways of analysing emotional meanings, along with a better theory of love.*

4.5 Power and solidarity in different forms constitute every complex social relationship and group. Power needs and rests on relations of solidarity, and vice versa. But, in further-from-equilibrium conditions, power can be opposed to solidarity and be a catalyst for exponentially exploding conflict or love.

- *Brown and Gilman's seminal sociolinguistic work established a solid basis for this theme in linguistics. Many signifying systems are recruited to carry these complex primary social meanings. Power and solidarity should always be estimated and given fuzzy values for analysis.*

4.6 The critical project of CDA and social semiotics has been called 'unscientific'. However, science includes diagnosis of dangerous, dysfunctional conditions. Social semiotics has a significant role in analysing social dysfunction (e.g., racism, injustice, war, suicide) and proposing and evaluating remedies (e.g., fuzzy logic, both–and thinking, complexity analysis).

- *Some kinds of linguistics already include normative models, as in Grice and Bateson's work and in speech therapy. Analysis of dysfunction is the other side of the coin of functional analysis.*

5   Material conditions

5.1 Every semiotic mode operates and has effects as it connects with one or more perceptual system(s), always with its basis in physiological systems, themselves ultimately with physical and chemical basis. Semiotic modes act like natural prosthetics of the senses or like prosthetic devices added on to more basic semiotic modes. As McLuhan observed, these prosthetic structures built onto other structures can enhance, distort or limit the production and circulation of meaning.

- *Linguistics analyses auditory systems, acoustic, phonetic and phonological. The same principle can be applied to all other semiotic modes, integrated with studies of meaning in a multimodal approach.*
- *The material basis of semiotic systems should be understood as the unpredictable intersection of incommensurably different domains of system, physical, biological, social and semiotic, which together produce unexpected effects.*

5.2 Digital technologies are distinct from digital meanings. They mainly use material devices with many material properties (extreme speed, unimpeded movement over great distances, mass dissemination, economical storage, tendency to exponential growth). These combine to produce the technological complex of the 'digital revolution'. This technological complex is inserted into political and economic systems which shape and are shaped by them. The unpredictable future of such technologies will be shaped by efforts of those who are currently dominant, politically and economically, and those who resist or diverge.

- *The task for critical social semiotics in the digital age is to understand linguistic, semiotic and social dimensions of that struggle better and to forge new paths for a more just society.*

References

ABC (Australian Broadcasting Commission) (2008) 'The girl least likely', 15 September, www.abc.net.au/austory/content/2007/s2365960.htm.

Adamic, L. A., and Huberman, B. A. (2000) 'Power-law distribution of the world wide web', *Science*, 287(5461): 2115.

Adams, M. (1994) *Beginning to Read: Thinking and Learning about Print*. Cambridge, MA: MIT Press.

Agnew, J. (2003) *Geopolitics: Revisioning World Politics*. London: Routledge.

Allen, G. (2000) *Intertextuality*. London: Routledge.

Althusser, L. (1971) *Ideological State Apparatuses*. London: New Left Books.

Aristotle (1933, 1935) *Metaphysics*, Vols. I and II, ed, trans. H. Tredennick. Cambridge, MA: Harvard University Press.

Aristotle (1951) *The Poetics*, ed. and trans. S. H. Butcher. New York: Dover.

Austin, J. (1962) *How to Do Things with Words*. Oxford: Oxford University Press.

Australian Government (2011) *Funding Rules for Federation Fellowships*.

Bak, P. (1996) *How Nature Works*. New York: Springer.

Bakhtin, M. M. (1981) *The Dialogic Imagination: Four Essays*, ed. M. Holquist. Austin and London: University of Texas Press.

Bandler, R., and Grinder, J. (1975) *The Structure of Magic*, Vol. I. Palo Alto, CA: Science and Behaviour Books.

Barthes, R. (1977) *Music–Image–Text*, ed. S. Heath. London: Fontana.

Bateson, G. (1973) *Steps to an Ecology of Mind*. London: Paladin Books.

Baudrillard, J. (1995) *The Iraq War Did Not Take Place*. Bloomington: University of Indiana Press.

Berger, P., and Luckmann, T. (1966) *The Social Construction of Reality*. Harmondsworth: Penguin.

Berlin, B., and Kay, P. (1969) *Basic Color Terms*. Berkeley: University of California Press.

Bernstein, B. (1971) *Class, Codes and Control*. London: Routledge.

Bernstein, B. (1981) 'Codes, modalities and the process of cultural reproduction: a model', *Language and Society*, 19: 327–63.

Bhabha, H. (1994) *The Location of Culture*. London and New York: Routledge.

Bilal, I. R. (2013) 'With Bilal Ibne Rasheen (2010)', in J. R. Martin, *Interviews with M. A. K. Halliday: Language Turned Back on Himself*. London: Bloomsbury.

Blommaert, J. (2005) *Discourse: A Critical Introduction*. Cambridge: Cambridge University Press.

Boas, F. (1911) 'Introduction: Handbook of American Indian languages', *Bulletin of the Bureau of American Ethnology*, 40: 1–83.

Bonfil, G. (1987) *México profundo: una civilización negada*. Mexico City: SEP.

Bourdieu, P. (1972) *Outline of a Theory of Practice*. Cambridge: Cambridge University Press.

Bourdieu, P. (2003) *Counterfire: Against the Tyranny of the Market*. London: Verso.

Bourdieu, P. (2010) *Distinction*, trans. R. Nice. London: Routledge.

Bradley, M., and Lang, P. (1999) *Affective Norms for English Words*, Technical report C-1. Center for Research in Psychophysiology, University of Florida.

Braudel, F. (1996) *The Mediterranean and the Mediterranean World in the Age of Philip II*. Berkeley: University of California Press.

Breivik, A. (2011) *2083: A European Declaration of Independence*, https://sites.google.com/site/knightstemplareurope/2083.

Brown, R., and Ford, M. (1961) 'Address in American English', *Journal of Abnormal and Social Psychology*, 62: 375–85.

Brown, R., and Gilman, A. (1960) 'The pronouns of power and solidarity', in T. Sebeok (ed.), *Style in Language*. Cambridge, MA: MIT Press, pp. 253–76.

Brynjolfsson, E., and McAfee, A. (2012) *Race against the Machine*. Lexington, MA: Digital Frontier Press.

Buddha (1948) *The Living Thoughts of Gotama, the Buddha*, ed. K. Coomaraswamy and I. B. Horner. London: Cassell.

Bühler, K. (2011) *A Theory of Language*. Amsterdam: John Benjamins.

Butt, D., Moore, A., Henderson-Brooks, C., Haliburn, J., and Meares, R. (2007) 'Dissociation, relatedness, and "cohesive harmony": a linguistic measure of degrees of "fragmentation"?', *Linguistics and the Human Sciences*, 3(3): 263–93.

Campbell, J. (1988) *The Hero with a Thousand Faces*. Princeton, NJ: Princeton University Press.

Carbó, T. (2001) 'Regarding reading: on a methodological approach', *Discourse & Society*, 12(1): 59–89.

Carbó, T. (2004) 'Parliamentary discourse when things go wrong: mapping histories, contexts, conflicts', in P. Bayley (ed.), *Cross-Cultural Perspectives in Parliamentary Discourse*. Amsterdam: John Benjamins, pp. 301–37.

Carbó, T. (2007) 'Introducción: la elocuencia de los cuerpos', *Estudios de Lingüística Aplicada*, 46: 13–30.

Carroll, J. (1956) 'Introduction', in *Language, Thought and Reality: Selected Writings of Benjamin Lee Whorf*. Cambridge, MA: MIT Press.

Chalker, S., and Weiner, A. (1998) *Oxford Dictionary of English Grammar*. 2nd edn, Oxford: Oxford University Press.

Chomsky, N. (1957) *Syntactic Structures*. The Hague: Mouton.

Chomsky, N. (1965) *Aspects of the Theory of Syntax*. Cambridge, MA: MIT Press.

Chomsky, N. (1968) *Language and Mind*. New York: Harcourt, Brace & World.

Chomsky, N. (1969) *American Power and the New Mandarins*. Harmondsworth: Penguin.

Chomsky, N. (1995) *The Minimalist Program*. Cambridge, MA: MIT Press.

Chomsky N. (1999) *Profit over People: Neoliberalism and Global Order*. New York: Seven Stories Press.

Clifford, J., and Marcus, G. E. (eds) (1986) *Writing Culture: The Poetics and Politics of Ethnography*. Berkeley: University of California Press.

Cohen, S. (1972) *Folk Devils and Moral Panics: The Creation of the Mods and Rockers*. London: MacGibbon & Kee.

Coronado, G. (2009) 'From autoethnography to the quotidian ethnographer', *Qualitative Research Journal*, 9(1): 123–9.

Coronado, G. (2014) 'De la profundidad a la superficie cultural: lucha de significados y migración', *Desacatos*, 46: 140–55.

Coulson, S. (2001) *Semantic Leaps*, Cambridge: Cambridge University Press.

Courpasson, D. (2000) 'Managerial strategies of domination: power in soft bureaucracies', *Organization Studies*, 21(1): 141–61.

Crain, S. (2012) *The Emergence of Language*. Cambridge: Cambridge University Press.

Cruse, A. (2004) *Meaning in Language*. Oxford: Oxford University Press.

Crutzen, P. (2002) 'Geology of mankind', *Nature*, 415(6867): 23.

Cunneen, C., and Stubbs J. (2004) 'Cultural criminology and the engagement with race, gender and post-colonial identities', in J. Ferrell, K. Hayward, W. Morrison and M. Presdee (eds), *Cultural Criminology Unleashed*. London: GlassHouse, pp. 97–108.

Davidson, P., and Griffin, R. (2003) *Management: Australia in a Global Context*. 2nd edn, Brisbane: John Wiley.

Davis, J. (1982) *Kullark: the Dreamers*. Sydney: Currency Press.

Deleuze, G., and Guattari, F. (1988) *A Thousand Plateaus: Capitalism and Schizophrenia*. London: Athlone Press.

Denzin, N., and Lincoln, Y. (2008) *Qualitative Research*. Thousand Oaks, CA: Sage.

Derrida, J. (1976) *Of Grammatology*, trans. G. C. Spivak. Baltimore and London: Johns Hopkins University Press.

Derrida, J. (1988) Afterword, in *Limited Inc*. Evanston, IL: Northwestern University Press.

Douglas, M. (1970) *Purity and Danger*. Harmondsworth: Penguin.

Durkheim, E. (1952) *Suicide: A Study in Sociology*. London: Routledge & Kegan Paul.

Eco, U. (1976) *A Theory of Semiotics*. Bloomington: Indiana University Press.

Eco, U. (2014) *From the Tree to the Labyrinth*. Cambridge, MA: Harvard University Press.

Edelman, G. (1988) *Topobiology: An Introduction to Molecular Embryology*. New York: Basic Books.

Eliot, T. S. (1963) *Collected Poems*. London: Faber & Faber.

Empson, W. (1930) *Seven Types of Ambiguity*. London: Chatto & Windus.

Fairclough, N. (1989) *Language and Power*. London and New York: Longman.

Fairclough, N (ed.) (1992) *Critical Language Awareness*. London: Longman.

Feshbach, S. (1976) 'The role of fantasy in response to television', *Journal of Social Issues*, 32(4): 71–85.

Fillmore, C. (2003) *Form and Meaning in Language*. Stanford, CA: CSLI.

Fiske, J., Hodge, B., and Turner, G. (1987) *Myths of Oz: Reading Australian Popular Culture*. Sydney: Allen & Unwin.

Foucault, M. (1971) 'Orders of discourse', *Social Science Information*, 10(2): 7–30.

Foucault, M. (1972) *The Archaeology of Knowledge*. London: Tavistock.

Foucault, M. (1977) *Discipline and Punish*. Harmondsworth: Penguin.

Foucault, M. (1978) *The History of Sexuality*, Vol. 1: *An introduction*. New York: Vintage.

Foucault, M. (1980) *Power/Knowledge: Selected Interviews and Other Writings, 1972–1977*. Brighton: Harvester.

Foucault, M. (1983) *This is Not a Pipe*. Berkeley: University of California Press.

Fowler, R., Hodge, B., Kress, G., and Trew, T. (1979) *Language and Control*. London: Routledge & Kegan Paul.

Frazer, N. (2003) 'From discipline to flexibilization?', *Constellations*, 10(2): 160–71.

Freud, S. ([1925] 1961) 'Negation', *Standard Edition of the Complete Psychological Works*. London: Hogarth Press, Vol. 19, pp. 235–9.

Gabriel, Y. (ed.) (2000) *Myths, Stories and Organizations*. Oxford: Oxford University Press.

Gadamer, H. G. (1989) *Truth and Method*. 2nd edn, London: Sheed & Ward.

Gee, J. P. (2010) *How to Do Discourse Analysis*. London: Routledge.

Geertz, C. (1973) *The Interpretation of Culture*. New York: Basic Books.

Gell-Mann, M. (1994) *The Quark and the Jaguar: Adventures in the Simple and the Complex*. London: Little, Brown.

Giddens, A. (1987) 'Structuralism, post-structuralism and the production of culture', in Giddens and J. H. Turner (eds), *Social Theory Today*. Cambridge: Polity, pp. 195–223.

Goffman, E. (1959) *The Presentation of Self in Everyday Life*. Harmondsworth: Penguin.

Gopnik, A. (2009) *The Philosophical Baby*. New York: Farrar, Straus & Giroux.

Graddol, D. (2006) *English Next: Why Global English May Mean the End of 'English as a Foreign Language'*. London: British Council.

Gramsci, A. (1971) *Selections from the Prison Notebooks*, ed. and trans. Q. Hoare and G. N. Smith. London: Lawrence & Wishart.

Greenberg, J. (1963) 'Some universals of grammar with particular reference to the order of meaningful elements', in Greenberg (ed.), *Universals of Language*. Cambridge, MA: MIT Press.

Grice, P. (1991) *Studies in the Way of Words*. Cambridge, MA: Harvard University Press.

Habermas, J. (1975) *Legitimation Crisis*. Boston: Beacon Press.

Habermas, J. (1990) *Moral Consciousness and Communicative Action*. Cambridge: Polity.

Hall, S. (1996) 'Introduction: who needs identity?', in Hall and P. Du Gay (eds), *Questions of Cultural Identity*. London: Sage, pp. 1–17.

Halliday, M. (1956) 'Grammatical categories in modern Chinese', *Transactions of the Philological Society*, 55: 177–224.

Halliday, M. (1970) 'Functional diversity in language', *Foundations of Language*, 6: 322–61.

Halliday, M. (1975) *Learning How to Mean*. London: Edward Arnold.

Halliday, M. (1976) *System and Function in Language: Selected Papers*, ed. G. Kress. Oxford: Oxford University Press.

Halliday, M. (1978) *Language as Social Semiotic*. London: Edward Arnold.

Halliday, M. (1985) *Introduction to Functional Grammar*. London: Edward Arnold.

Halliday, M., and Hasan, R. (1976) *Cohesion in English*. London: Longman.

Hanisch, C. 2009 *Women of the World Unite: Writings by Carol Hanisch*, www.carolhanisch.org/index.html.

Haraway, D. (1991) 'A cyborg manifesto: science, technology, and socialist-feminism in the late twentieth century', in *Simians, Cyborgs and Women: The Reinvention of Nature*. London: Routledge, pp. 149–81.

Hardt, M., and Negri, A. (2000) *Empire*. Cambridge, MA: Harvard University Press.

Harris, R. A. (1993) *The Linguistics Wars*. Oxford: Oxford University Press.

Harris Z. (1950) 'Concurrence and transformation in linguistic structure', *Language*, 33(3): 283–340.

Harvey, D. (1991) *The Condition of Postmodernity*. Oxford: Blackwell.

Harvey, D. (2005) *A Short History of Neoliberalism*. Oxford: Oxford University Press.

Hegel, G. W. F. ([1807] 1977) *The Phenomenology of Spirit*, trans. A. V. Miller. Oxford: Oxford University Press.

Heidegger, M. (1971) *On the Way to Language*. San Francisco: Harper & Row.

Herman, E., and Chomsky, N. (2002) *The Manufacture of Consent*. New York: Pantheon Books.

Hodge, B. (2011) 'Museums and attacks from cyberspace: non-linear communication in a postmodern world', *Museum and Society*, 9(2): 107–22.

Hodge, B., and Kress, G. (1974) 'Transformations, models, and processes: towards a more usable linguistics', *Journal of Literary Semantics*, 3(1): 5–22.

Hodge, B., and Kress, G. (1988) *Social Semiotics*. Cambridge: Polity.

Hodge, B., and Kress, G. (1993) *Language as Ideology*. 2nd edn, London: Routledge.

Hodge, B., and Louie, K. (1998) *The Politics of Chinese Language and Culture*. London: Routledge.

Hodge, B., and Matthews, I. (2011) 'Complexity theory and engaged research: critical incidents in the Sydney rail system', *Continuum*, 25(6): 887–901.

Hodge, B., and O'Carroll, J. (2006) *Borderwork in Multicultural Australia*. Sydney: Allen & Unwin.

Hodge, B., and Tripp, D. (1986) *Children and Television: A Semiotic Approach*. Stanford, CA: Stanford University Press.

Hodge, B., Coronado, G., Duarte, F., and Teal, G. (2010) *Chaos Theory and the Larrikin Principle: Working with Organisations in a Neo-Liberal World*. Copenhagen, Liber.

Hofstede, G. (2001) *Culture's Consequences: Comparing Values, Behaviours, Institutions and Organizations across Nations*. Thousand Oaks, CA: Sage.

Homer (1974) *The Odyssey*, trans. A. Cook. New York: W. W. Norton.

Hudson, J. (2013) 'Exclusive: after multiple denials, CIA admits to snooping on Noam Chomsky', *Foreign Policy*, 13 August.

Hughes, H., and Hughes, M. (2014) *Indigenous Education 2014*. Sydney: Centre for Independent Studies.

Hulme, M. (2009) *Why We Disagree about Climate Change*. Cambridge: Cambridge University Press.

Hymes, D. (1972) *On Communicative Competence*. Philadelphia: University of Pennsylvania Press.

Ivancic, L., Perrens, B., Fildes, J., Perry, Y., and Christensen, H. (2014) *Youth Mental Health Report*. Mission Australia and Black Dog Institute, http://apo.org.au/resource/youth-mental-health-report-2014.

Jablonka, E., and Lamb, M. J. (2005) *Evolution in Four Dimensions: Genetic, Epigenetic, Behavioral, and Symbolic Variation in the History of Life*. Cambridge, MA: MIT Press.

Jakobson, R. (1962) *Selected Writings*, Vol. I: *Phonological Studies*, ed. R. Stephen. The Hague: Mouton.

Jakobson, R., and Halle, M. (1956) 'Phonology and phonetics', in *Fundamentals of Language*. The Hague: Mouton, pp. 4–51.

Jerne, N. (1984) 'The generative grammar of the immune system', Nobel lecture, 8 December, www.nobelprize.org/nobel_prizes/medicine/laureates/1984/jerne-lecture.pdf.

Johnson, T., and Grim, B. (2013) *The World's Religions in Figures*. Hoboken, NJ: Wiley-Blackwell.

Jones, W., and Cannon, G. H. (1993) *The Collected Works of Sir William Jones*. New York: New York University Press.

Karttunen, L. (1974) 'Presupposition and linguistic context', *Theoretical Linguistics*, 1(1–3): 181–94.

Kress, G. (2010) *Multimodality: A Social Semiotic Approach to Contemporary Communication*. London: Routledge.

Kress, G., and Hodge, R. (1979) *Language as Ideology*. London: Routledge & Kegan Paul.

Kress, G., and Van Leeuwen, T. (2001) *Multimodal Discourse*. Oxford: Oxford University Press.

Kress, G., and Van Leeuwen, T. (2006) *Reading Images: The Grammar of Graphic Design*. 2nd edn, London: Routledge.

Kristeva, J. (1980) *Desire in Language: A Semiotic Approach to Literature and Art*. New York: Columbia University Press.

Kristeva, J. (1982) *The Powers of Horror: An Essay on Abjection*. New York: Columbia University Press.

Kuhn, T. (1962) *The Structure of Scientific Revolutions*. Chicago: University of Chicago Press.

Labov, W. (1970) 'The logic of non-standard English', in J. Alatis (ed.), *Georgetown Monographs on Languages and Linguistics*, 22: 1–43.

Labov, W. (1972) *Sociolinguistic Patterns*. Oxford: Blackwell.

Labov, W. (2013) *The Language of Life and Death: The Transformations of Experience in Oral Narrative*. Cambridge: Cambridge University Press.

Lakoff, G. (1968) 'Adverbs and the concept of deep structure', *Foundations of Language*, 4(1): 4–29.

Lakoff, G. (2004) *Don't Think of an Elephant*. White River Junction, VT: Chelsea Green.

Lakoff, G., and Johnson, M. (1980) *Metaphors We Live By*. Chicago: University of Chicago Press.

Latour, B. (2005) *Reassembling the Social: An Introduction to Actor-Network-Theory*. Oxford: Oxford University Press.

Law, J. (2004) *After method*. London: Routledge.

Le Guin, U. (1975) 'Winter's king', in *The Wind's Twelve Quarters*. London: Victor Gollancz.

Lefebvre, H. (1947) *The Critique of Everyday Life*. London: Verso.

Lenin, V. ([1903] 1938) 'Materialism and empirio-criticism', *Selected Works*, Vol XI. Moscow: Foreign Languages Publishing House.

Lenin, V. ([1902] 1947) *What is to be Done?* Moscow: Progress.

Lévi-Strauss, C. (1963) *Structural Anthropology*. New York and London: Basic Books.

Lewis, C., and Short, C. ([1879] 1922) *A Latin Dictionary*. Oxford: Clarendon Press.

Lewis, P., and Evans, R. (2013) *Undercover: The True Story of Britain's Secret Police*. London: Faber & Faber.

Liddell, H., and Scott, R. (1849) *A Greek–Engish Lexicon*. Oxford: Oxford University Press.

Lorenz, E. (1993) *The Essence of Chaos*. Seattle: University of Washington Press.

Lovelock, J. (2000) *Gaia: A New Look at Life on Earth*. Oxford: Oxford University Press.

Lyons, J. (1970) *Chomsky*. London: Fontana.

Lyotard, J.-F. (1984) *The Postmodern Condition: A Report on Knowledge*. Minneapolis: University of Minnesota Press.

McCauley, J. (1976) *Grammar and Meaning*. New York: Academic Press.

McGregor, W. (2009) *Linguistics: An Introduction*. London: Continuum.

McLuhan, M. (1964) *Understanding Media*. London: Routledge.

Mandelbrot, B. (1977) *The Fractal Geometry of Nature*. New York: W. H. Freeman.

Mandelbrot, B. (1993) 'The fractal geometry of nature', in N. Hall (ed.), *The New Science Guide to Chaos*. Harmondsworth: Penguin.

Margulis, L. (1998) *Symbiotic Planet: A New View of Evolution*. New York: Basic Books.

Martinelli, A. (2014) 'The ISA's contribution to global democratic governance', *Global Dialogue*, 4(4), http://isa-global-dialogue.net/the-isa-at-65-the-isas-contribution-to-global-democratic-governance.

Marx, K. (1971) *Early Texts*, trans. D. McLellan. Oxford: Blackwell.

Marx, K. ([1849] 1972) *Capital*, trans. E. Paul and C. Paul. London: Dent.

Marx, K., and Engels, F. (1970) *Selected Works in One Volume*. London: Lawrence & Wishart.

Marx, K., and Engels, F. ([1845] 1976) *The German Ideology*. London: Lawrence & Wishart.

Mey, J. (1985) *Whose Language? A Study in Linguistic Pragmatics*, 3 vols. Amsterdam: John Benjamins.

Miller, G. (1979) 'Images and models, similes and metaphors', in A. Ortony (ed.), *Metaphor and Thought*. Cambridge: Cambridge University Press, pp. 202–50.

Mills, C. W. (1959) *The Sociological Imagination*. Oxford: Oxford University Press.

Morris, C. (1971) *A General Theory of Signs*. The Hague: Mouton.

Morrison, A. ('Afferbeck Lauder') (1965) *Let Stalk Strine*. Sydney: Ure Smith.

Mulvey, L. (2009) *Visual and Other Pleasures*. Basingstoke: Palgrave Macmillan.

Nakamura, D., and Branigin, W. (2011) 'In quiet appearance, Loughner answers charges', *Washington Post*, 10 January.

Newman, P. (2009) 'Fieldwork and field methods in linguistics', *Language Documentation & Conservation* 3(1): 112–24.

Newton, I. ([1687] 1999) *The Principia: Mathematical Principles of Natural Philosophy*. Berkeley: University of California Press.

Nietzsche, F. (1946) *The Birth of Tragedy*. New York: Doubleday.

Nowotny, H., Scott, P., and Gibbons, M. (2001) *Rethinking Science*. Cambridge: Polity.

Orwell, G. ([1949] 2011) *1984* Rockville, MD: Wildside Press.

Partridge, E. (1966) *Origins*. London: Routledge & Kegan Paul.

Pauksztat, B., Van Duijn, M., and Wittek, R. (2011) 'A "special attachment"? Voice and the relational aspect of loyalty', *International Sociology*, 26(4): 524–46.

Pauwels, A., and Winter, J. (2006) 'Gender inclusivity, or "Grammar rules OK"?', *Language and Education*, 20(2): 128–40.

Peirce, C. S. (1956) *Selected Writings*. Chicago: University of Chicago Press.

Piaget, J. (1956) *The Language and Thought of a Child*. New York: Harcourt, Brace.

Pike, K. (1993) *Talk, Thought and Thing*. Dallas: Summer Institute of Linguistics.

Piller, I. (2011) *Intercultural Communication*. Edinburgh: Edinburgh University Press.

Plato (1892) 'Cratylus', in *The Dialogues of Plato*, trans. M. A. Jowett. 3rd edn, New York and London: Macmillan, pp. 323–89.

Poincaré, H. (1993) *New Methods of Celestial Mechanics*, 3 vols, ed. D. L. Gorrof. Woodbury, NY: American Institute of Physics.

Prigogine, I., and Stengers, I. (1984) *Order Out of Chaos*. London: Fontana.

Putnam, R. D. (2000) *Bowling Alone: The Collapse and Revival of American Community*. New York: Simon & Schuster.

Robertson, R. (1992) *Globalization: Social Theory and Global Culture*. London: Sage.

Rochester, S., and Martin, J. R. (1979) *Crazy Talk*. New York: Plenum Press.

Rosch, E. (1978) 'Principles of categorization', in Rosch and B. Lloyd (eds), *Cognition and Categorization*. Hillsdale, NJ: Lawrence Erlbaum.

Rundle, G. (2008) *USo8: Wondering where America's at from the Extended Stay Hotel*, 24 January, www.crikey.com.au/2008/01/24/us08-wondering-where-americas-at-from-the-extended-stay-hotel/?wpmp_switcher=mobile.

Ruthrof, H. (2015) 'Implicit deixis', *Language Sciences*, 47: 107–16.

Sacks, H., Schegloff, E. A., and Jefferson, G. (1974) 'A simplest systematics for the organization of turn-taking for conversation', *Language*, 50: 696–735.

Said, E. (1978) Orientalism. Harmondsworth: Penguin.

Sapir, E. (1921) *Language: An Introduction to the Study of Speech*. Oxford: Harcourt, Brace.

Saussure, F. de (1974) *A Course in General Linguistics*, trans. W. Baskin. London: Fontana.

Schouten, P. (2008) 'Theory talk 13: Immanuel Wallerstein on world-systems, the imminent end of capitalism and unifying social science', 4 August, www.theory-talks.org/2008/08/theory-talk-13.html.

Shakespeare, W. ([1603] 1963) *The Tragedy of Hamlet Prince of Denmark*. New York: New American Library.

Shannon, C. E., and Weaver, W. (1949) *The Mathematical Theory of Communication*. Urbana: University of Illinois Press.

Shklovsky, V. (1991) *Theory of Prose*. Normal, IL: Dalkey Archive Press.

Silverstone, R. (1994) *Television and Everyday Life*. London: Routledge.

Smith, F. (2004) *Understanding Reading*. London: Routledge.

Spitzer, L. (1948) *Linguistics and Literary History*. Princeton, NJ: Princeton University Press.

Stein, S. (2011) 'NRA at CPAC: media turned Jared Loughner into a celebrity', *Huffington Post*, 10 February.

Steyvers, M., and Tenenbaum, J. B. (2005) 'The large-scale structure of semantic networks: statistical analyses and a model of semantic growth', *Cognitive Science*, 29(1): 41–78.

Sun Tsu (1963) *The Art of War*, trans. S. B. Griffith. New York: Oxford University Press.

Thompson, J. B. (1984) *Studies in the Theory of Ideology*. Berkeley: University of California Press.

Trew, T. (1979) 'Theory and ideology at work', in R. Fowler, B. Hodge, G. Kress and T. Trew, *Language and Control*. London: Routledge & Kegan Paul.

Trubetzkoy, N. (1969) *Principles of Phonology*. Berkeley: University of California Press.

Turner, V. (1974) *Dramas, Fields and Metaphors: Symbolic Action in Human Society*. Ithaca, NY: Cornell University Press.

Urry, J. (2005) 'The complexity turn', *Theory, Culture and Society*, 22(5): 1–14.

US National Commission on Terrorist Attacks (2004) *The 9/11 Commission Report*. New York: W. W. Norton.

van Dijk, T. A. (1972) *Some Aspects of Text Grammars: A Study in Theoretical Linguistics and* Poetics. The Hague: Mouton.

van Gennep, A. (1960) *The Rites of Passage*. Chicago: University of Chicago Press.

Voloshinov, V. (1973) *Marxism and the Philosophy of Language*. New York: Seminar Press.

Vygotsky, L. (1978) *Language and Thought*. Cambridge, MA: MIT Press.

Wallerstein, I. (1974) *The Modern World-System*, Vol. 1: *Capitalist Agriculture and the Origins of the European World-Economy in the Sixteenth Century*. New York: Academic Press.

Watson, J. D. (1970) *The Double Helix: A Personal Account of the Discovery of the Structure of DNA*. Harmondsworth: Penguin.

Watts, D. (1999) *Small Worlds*. Princeton, NJ: Princeton University Press.

Weber, M. (1947) *The Theory of Economic and Social Organization*, trans. A. M. Henderson and T. Parsons. New York: Oxford University Press.

Whorf, B. (1956) *Language, Thought and Reality: Selected Writings of Benjamin Lee Whorf*, ed. J. Carroll. Cambridge, MA: MIT Press.

Wiener, N. (1948) *Cybernetics: or, Control and Communication in the Animal and the Machine*. Cambridge, MA: MIT Press.

Williams, R. (1976) *Keywords: A Vocabulary of Culture and Society*. London: Collins.

Williams, R. (1977) *Marxism and Literature*. Oxford: Oxford University Press.

Wittgenstein, L. (1968) *The Philosophical Investigations*, ed. G. Pitcher. Melbourne: Macmillan.

Wittgenstein, L. (1969) *On Certainty*. New York: Harper & Row.

Wittgenstein, L. ([1921] 1971) *Tractatus Logico-Philosophicus*. 2nd edn, London: Routledge & Kegan Paul.

Wittgenstein, L. (2001) *Philosophical Notebooks*. Oxford: Oxford University Press.

Zadeh, L. (1973) 'Outline of a new approach to the analysis of complex systems and decision processes', *IEEE Transactions on Systems, Man, and Cybernetics*, 3(1): 28–44.

Zapata, D. (2008) http://dushkablog.blogspot.com.au.

Zipf, G. (1949) *Human Behaviour and the Principle of Least Effort*. Cambridge, MA: Addison-Wesley.

Index